Inside the Welfare State

British Politics and Society

SERIES EDITOR: PETER CATTERALL

Popular Newspapers, the Labour Party and British Politics
James Thomas

In the Midst of Events
The Foreign Office Diaries and Papers of Kenneth Younger, February 1950–October 1951
Edited by Geoffrey Warner

Strangers, Aliens and Asians
Huguenots, Jews and Bangladeshis in Spitalfields 1666–2000
Anne J. Kershen

Conscription in Britain 1939–1964
The Militarization of a Generation
Roger Broad

German Migrants in Post-War Britain
An Enemy Embrace
Inge Weber-Newth and Johannes-Dieter Steinert

The Labour Governments 1964–1970
Edited by Peter Dorey

Government, the Railways and the Modernization of Britain
Beeching's Last Trains
Charles Loft

Britain, America and the War Debt Controversy
The Economic Diplomacy of an Unspecial Relationship, 1917–1941
Robert Self

Reginald McKenna
Financier among Statesmen, 1863–1916
Martin Farr

Inside the Welfare State
Foundations of Policy and Practice in Post-War Britain
Virginia A. Noble

Inside the Welfare State

Foundations of Policy and Practice in Post-War Britain

Virginia A. Noble

Routledge
Taylor & Francis Group
New York   London

First published 2009
by Routledge
270 Madison Ave, New York, NY 10016

Simultaneously published in the UK
by Routledge
2 Park Square, Milton Park, Abingdon, Oxon OX14 4RN

Routledge is an imprint of the Taylor & Francis Group, an informa business

Library of Congress Cataloging in Publication Data
Noble, Virginia A., 1963–
   Inside the welfare state : foundations of policy and practice in post-war Britain /
Virginia A. Noble.—1st ed.
      p. cm.—(British politics and society)
   Includes bibliographical references and index.
   1. Public welfare—Great Britain—History—20th century.   2. Great Britain—Social
policy.   I. Title.
   HV245.N67 2008
   361.6'5094109044—dc22
   2008021723

ISBN10: 0-415-70187-2 (hbk)
ISBN10: 0-203-88731-X (ebk)

ISBN13: 978-0-415-70187-7 (hbk)
ISBN13: 978-0-203-88731-8 (ebk)

Contents

Acknowledgments

Many thanks to Judith Bennett, Stacy Braukman, D'Arcy Brissman, David Carter, Sally Clark, Kirsten Delegard, Eve Duffy, Natalie Fousekis, Cynthia Herrup, Ben Holtzman, Caroline Light, Christa McGill, Kathy Newfont, Stephanie Rambler, Don Reid, Richard Soloway, Sarah Theusen, Susan Thorne, Anne Whisnant, and the John Hope Franklin Humanities Institute at Duke University, Durham, NC.

Introduction

This book is about the practices and policies that determined how welfare was actually provided in Britain between 1948 and 1965. While legislation enacted in the 1940s set out the framework for post-war welfare provision, crucial terms and conditions of participation in the welfare state were often determined elsewhere, in decisions made by bureaucrats and in the interactions between those claiming benefits and those dispensing them. Very soon after the Second World War, the practice of welfare provision became an ongoing exercise in defining and enforcing certain connections among individuals, families, and the labor market—a project that invariably revolved around gendered notions of proper conduct. And as immigration increased in the 1950s, race, too, became a prominent determinant of welfare practice. In a wide variety of contexts in the two decades after the war, central and local governments developed policies and practices to prescribe domestic and employment roles, reform attitudes and conduct, and deter dependence on the state.

To understand why and how gender and race shaped social policy in the second half of the twentieth century, we need to know how the social security legislation of the 1940s was interpreted, elaborated, and applied. We also need to compare the experience of women and men in various contexts of welfare provision, an undertaking that has not had much momentum in either the literature on women's status in the welfare state or more general welfare studies. Since gender is relational—constructions of masculinity and femininity are interdependent—it is important to consider how the gendered expectations of those controlling welfare benefits involved both women and men. Race also became a stratifying feature of welfare distribution, reflecting growing anxieties about South Asian, African, and West Indian immigration in the 1950s and 1960s. This study, therefore, focuses on some of the policies and practices of welfare distribution in the first two decades of the post-war welfare state's life. I examine the different conditions imposed on different groups of claimants in three ostensibly gender- and race-neutral welfare programs: national insurance (focusing on unemployment benefit), means-tested national assistance (which replaced poor relief), and temporary housing for the homeless in London. I consider both the policymaking of upper-level officials and the practices of "street-level bureaucracy," where policy was translated into social reality.[1] Drawing primarily on examples from the London area, I use specific cases to illustrate how this crucial period in the forging of the modern welfare state affected individual lives and shaped collective social experience.

Government programs for social welfare, of course, were not an invention of the post-war era. The Poor Law had obliged local government to provide some modicum of relief since the sixteenth century, and in the early twentieth century, Parliament created new responsibilities for central government. Between 1906 and 1914, legislation introduced maternal and child health measures, old-age pensions, and contributory sickness and unemployment benefits. By the Second World War, the British government had considerable experience experimenting with various social welfare measures. The spate of legislation enacted in the 1940s, though, signaled a new commitment to collective provision and economic management by the state that changed the scope and character of social and economic policy. The measures of the 1940s coalesced into the institution that came to be known as the modern welfare state.

Although the legislation that emerged in the mid-1940s had much in common with what had come before, it was distinct in its self-conscious effort to define itself by two new reference points: first, the commitment to the social reconstruction that was to heal the wounds of World War II; and second, the resolution to prevent the mass unemployment and ineffective relief efforts of the 1930s. By all accounts, the government's response to the problem of unemployment in the 1930s had been woefully inadequate, and the humiliating abuses of the means test—which required an applicant to prove that the combined resources of the household were inadequate for survival—became a powerful symbol of the failures of government aid.

The social and economic legislation of the 1940s was wide-ranging. The 1944 Education Act raised the minimum school-leaving age to fifteen and made state education in secondary schools free. The Family Allowances Act of 1945 provided flat-rate family allowances for each child after the first. The National Insurance Act of 1946 integrated and extended previous social insurance schemes and provided flat-rate benefits for retirement, sickness, unemployment, and widowhood. Workers secured their rights to national insurance through mandatory contributions to the insurance fund. The National Health Service, in many ways the most popular welfare measure, was created in 1948 to provide free universal health care. And the National Assistance Act of 1948 replaced the Poor Law, providing means-tested aid to the poor.

The sheer scale of the post-war project—which eventually included not only social security and health care, but the nationalization of several industries—led some scholars to see it as a political victory of the organized working class, an inevitable product of the forward march of social democracy.[2] Others have viewed it as an entirely different mechanism of class interest, one which served the interests of capital by guaranteeing the health and socialization of laborers, exercising social control over the working class, or appeasing dissatisfied workers who might otherwise embrace radical politics.[3] The post-war welfare state has also been cast as a victory for the middle class, who for the first time enjoyed inclusion in the insurance-based programs that had previously only been available to the working class.[4]

Class, however, was not the only social relationship to inform the creation of the post-war welfare state. The importance of gender in the ideological grounding of post-war social policy is particularly evident in the 1942 Beveridge Report, often described as the blueprint for the modern welfare state. The report, the product of an interdepartmental committee chaired by William Beveridge, set out a detailed plan of government action designed to end poverty, remove the stigma of public assistance, create full employment, and spark unprecedented economic growth.[5] Relying on the principles of Keynesian economics, the state would stimulate employment through public spending. But the most potent symbol of citizenship in the new Britain would be social security—that is, security from loss of wages. Beveridge concluded that the solution to poverty lay in the resuscitation of national insurance, and he proposed a comprehensive, integrated, and adequately funded scheme that would allow benefits for wage-interruption as a matter of right, without requiring recipients to prove they could not otherwise survive.[6]

In explaining the foundations of national insurance, the Beveridge Report celebrated the virtues of the marital partnership, in which wives were rewarded for their valuable unpaid labor with their husbands' guaranteed economic support. Married women (even those who earned wages) did not need to be insured against economic risk, Beveridge argued, because in all situations—in sickness, unemployment, and old age—they were supported by their husbands. Most married women were not employed, he added, and those who did work were merely supplementing their husbands' wages, which were adequate for family support. With this conception of the family economy, Beveridge saw no reason to protect married women against loss of wages, and, therefore, no need to guarantee their direct inclusion in the system of national insurance. Husband and wife were to be treated as a team for the purposes of national insurance. Thus, he claimed, national insurance coverage was truly universal, for even though married women were unlikely to be direct participants in the welfare state's extension of "social citizenship," they could vicariously enjoy participation through their husbands.

These assumptions about the economic relationships inscribed in marriage had important significance for the terms of participation in national insurance set out in the National Insurance Act of 1946. All men and single women qualified for national insurance benefits by having mandatory contributions deducted from their wages. When women married, they lost credit for all insurance contributions made during employment while single. When men could not work, they received a joint benefit for themselves and their wives and children. Because the insurance scheme was entirely based on contributions from wages, unemployed married women were not insured at all. Married women who did earn wages were presumed not to need national insurance, but could elect to participate. The unemployment and sickness benefits they received, however, were substantially less than those paid to men and single women. Also, if these women did not make contributions during at least half of their married lives, they could not receive retirement pensions.

This marginalization of married women in the preferred form of social security—national insurance—has been noted by some scholars of social policy, who have offered trenchant critiques of the Beveridge Report's reinforcement of women's dependent position within families. In the first lengthy work on women's status in the British welfare state, Elizabeth Wilson expanded the socialist critique of social policy to include gender, arguing that post-war programs were designed to ensure that women continued to perform the unpaid domestic labor that reproduced the work force from day to day and generation to generation. Wilson emphasized that the Beveridge Report's clear approbation of women's domestic roles formed the basis of an exploitative post-war welfare state that reinforced the sexual division of paid and unpaid labor.[7] Wilson's conclusion that female dependency was built into the legislative terms of post-war welfare, particularly in national insurance, has been widely accepted, though her attribution of this dependency to capitalist relations of production has not.[8]

William Beveridge did not foresee the significant increase in married women's employment, much of it part-time work, which began in the 1950s. The growing economy drove unemployment rates down, and women streamed into the labor force to satisfy the demand for workers. Whereas only about 12% of married women worked in 1931, by 1965, about 45% of married women were employed.[9] Even if Beveridge had known of the impending changes in the labor market, he may not have revised his conception of national insurance. Women's employment in the 1950s, while desirable for expanding production, was still seen as peripheral in the economies of individual families. Governments in the 1950s and 1960s saw no need to insure women's wages in the same way as men's; thus, the basic structure of national insurance remained the same.

Another of Beveridge's assumptions—that national insurance benefits would be paid at a level adequate for subsistence—proved to be far more vexing for officials. The Treasury's reluctance to fund the program, along with the political resistance to increasing the contributions from workers and employers, resulted in benefits for unemployment, sickness, and old age that did not meet basic needs. Recipients who lacked other income or resources were forced to apply for means-tested national assistance to "top up" their insurance benefits. Benefit levels did not keep pace with inflation, and throughout the 1950s and 1960s, the number of people receiving both national insurance and national assistance continued to rise. Rather than slowly disappearing, as Beveridge had predicted, means-tested relief assumed increasing importance in social provision after the war. And like the national insurance legislation, the terms of the National Assistance Act of 1948 also enforced the male breadwinner–female dependent norm. Only husbands could claim assistance for their families. Wives were included as dependents in calculating the amount of the allowance, but could not be paid directly. If a husband worked full-time, the family received no assistance, regardless of need.

Despite the inadequacy of insurance benefits, the booming economy temporarily obscured flaws in the welfare state. Seebohm Rowntree's well-publicized survey of poverty in York in the early 1950s uncovered remarkably little deprivation, and politicians were quick to proclaim that the welfare state had abolished want.[10] It was not until the mid-1960s that more critical appraisals of social policy gained currency. In 1965, Brian Abel-Smith and Peter Townsend challenged the notion that poverty had virtually been eliminated. In *The Poor and the Poorest*, published in 1965, Abel-Smith and Townsend claimed that the number of people living in poverty had actually increased between 1953 and 1964.[11] This "rediscovery of poverty" raised questions about the efficacy of welfare programs and spurred further investigation of the lives of the poor. Homelessness, the responsibility for which primarily fell to local authorities, was increasingly evident, particularly in urban areas, and the BBC docudrama, "Cathy Come Home," drew public attention to the problem in 1966. The most surprising revelation of the mid-1960s, however, was that many children were still living in poverty. Pressure groups, most notably the Child Poverty Action Group, which had been formed in 1965, complained about the inadequacy of government benefits and the demeaning treatment of recipients of means-tested relief.

The 1960s witnessed not only a new awareness of poverty, but a growing unease about the state's ability to prevent and relieve it. The uncertainty about the government's role resulted from the deteriorating economic climate, which produced higher rates of unemployment and lower revenues to fund social provision. By the mid-1970s, the once robust post-war economy was a shadow of its former self. Exacerbated by the oil crisis of 1973–1974, inflation collided with contracting production. Full employment, which Beveridge had declared to be a prerequisite for the welfare state, slipped out of reach. The Keynesian demand management techniques that had been so popular in the 1950s fell out of favor, as politicians began to see government retrenchment, rather than spending, as the solution to the country's economic woes.

The economic malaise had repercussions for social policy. As Peter Golding and Sue Middleton argue, "the crisis in the British economy [had] become the occasion for a social derision of the poor so punitive as to threaten the very props of the welfare state."[12] Economic insecurity resulted in a backlash against the unemployed, manifested in a generalized dissatisfaction with a welfare state that supported the unworthy. When Margaret Thatcher came to power in 1979, she exploited and magnified popular resentments of the "undeserving" needy, and this hostility found expression in public policy.[13] The 1980 Social Security Act cut the value of insurance-based unemployment and sickness benefits by 5%, abolished the earnings-related additions that had been implemented in 1966, phased out the child dependent's additions, restricted future increases in benefit amounts, and made all the benefits taxable.[14] Women experienced special difficulties in claiming unemployment benefit. Part-time workers, most of whom were female, had to demonstrate that they had a "reasonable chance" of finding part-time work in their local area. In addition, officials required women with children to prove that they could arrange for childcare if they found employment. If officials were not satisfied that childcare could be secured, benefits were terminated.[15] The Thatcher government also tried to rein in spending on means-tested relief. In 1986, the additional weekly grants paid to recipients who had exceptional needs, such as the disabled, were brought under tighter control. In addition, one-time grants for urgent needs, such as winter clothing, were replaced by loans that were repaid out of future weekly benefits.[16]

Prime Minister John Major's government continued Margaret Thatcher's work in the 1990s. In 1996, unemployment benefit was converted to the "jobseekers allowance," which reduced the time during which claimants could receive non-means-tested benefit from one year to six months. Moreover, claimants received the allowances only if they satisfied rigorous standards in their job searches and, if directed, completed training on motivation and appropriate appearance. As Conservative leaders acknowledged, these measures aimed to sanction the workshy and force the unemployed to take whatever work could be found.[17] John Major's government also tried to cut spending on means-tested relief. Lone mothers formed the fastest growing class of recipients of means-tested aid, and the government was loath to support them. In an effort to move these women off the rolls, the government launched a campaign in the early 1990s to force absent fathers to support their biological children. When this effort, criticized for its heavy-handedness and poor results, failed, the government began pressuring lone mothers to enter the labor market. As Kathleen Kiernan, Hilary Land, and Jane Lewis point out, social policy concerning lone motherhood has been largely determined by the belief that it is a moral problem and that reducing or withholding benefits is an effective way to change behavior.[18]

This book bridges the gap between, on one hand, the considerable scholarship on the gradual emergence of collective provision between 1900 and 1948; and on the other, accounts of the crisis of welfare from the 1970s on.[19] It provides historical perspective for the empirical studies detailing the policy changes of the last quarter of the twentieth century that restricted access to assistance and reduced the value of benefits.[20] Like the general welfare state literature, the scholarship on gender and social policy in the early post-war period is also underdeveloped. Historical accounts focus on the debates leading up to the Family Allowances Act of 1945 and the Beveridge Report of 1942, which laid out the blueprint for post-war welfare.[21] Social policy studies have mostly considered the "crisis" period of welfare in the last quarter of the century, detailing benefit reductions and exclusions that have hurt women.[22] These works have revealed some of the gendered assumptions embedded in the overall project of welfare. However, we still have little knowledge of how gender operated in the actual implementation of post-war welfare, particularly prior to 1975. And there has been very little work on the ways gendered assumptions affected men. This book builds on previous scholarship by analyzing how welfare administrators envisioned gender roles and how they devised their own innovative methods of incorporating these roles into the emerging post-war welfare state.

Much has been written about the resistance to Africans, Asians, and West Indians who came to Britain and the myriad cultural and social forms of racism that have appeared over the last sixty years. However, there have not been detailed, empirical examinations of the role of welfare in both shaping whites' perceptions of non-white residents and in creating hierarchies of social citizenship in the 1950s and 1960s. Here, I undertake a preliminary examination of the intersection of race, citizenship, and welfare. Whereas the template of female dependency was well established in social policy, race had not been a prominent structuring feature of welfare before the large-scale immigration of the post-war period. Opposition to the presence of blacks and Asians after the war, however, was bound up with questions of national identity and citizenship, and the welfare state quickly became a site in which post-imperial anxieties about race were played out.

Inside the Welfare State, therefore, focuses on welfare distribution between 1948 and 1965, a period when its development was free of the pressures of high unemployment and economic decline that would become so determinative later. The practice of welfare in these years was shaped not by economic crisis, but by the conflict between the state's promise to provide universal social citizenship and the state's interest in protecting certain gendered dependencies and obligations that might be undermined by government assistance. Welfare administration was also influenced by the reluctance to extend full citizenship to black and Asian immigrants. Post-war social policy developed in a context of ambitious promises from politicians, matched by the high expectations of the public. The war had intensified the popular belief that collective betterment could be achieved through government, that the state had a responsibility to promote and protect the well-being of its citizens. Public enthusiasm for this general notion was just as important in institutionalizing the welfare state as support for particular programs. In the first two decades of the post-war welfare state's existence, the public took to heart the rhetoric surrounding the new programs. People embraced a range of services and benefits as rights to which they were entitled—health care, higher levels of education, pensions, benefits for unemployment, sickness, and maternity.[23] Politicians recognized the electorate's strong attachment to the welfare state and acted accordingly. Peter Thorneycroft's resignation as Chancellor in 1958, precipitated by his attempts to curb social spending, demonstrates the seriousness with which governments took the public's commitment to the welfare state.

Ian Gough, drawing on the theory of Antonio Gramsci, argues that a crucial function of the British welfare state has been to provide "legitimation" of the social relations of a capitalist society by relieving its worst abuses and by creating an atmosphere of social justice.[24] The post-war welfare state performed this task admirably, generating rhetoric (but not the reality) of universalism, hopes for raised living standards, and promises of the destigmatization of state aid. The "social wage," as it would later be called, added the fruits of an integrated welfare state—health care, social security, better housing and education—to earnings from employment. The costs of social well-being were partially collectivized, thereby reducing the hardships that arose from the inequalities of capitalism. The possibilities of welfare, though, have been limited by another necessary function of the state—the protection of capitalist accumulation. The tension between maintenance of the economic *status quo* and progressive reform has created problems in defining the mission of the welfare state. This tension was particularly evident in the 1970s and 1980s, when economic decline made it increasingly difficult to maintain the spiraling cost of social services while assuring significant profits in the private sector. The task for policymakers and administrators has been to maintain a balance between public demands for social provision and the smooth functioning of the capitalist economy.

The accommodation of capitalist production, however, was not the only structural constraint built into the welfare state. The design of post-war welfare, like the various systems of relief and insurance that preceded it, reinforced and perpetuated women's economic dependence within families and their disadvantaged position in the labor market. The confirmation of men's obligations as breadwinners and women's special role as keepers of the home was expressed unequivocally by Beveridge and echoed in the basic terms of welfare state legislation, which, for the most part, made national insurance and national assistance available to married women only as dependents of their husbands. But the patriarchal imperatives of welfare, like the capitalist ones, ran up against the broadly legitimating character of the new welfare state. In contrast to the relief systems in place before the war, inextricably linked in popular memory with the means test and humiliation, the post-war settlement celebrated social rights and common citizenship. These general themes, ubiquitous in the government's promotion of the post-war settlement, were not articulated in gender-specific terms, but instead stressed destigmatization and universality. It was possible, then, for women and men to make claims on the welfare state after the war that were inconsistent with the gendered roles and responsibilities envisioned by its architects and administrators. The decisions and practices regarding these unanticipated and unwelcome claims reveal how deeply gender was embedded in the ongoing processes of welfare-state formation.

Claims on the welfare state by black and Asian immigrants were similarly unanticipated and unwelcome. As the number of non-white British residents grew during the 1950s, so did opposition to their presence. In debates about immigration from the colonies and the Commonwealth, the new British welfare state was cast as a magnet that drew immigrants to the United Kingdom. Black and Asian British subjects were not viewed as real Britons entitled to the full benefits of citizenship, especially the social citizenship of the welfare state. Moreover, the unsubstantiated but common belief that these newcomers took advantage of the welfare system led to practices that discriminated against many Africans, Indians, Pakistanis, and West Indians who turned to the state for assistance.

The practice of welfare provision was, therefore, in a state of flux in the 1950s and 1960s, as officials sought to reconcile the new welfare state's message of unqualified inclusion with the deeply ingrained norms that militated against providing state aid to men of working age, to women who had even a tenuous connection to a male wage-earner, or to non-whites who did not have an authentic "British" identity. Local and central government officials were simply unprepared for the claims of various groups of poor people—lone mothers, unemployed men not supporting their dependents, "coloured" immigrants, and homeless families—who, in one way or another, had violated gender or racial norms and were therefore not desirable recipients of the state's largesse. The task of administering welfare was further complicated by the dramatic increase in the number of women in paid employment after the war, a development unanticipated by Beveridge or those who enacted welfare legislation. Since national insurance had been promised as a reward for wage-earners, officials had to determine the conditions under which employed women would have access to its benefits. By the mid-1960s, clear patterns in practice and policy had emerged, both in national insurance and means-tested programs. The patterns did not arise from party politics; rather, the trends began in the Labour government of 1945–1951, moved through the Conservative governments of 1951–1964, and continued in the first years of the Labour government that came to power in 1964.

In various contexts, the government maintained its affirmation of women's primary role as capable domestic workers who should be dependent, for the most part, on male wage-earning. This had been the premise of the Beveridge's conception of national insurance and the organizing principle of post-war social security. However, officials also adjusted their policies to take account of the benefits married women could provide for the labor market in an expanding economy. Upper-level officials, for example, began to see unemployment benefit as a means of rewarding married women who tried to combine domestic and part-time paid labor. Because there was usually a wage-earning husband in the home, payment of unemployment benefit to an insured woman for a limited period did not compromise the male breadwinner principle. The government was far less comfortable, though, providing open-ended assistance to women with children who turned to the government because they had no other source of income, and it went to great lengths to redirect their claims for support.

As a matter of both ideology and policy, women's dependence was intertwined with men's independence. This binary opposition meant that policies encouraging women to rely on men only made sense if other policies insisted on men's reliability as wage-earners. Officials tried to limit governmental responsibility for the maintenance of poor women who did not have the support of a male breadwinner as much as possible, while also restricting the state's long-term obligations to poor unemployed men and their families.[25] By turning obligations of support away from the state and toward individual men, the welfare state not only maintained work incentives for men, but also reaffirmed the traditional family economy.

The early post-war period is notable for the innovative and wide-ranging, though often unsuccessful, methods employed in pursuit of these goals. Fusing the rationales of the Poor Law and the technologies of the modern bureaucratic state, various government branches used rewards, rehabilitation, training, expertise, surveillance, litigation, and threats to shape behavior and conduct. These efforts were intended to instill or reinforce appropriately gendered standards of domesticity and breadwinning, as well as curtail the state's role in providing cash benefits and other support to non-white immigrants. The emphasis on retrenchment undermined the message of universality and inclusion that had led undesirable constituents to the welfare state in the first place. Because of this conflict between rhetoric and practice, deterrence was an increasingly valued commodity in the economy of welfare distribution in the 1950s and 1960s: if unwelcome claimants voluntarily chose to forego or abandon their claims, the government could maintain that they did so because they did not need the state's help. The fragile illusion of consensus and fulfilled need that protected the welfare state's legitimacy could be preserved, temporarily at least. This illusion was subsequently shattered, however, first from the left in the 1960s—in the form of the rediscovery of poverty—and then from the right in the 1980s—with the claim that the welfare state created the need it served. In the 1980s and 1990s, when fiscal and political pressures altered the terms of discourse about welfare, the kind of legitimation it required changed entirely, and the harsh realities of practice no longer needed to be obscured. The coercive features of welfare distribution that had been established early on were intensified and openly displayed as important objectives of social policy.

To sort out the early post-war welfare state's efforts to define women's and men's roles in families and the labor market, *Inside the Welfare State* begins with national insurance—the centerpiece of social security in the new welfare state that provided retirement pensions, unemployment benefit, and sickness benefit for eligible workers. Chapter 1 investigates the government's responses to the dramatic rise in women's employment in the 1950s and 1960s, a phenomenon that raised issues concerning national insurance that had not been anticipated by Beveridge or the members of Parliament who passed the National Insurance Act in 1946. In the 1950s, the government made national insurance more exclusive by declaring part-time employees working fewer than eight hours a week, most of whom were women, ineligible for coverage. Government officials and employers agreed that the women affected by the policy change were dependent on men and therefore did not need to be insured. Women's access to the social citizenship offered by national insurance was thus restricted by assumptions about their peripheral role in family economies. An analysis of the approximately 1,500 contested claims for unemployment benefit in the London area between 1948 and 1963 shows that lower level officers viewed married women's claims for unemployment benefit with suspicion. At the higher levels of officialdom, however, the 1950s and 1960s saw an increased willingness to grant unemployment benefit to insured women whose commitment to domestic responsibilities interfered with employment opportunities. Responding to a changing labor market that increasingly relied on the employment of married women, the deputy commissioners who adjudicated claims for benefit rewarded women who not only entered the labor force, but also demonstrated that obligations to husband and family were paramount. The dominant themes in the deputy commissioners' decisions on men's claims were quite different. Men were far more likely than women to leave or refuse jobs because of poor pay or conditions, and the deputy commissioners were unwilling to give legitimacy to such complaints by awarding full benefits.

Chapter 2 assesses efforts to constrain the growth of the welfare state by considering the national assistance program, which faced a dramatic increase in the number of lone women (separated and divorced women and unmarried mothers) applying for means-tested assistance in the 1950s and 1960s. Officials at the National Assistance Board (NAB) were surprised and dismayed that such women would turn to the state for aid. Administrators devised various forms of persuasion, coercion, and intimidation to compel women to look to estranged husbands, cohabitees, or, in some cases, other family members, for support. The NAB invoked legal principles from the Poor Law and tried to extend the reach of family law precedents in order to force men to support estranged spouses. Officials were unable, however, to stem the tide of women who sought assistance.

Chapter 3 considers unemployed men's claims for means-tested assistance. For fiscal and ideological reasons, the NAB placed great emphasis on discouraging men with families from lingering on the national assistance rolls. In the 1950s and 1960s, the NAB developed several techniques to keep men of working age off assistance, combining old Poor Law tactics and new measures of the bureaucratic state to shore up masculinity. Programs to instill discipline and respectability did little to improve employment rates among the men, many of whom had physical and/or mental disabilities. The programs were effective, though, in deterring men from applying for assistance. Deterrence became a central objective in social policy.

Chapter 4 explores the ways in which the welfare state constituted different forms of social citizenship for black and Asian immigrants. Unfounded fears that immigrants abused national assistance fueled the drive to restrict immigration, and also caused NAB officials to treat "coloured" applicants as a separate class requiring additional monitoring and different conditions of assistance. NAB administrators encouraged immigrants who were seen as a burden on public funds to return home. They restricted rent allowances in ways not employed when dealing with whites. And they kept a particularly close watch on unmarried black women who received assistance.

Chapter 5 examines temporary housing for the homeless in London after the Second World War. The London County Council conditioned the provision of temporary accommodation for poor families on respectability, focusing on the domestic practices of women and the work ethic of men. In the late 1940s, the London County Council implemented programs to train and rehabilitate "problem families." Mother and baby homes, usually run by voluntary organizations, also supplied temporary housing for unmarried mothers; there, too, the focus was on rehabilitation and domestic training. The supply of temporary housing for homeless unemployed men, low on the list of the welfare state's priorities, contracted during the 1950s and 1960s. The NAB gradually closed its facilities for male vagrants, and the supply of private lodging houses dwindled.

The Epilogue places the developments of the 1950s and 1960s in a broader perspective, linking them to the attitudes and policies of both the Conservative governments of the 1980s and early 1990s and the two Labour governments that followed. Ironically, the very state that Margaret Thatcher was so determined to "roll back" in the 1980s had institutionalized some of her most cherished values thirty years earlier. And despite the fact that, in the 1980s, the Labour Party roundly criticized Conservative attempts to dismantle the welfare state, since coming to power in 1997, Labour leaders have embraced the essence of Conservative claims, although wrapping them in gentler rhetoric. Redemption of the welfare state, says New Labour, lies in persuading individuals to meet more of their own needs by relying on the labor market and their families. Though it has been politically expedient for Tony Blair and Gordon Brown to treat this approach as a break with the past—just as the New Right did—these principles have been at the very core of the post-war welfare state since its inception. Although not acknowledged by New Labour, the techniques for achieving their goals for the welfare state owe a great deal to the methods employed in the 1940s, 1950s, and 1960s.

The demands placed on the diverse branches of the welfare state in the 1950s and 1960s were an unintended consequence of its post-war refashioning. Officials responded by trying to enforce gender roles that allowed some room for women's participation in the post-war economy, but primarily emphasized women's domesticity and dependence and men's wage earning. Exaggerated fears of black and Asian reliance on welfare benefits produced restrictive conditions on their access to assistance. The continuing process of building a welfare state, of determining when and how to provide aid, cemented gender and race into the practice of welfare.

1 Limits and Possibilities of Social Citizenship

The Gendered Boundaries of National Insurance and Unemployment Benefit

In its 1951 election manifesto, the Labour Party congratulated itself on the extension of social security, through the National Insurance Act of 1946, to all British citizens. Juxtaposing the post-war welfare state against the inadequate social policies of the 1930s, Labour basked in the glow of its revolutionary achievement:

> [In the inter-war years] millions suffered from insecurity and want. Now we have social security for every man, woman and child....Now we have a national insurance system covering the whole population. . . . [1]

Such characterizations of national insurance—as a universal, comprehensive system that would protect all British citizens against loss of income—predominated in the optimistic political climate of the 1940s and 1950s. Some historians have echoed the Labour Party's assessment, with Peter Baldwin going so far as to describe the expansion of state welfare after the war as "an historic event equivalent in importance and stature to the French and Russian Revolutions."[2] Rodney Lowe contends that the national insurance system that emerged after the war:

> transformed the fundamental nature of the relationship between the state and its citizens. . . . For the first time in history *all* citizens were to be insured 'from the cradle to the grave' against *every* eventuality which might lead to the inadvertent loss of their income.[3]

As has been pointed out by other scholars, however, the citizenship that accompanied national insurance was far from universal. It could only be secured through fairly regular employment, which meant that many women could not participate. National insurance was for wage-earners, and women who did not have paid work could only benefit as dependents of their husbands, not in their own right. Female dependency on male breadwinners was thus reinforced, and many women experienced the much-touted citizenship in post-war national insurance only derivatively, if at all.[4] This assessment, which focuses on the basic terms of the National Insurance Act of 1946, certainly captures the negative effect of a wage-based social security system on women as a group. Less attention has been paid, however, to the prospects of *employed* women—particularly married women—in the newly restructured welfare state. On what terms were working women covered by national insurance, and, if insured, on what terms were they granted benefits?

In this chapter, I focus on employed women's eligibility for national insurance and their claims for one of its primary rewards, unemployment benefit. Defining women's rights in the new welfare state was an ongoing, dynamic process that grew out of the shifting policies and practices of the officials who administered benefit programs. After the war, economic growth and increased female labor force participation changed the context in which policymakers determined the conditions under which working women participated in and benefited from the welfare state. Officials continually assessed the meaning and value of women's employment: they rewarded work they deemed as significant with insured status and refused to insure work they considered marginal. The results for women were mixed. After 1946, more and more women found themselves uninsured, but insured women found that some of the barriers to claiming benefits during unemployment gradually eroded.

GENDER AND UNEMPLOYMENT BEFORE WORLD WAR II

Aid for the unemployed has been provided by charities, churches, friendly and other mutual aid societies, and trade unions. Until the early twentieth century, however, poor relief administered by local authorities was the only governmental remedy for the hardships caused by unemployment. The Poor Law guardians had far-reaching discretion in deciding who deserved aid, and in the nineteenth century, the conventions of Victorian morality weighed heavily on their choices. Unemployment tended to be seen as an individual failing, rather than an unavoidable feature of a capitalist economy, and those dispensing relief were often reluctant to subsidize what they viewed as idleness. However, by the early twentieth century, these attitudes softened as policymakers began to see unemployment as a structural, social problem that required a coordinated response from the state. The 1911 Unemployment Insurance Act marked the first attempt by the national government to address the problem of unemployment in a systematic fashion.[5] The scheme required the workers it covered to make weekly, flat-rate contributions to the insurance fund, contributions that were matched by employers and the government. When unemployed, those workers could draw a flat-rate benefit (all received the same weekly benefit, regardless of their previous wages). But the 1911 Act created a selective system that covered only 2.25 million workers. State-sponsored unemployment insurance offered protections to employees in a few trades in which unemployment was thought to be temporary and relatively predictable; trades character-ized by cyclical unemployment.

Despite the narrowness of coverage, the 1911 Act has been hailed as an important first step in the evolution of the welfare state, significant because "the national Government of Great Britain entered for the first time the life of the ordinary, adult, male able-bodied workman."[6] The Act's focus on male workers was not controversial or even noteworthy to contempo-raries, nor has it been the subject of discussion in much of the literature on the British welfare state. From the inception of unemployment insurance, its intended beneficiaries were male breadwinners; accordingly, the 1911 Act excluded trades in which large numbers of women were employed. [7] Between 1911 and the Second World War, the scope of unemployment insurance expanded to include more and more workers, but the under-standing that benefits were primarily for men remained a constant theme in policy and practice.

The gendering of unemployment benefit continued in the economic dis-locations that followed World War I. After the war, social policy worked in tandem with the labor market to marginalize women's positions as paid workers and ensure their dependence within families. In 1919, thou-sands of displaced female workers lost the "out-of-work donation" pro-vided to former war-industry workers because they refused low-paying jobs in laundry work or domestic service. Officials reasoned that these women should be penalized for refusing "suitable work," a rationale that rarely surfaced in the consideration of men's cases. Throughout the 1920s and 1930s, women applying for unemployment benefit could be forced to undergo training in domestic service. Women found their claims for ben-efit denied at a much higher rate than men's, and these practices severely undermined women's ability to claim unemployment in their own right as workers.[8] The overall effect of the unemployment insurance scheme, which, by the early 1920s, included dependents' allowances, was to ben-efit women (even those who had been wage-earners) only indirectly, as dependents of their husbands.[9]

Though industrial needs during World War I had allowed women to break into male jobs, employers and trade unions quickly re-established the sexual division of paid work after the war. In addition, the "marriage bar" to female employment persisted throughout the 1920s in many areas and in many industries, often with governmental and union sup-port.[10] Many employers either refused to employ married women or fired them first, regardless of seniority. Women's employment, viewed through the lens of the male breadwinner norm, was seen as marginal, and was certainly not a priority in unemployment relief policy.[11] Throughout the 1920s, women, far more often than men, were disqualified from receiv-ing benefits because they were not "genuinely seeking work." A woman could not possibly want a job, insurance officers claimed, if her husband was employed.[12]

The economic depression of the late 1920s and 1930s strained the unemployment insurance system almost to the breaking point, which compounded the difficulties women faced in claiming benefits. When pressure on the unemployment insurance fund triggered a scramble to cut costs, married women's benefits were the first target. After an investigation by a Royal Commission, Parliament passed the Anomalies Act of 1931, which formalized and intensified the discriminatory treatment married women had received since the First World War. Under the 1931 Act, married women had to prove not only that they were actively seeking work, but that local industries regularly hired married women. Accordingly, a woman who had worked and made compulsory contributions to the insurance fund, but lost her job when she married, was likely to face an uphill battle in trying to claim benefit. For local insurance officials, employers' discrimination against married women constituted proof that they were unemployable. Those women who did not have a "reasonable expectation" of finding work were denied benefit. Because of the Anomalies Act, 48% of women's claims were denied in the last quarter of 1931, as compared to 4% of men's.[13] Governments of the 1930s were reluctant to treat married women as citizens who had legitimate claims on unemployment funds.[14]

Men did not face the insurmountable obstacles of the Anomalies Act, but they did have to deal, as women did, with the despised means test. The 1934 Unemployment Act imposed a household (rather than an individual) means test on the long-term unemployed. If the total household income was considered to be adequate for subsistence, an unemployed individual could not receive benefit. Officials' intrusive and demeaning investigations of household finances became infamous in the 1930s, as did the poverty that was exacerbated by the denial of claims. The ineffective relief of unemployment in the 1930s was seared into popular memory, symbolized by the humiliated male breadwinner who was reduced to dependence on family members, even children.[15] J. B. Priestly's 1934 description of the crisis of working-class masculinity wrought by unemployment was typical of contemporary accounts: unemployed men "felt defeated and somehow tainted. Their self-respect was shredding away. Their very manhood was going."[16] The benefit rate was about half the value of the average wage, so that even those who received unemployment benefit lived at or near the poverty line.[17]

The hardships of the 1930s were to have a tremendous impact on the reshaping of the welfare state after World War II. The widely held conviction that the unemployed had been treated badly made a more effective, less stigmatizing system of social security a political necessity. The willingness of the electorate and politicians to allow an increased role for the state in the provision of social security also grew out of the experience of the war itself. Domestic and social issues had been tabled, for the most part, in order to secure a military victory, and the deprivations of the war left a craving for security and a renewed appreciation of the virtues of mutual aid. Politicians of both parties realized the nation was ready to turn its attention inward. The war had also accustomed the public to unprecedented governmental involvement in innumerable features of everyday life. From economic central planning to food rationing to civilian defense, the state was a ubiquitous presence; thus, the notion of a greatly expanded network of government agencies to deal with health and welfare was not as alarming as it might previously have been.

THE BEVERIDGE REPORT'S INFLUENCE
ON NATIONAL INSURANCE

Even during the war, the coalition government began exploring the possibilities for a comprehensive scheme of social security that would prevent the poverty caused by unemployment, illness, disability, and old age. In 1942, an interdepartmental committee issued the famous Beveridge Report (named for committee chairman William Beveridge), which would become the blueprint for the post-war welfare state.[18] Beveridge described the report's proposal for social security as "a plan to win freedom from want by maintaining incomes."[19] His concept of the relationship between the state and its citizens was crucial in the ideological grounding of post-war social policy.

The Beveridge Report's plan for social insurance was translated, in modified form, into legislation in the National Insurance Act of 1946. The Act integrated various insurance-based benefits into one system that would be funded by contributions from employees, employers, and the government. National insurance occupied a privileged place in the new welfare state because its benefits were not accompanied by demeaning inquiries to verify need. The new scheme operated on the same principle as prior unemployment insurance arrangements, but it extended coverage, in theory, to all workers (previously only certain trades and certain income levels had been covered). In addition, by virtue of their contributions through employment, insured workers would enjoy sickness, old age, and maternity benefits as well. The Beveridge Report's implicit linking of citizenship and welfare state rights—particularly participation in national insurance—reflected the popular sentiment that the state should act to ensure the security of its people. Mass-Observation surveys in the 1940s revealed a widely held belief that misfortunes such as unemployment were not the result of individual failings, and that the state was obliged to provide relief, "not as a favour but as a *right*."[20]

The necessary inclusion of welfare rights in citizenship also found theoretical expression in the work of prominent academics in the 1940s and 1950s. In 1949, influential social policy scholar, T. H. Marshall, outlined a theory of modern citizenship that focused on social rights. Citizenship in the twentieth century, Marshall argued, was dependent on the extension of welfare rights that derived from the state. These rights had intrinsic value in providing social security, but were also necessary for the meaningful exercise of civil and political rights.[21] The notion of social citizenship in the welfare state centered on national insurance, which posited a contract of mutual obligation between the state and it citizens. "Social security," Beveridge insisted, "must be achieved by co-operation between the State and the individual. The State should offer security for service and contribution."[22] Workers secured their rights through mandatory contributions to the insurance fund. In return, national insurance supplied benefits for wage-earners who lost income because of unemployment, sickness, or old age.

Despite the implication that the right to participate in national insurance was open to all citizens, the terms and conditions of social citizenship were, in fact, determined by sex and marital status.[23] The Beveridge Report, on which the 1946 National Insurance Act was based, had proposed drastic limitations on married women's direct participation in national insurance. Beveridge reasoned that the vast majority of married women did not need insurance against loss of income because they did not earn wages. Extrapolating from the 1931 census, Beveridge estimated that only one in seven married women engaged in paid work in 1941. Even employed women did not need to be insured against wage loss, he contended, because their earnings were not required for the family's subsistence. In times of unemployment, a married woman could always rely on her husband's earnings or his benefit if his earnings had been interrupted. Beveridge observed that social practice and law prescribed women's dependence; social policy, he concluded, operated most effectively by reinforcing those arrangements. "All women by marriage acquire a new economic and social status, with risks and rights different from the unmarried," Beveridge wrote. "On marriage a woman gains a legal right to maintenance by her husband . . . she undertakes at the same time to perform vital unpaid service."[24] Married women were primarily domestic workers, not wage-earners; therefore, they should not share men's direct connection to the welfare state. This thinking mirrored the rationale behind the punitive unemployment insurance policies of the 1920s and 1930s—that is, that women should be supported by their husbands rather than the state in times of unemployment.

Beveridge contended that the basic structure of national insurance should reflect marital dependencies; he thus proposed that married women earning wages be given the option not to participate in national insurance. The National Insurance Act included this provision. This was a departure from previous schemes, which had required married women's participation. Married women who did choose to participate, he added, should receive lower benefits than other workers. The Trades Union Congress (TUC) was, on the whole, satisfied with Beveridge's plan for national insurance, and it voiced no objection to married women's marginalized position in the proposed scheme.[25] Concerned with protecting the interests of its predominantly male constituency, the TUC had consistently objected to social policies, such as generous family allowances, that might undermine workers' claim for a family wage from employers.[26] The structure of Beveridge's national insurance, which designated the male breadwinner as the family's wage-earner and the recipient of government benefits for income loss, did not disturb the foundation of the family wage on which the labor movement relied, and therefore, TUC leaders were happy to lend their support to Beveridge's plan.

The National Council of Women voiced the only strong dissent to the Beveridge Report's proposal for married women. Noting that the plan made married women second-class citizens in the welfare state, the Council argued that discrimination based on marital status subverted any possibility of women's economic equality and independence.[27] Their vehement objections, however, fell on deaf ears. Civil servants and members of Parliament, well aware that the Report's treatment of married women would provoke no serious political opposition, ignored the Council's complaints. Discussions among civil servants between 1943 and 1946 indicated that many wanted to remove married women from national insurance altogether. Such an outright exclusion was thought to be "politically impracticable,"[28] however, and did not appear in the final legislation.

GENDERED EFFECTS OF THE BEVERIDGE REPORT AND THE NATIONAL INSURANCE ACT

Allowing married women to opt out of national insurance fundamentally altered their relationship to the welfare state. Though cast in both the Beveridge Report and the 1946 Act as a favorable concession, optional participation for married women had significant symbolic and practical disadvantages. Symbolically, making married women's participation optional placed them outside the boundaries of an insurance scheme purportedly based on universal, compulsory participation and social solidarity. Moreover, their financial dependence on their husbands during periods of unemployment was reinforced. In the early 1950s, about 60% of employed married women who otherwise would have been eligible for national insurance opted out.[29] By 1962, two-thirds of the 4.5 million married women who worked opted out of national insurance.[30] Opting out meant that the flat-rate weekly contribution was avoided, not a small consideration for low-wage workers. A woman's weekly insurance contribution was just under 6 shillings (s.): about one-seventh of what she would earn working a 20-hour week (just over £2) in a typical department store in the West End of London.[31] The decision to opt out was not so much a rejection of welfare state protections as it was a sign of the more immediate need for a larger wage packet, an imperative that undoubtedly would have caused many other workers, particularly low-wage-earners, to opt out of the scheme had they been given the choice.

A welfare state that, in theory, universally rewarded employment with national insurance, was, in practice, a much more complicated and stratified system based on the mandatory inclusion of some workers and the marginalization of others. The process of marginalization was highly gendered, as it was usually women who were identified as the workers who did not require welfare state protections.[32] Ironically, as the post-war welfare state was taking shape, women were becoming more numerous and visible in the labor market. Contrary to Beveridge's expectations, married women's employment expanded dramatically and continuously throughout the 1950s. Whereas only one in eight married women had worked in 1931, by 1951 one in four (a total of three million) did. By 1957, almost four million married women—nearly one-third of all married women—were employed.[33] The proportion of married women who worked continued to increase in the 1960s; in 1965, about 45% of married women were employed.[34]

For the most part, married women worked to keep their families out of poverty or to maintain a reasonable standard of living. In Viola Klein's 1957 survey of employed married women, 73% of the women interviewed indicated that they took on employment primarily for financial reasons. The motivation of economic necessity was most evident among working-class women. Of employed women married to manual laborers (both skilled and unskilled), 79% worked primarily to provide needed income.[35] Women's paid work, then, was important in the family economy, as maintenance of a stable standard of living depended on women's wages. For some, earnings warded off abject poverty. For others, maintaining a "proper" standard of living—always a relative concept—required wages from both husband and wife. Because of the relaxation of war-time rationing and the increased availability of mass-produced consumer goods, what previously had been luxuries became necessities in the 1950s. Two-income families were able to buy more furniture, rent a larger flat, or perhaps purchase a car. More money was required to live, and women's wages were essential. Beveridge had contended that married women's earnings were superfluous and therefore did not need to be covered by national insurance. However, the family economy of the 1950s belied that notion, as married women worked to sustain a decent standard of living.

Employers and policymakers alike agreed that, given the choice, married women would opt out of insurance. Many women were undoubtedly relieved not to have their already meager wages reduced by an insurance contribution. Still, many married women were eager to be insured, acutely aware that the equilibrium of the household budget depended on protection of their wages. Overall, a full 40% of married women, hardly an insignificant minority, did choose to participate in national insurance in the early 1950s.[36] The desire for insurance protection was not confined to full-time workers or high wage-earners. A woman in South London, for example, earned only £2 a week assisting her husband, who was the manager of a pub. She expected to have national insurance coverage, but Carlos & Thrale, the pub's owner, refused to include her among its insured employees. The company claimed that its contract of service was only with her husband and that she was therefore not a company employee eligible for national insurance. The woman fought the denial of coverage, appealing to the local national insurance officer for help. Because of its implications for a large class of "pub-wives," the case made its way to the upper reaches of the Ministry of National Insurance. In the meantime, Carlos & Thrale successfully pressured the woman to withdraw the appeal. The company's representative reported to the Ministry that she had "realized" that she was not employed by the company and wished to proceed no further with the claim.[37] In a similar case, Doris Bolton, who sewed garments at home, was denied national insurance coverage because the firm she worked for claimed she was not an employee with a contract of service. Like Carlos & Thrale, the company wanted to avoid paying national insurance contributions. Bolton contested the denial, but was unsuccessful.[38] Although employers stymied the claims of both of these women, their pursuit of national insurance suggests that its protections were not, as Beveridge and other policymakers assumed, irrelevant to married women.

PART-TIME WORK: INSURABLE OR INSIGNIFICANT?

Much of the growth in married women's employment was in part-time work. In 1951, about 25% of married women workers worked part-time (between four and thirty hours per week), and by 1957, between 40% and 50% worked part-time.[39] This development gave rise to new debates over who should benefit from national insurance. How much paid employment was required to make someone a first-class citizen in the welfare state? And, more generally, how should social policy be used to accommodate the needs of capital in a tight labor market? Under the initial regulations implementing the National Insurance Act of 1946, employees who worked fewer than four hours per week were excluded from national insurance because their employment was deemed "insignificant." Employees in cleaning or domestic services and those providing school meals, nearly all of whom were women, had to work eight hours per week to be eligible for national insurance. In a sustained lobbying campaign that spanned most of the 1950s, employers sought to expand the "insignificant employment" exception. Their objective, of course, was to cut costs. In addition to money supplied by general government funds and contributions from employees, national insurance was also funded by flat-rate contributions from employers. Whether an employee worked four hours per week or forty, the employer's contribution was the same.[40] In the early 1950s, various employer associations began to complain to government officials about their responsibility for insurance contributions for part-timers. The debate that ensued rapidly became an argument about women working in the post-war economy and their accompanying rights in the welfare state.

Married women constituted the vast majority of part-time workers in the 1950s and 1960s. In 1951, 95% of the 798,000 part-time employees were women, and of the female part-timers, 90% were married.[41] Part-time employment was most available in domestic service, office cleaning, and school and factory canteens.[42] But it was not limited to these areas. Part-time work spread across a range of industries, and provided labor necessary for a broad-based economic expansion. A survey of 120 employers in diverse businesses showed that all but fourteen of them used part-time employees in 1957. Shortages of full-time labor forced some employers to hire part-timers, while others, faced with fluctuating demand, depended on part-time labor to expand their workforces during peak periods.[43] Women worked part-time in clerical positions, in shops, and on the factory floor, where night shifts were fairly common. Though women worked part-time in many different settings, most of this work was unskilled and poorly paid: In 1957, two-thirds of part-timers held unskilled positions.[44]

Government officials from both the Ministry of Labour and the Ministry of National Insurance encouraged the employment of married women, emphasizing the desirability of part-time work that would not interfere with domestic responsibilities. It seemed to be the perfect solution to the labor shortage, a strategy that preserved domestic ideology but created space for redefined work roles. Married women could work without disruption of their duties at home, and employers could expand their businesses with the new-found pool of labor. To promote the hiring of married women, the government orchestrated conferences on the use of part-time labor and published testimonials of employers extolling the virtues of the part-time worker.[45] At the same time, a body of social scientific literature was emerging that examined the compatibility of employment and domestic responsibility for women. Alva Myrdal's and Viola Klein's 1956 book, *Women's Two Roles*, reported favorably on married women's employment:

> The pioneering days [of choosing between work and family] are now over. With them has gone the need for women to make a fatal decision between irreconcilable alternatives. The Gordian knot of a seemingly insoluble feminine dilemma has been cut. The technical and social developments of the last few decades have given women the opportunity to combine and to integrate their two interests in Home and Work.[46]

Married women were entering the labor force in record numbers, but employers continued to subject them to various forms of discrimination. Many firms were reluctant to promote married women, and managers were quite candid about the barriers to advancement in the 1950s. A representative of a company making scientific industrial instruments, for example, acknowledged that "promotion [of married women] would only be considered in exceptional circumstances." A manufacturer of electrical appliances noted that "promotion occurs infrequently," and a manager at a motor vehicle accessories plant stated categorically that "there is no opportunity for promotion to supervisory jobs for any women."[47] Employers routinely imposed additional requirements on women's participation in pension plans (e.g., additional years of service), and married women were sometimes excluded altogether. Additionally, in times of redundancy, married women were terminated first.[48] Part-timers were viewed as a distinct, and inferior, class of workers, employees "not really belonging to the regular establishment."[49]

Employers took advantage of women's part-time labor, but complained loudly about the cost of national insurance contributions. Employer associations hoped that the government might succumb to pressure to remove part-time work from the umbrella of national insurance altogether. Searching for weaknesses in the commitment to national insurance, employers astutely identified married women's labor as the area in which governmental concessions were most likely to be won. The employers' strategy was made possible by the government's own position that, though married women should be encouraged to work, they did not really need national insurance. The Ministry of Labour received more complaints from employers about their insurance contributions for part-time work than any other aspect of the national insurance scheme.[50] Employers paid contributions for all workers, even married women who opted out of national insurance. The cost of the national insurance contribution for part-time workers, employers argued, was out of proportion to the value of the services rendered: two half-time workers cost an employer twice as much in insurance contributions as one full-time employee.

The British Employers' Confederation proposed that employees working fewer than twelve hours be removed from the national insurance scheme and that the employer contribution be halved for those working between twelve and twenty-three hours per week. Other employer groups representing the sectors using part-time labor most heavily (retail, distributive, and service trades) made similar proposals.[51] Employers claimed that if their grievances were not addressed, they would stop hiring part-time workers and slow the economic boom. They also reassured officials that no one who actually needed national insurance would suffer as a result of being deprived of it. The vast majority of part-time workers, after all, were married women "for whom there was no question of hardship."[52]

Twenty percent of employees in the retail industry were part-timers, and retailers were especially aggressive in pressing their case. A representative of the Retail Distributive Trades Conference told the National Insurance Advisory Committee (NIAC) that national insurance contributions significantly deterred the hiring of part-time workers. If the burden on employers was relieved, he claimed, more part-timers would be hired and retail prices would fall.[53] London retailers, like many around the country, had come to rely on part-time workers for the peak shopping times—the lunchtime rush and Saturdays. Most were married women who were not able to accept full-time work. The personnel manager for Marks & Spencer in London told the NIAC that between 35% and 55% of all sales were made on Saturdays, which gave rise to a separate "Saturday staff," of married women, who, he claimed, had "no interest in their own personal insurability."[54] Private agencies providing part-time clerical labor joined the chorus of opposition to national insurance coverage for part-timers. Married women, they claimed, recoiled from the formalities of national insurance; the fear of endless forms and other bureaucratic intrusions, it was argued, deterred many women from working at all.[55] The squeamishness clerical agencies ascribed to married women, however, was misplaced. Married women, if they wished, could avoid all contributions and paperwork simply by opting out of national insurance. The placement agencies' real concern, it seems, had more to do with their client employers' aversion to the expense and bureaucracy than with the lack of sophistication of the women involved. Still, their claims about what women wanted contributed to the consensus in both governmental and business circles that women did not need national insurance.

Even the largest organization of trade unions, the TUC, agreed in principle that "marginal employments" should not be insured, but contended that the cut-off should be an eight-hour work week. Douglas Houghton, Member of Parliament and leader of the TUC delegation, assured the NIAC that employees who worked only a few hours per week did not rely on their earnings, nor did they want to be insured. He insisted, however, on the necessity of maintaining the insurance status of workers who might be dependent on wages. To be on the safe side, he asserted, anyone working more than eight hours per week should be covered.[56]

Leaders of middle-class women's organizations, steadfast in their belief that full-time work was inappropriate for mothers, considered part-time work the perfect accommodation of domestic duties and paid employment. Consequently, their primary objective in trying to influence national insurance policy was to maximize the part-time employment opportunities for married women. They took seriously the warnings from employers that without relief of their national insurance burden, part-time employment would stagnate or decline. In October 1957, the National Council of Women cited "the undesirability of the full-time employment of mothers of young children, the shortage of labor in certain occupations and the reluctance of employers to use part-time workers" as compelling reasons to ease the national insurance burden on employers who used part-timers. Both the National Council of Women and the British Federation of University Women lobbied the NIAC for a relaxation of the insurance requirements imposed on employers for part-time workers.[57]

From the beginning of the campaign to lighten contribution requirements for employers, government officials were skeptical about the dire
predictions of the employer lobby. After conferring with their local and
regional officials, top-ranking civil servants at the Ministry of Labour concluded that employers' national insurance contributions had very little, if
any, deterrent effect on part-time employment. Employers were hiring part-
timers steadily, out of necessity rather than choice. In some industries, such
as the Yorkshire textiles, filling out the labor force with part-time workers
was viewed as a temporary expedient in a time of labor scarcity. In other
businesses, such as shops and cleaning services, the use of part-time workers was a permanent and acceptable situation. In either case, relatively full
employment in the 1950s meant that employers were forced to rely on the
part-time labor of women. In addition, national insurance contributions
were not the only problem associated with part-time employees—there
were internal administrative and organizational difficulties as well. Apart
from having to pay insurance contributions, employers had to adjust sched-
uling to accommodate part-time workers. So although use of part-time
labor caused problems for many employers, they had no real alternative.
Economic expansion proceeded apace, and the labor market continued to
reach into previously untapped sectors of the population. Government officials, cognizant of this economic reality, focused on the consistent growth
of married women's employment. At the February 1957 meeting of the
NIAC, social policy stalwart, Richard Titmuss, emphasized the tremendous growth in married women's paid work. Between 1947 and 1956, he
noted, the number of employed married women had mushroomed from
1.5 million to 3.75 million, a 150% increase in just nine years.[58] Much
of this expansion was in part-time work, which undermined employers'
claims that the national insurance contribution for part-timers paralyzed
economic growth.

Given the sanguine economic picture, the National Insurance Advisory
Committee was willing to gamble that employers would continue to hire
part-time workers, even in the absence of any fundamental restructuring
of national insurance. Ministry officials were far more worried about what
might happen to labor market dynamics if employers had more incentives
to hire part-time employees. If employers did not have to pay insurance
contributions for part-time workers, would married women become more
desirable employees than male breadwinners? Officials were particularly
concerned that in an economic downturn employers might choose to
restructure their workforces around the employment of part-time women
for whom they would not have to make insurance contributions. This, of
course, would disadvantage male wage-earners. The potential damage to
men's breadwinning status and the resulting inversion of power in families
worried policymakers.[59]

Another powerful motivation lay behind the government's reluctance to
release employers from their responsibility for insurance contributions for

part-time workers. The Exchequer worried constantly about the integrity of the insurance fund, and national insurance officials were loath to give up the considerable revenues from contributions by both employers and employees for part-time work. Conspicuously absent from the list of governmental concerns about the proposed exclusion of part-time work was any hesitation about pushing an overwhelmingly female group of employees out of the national insurance program. This omission is hardly surprising, given the orthodoxy that married women had nothing to lose in the proposed withdrawal of insurance coverage. Government officials agreed with employers that their work did not need to be insured.

The government was not entirely unsympathetic to employers' grievances. Officials were willing to accommodate management demands in the interest of maximizing economic growth, as long as the long-term interests of male workers and the integrity of the national insurance fund were protected. So the debate over part-time employment returned to its starting point—how to define "marginal employments" that could harmlessly be exempted from insurance coverage. Defining all part-time work as marginal threatened the gendered equilibrium of the labor market—it would be too easy, especially in economic slumps, for part-time women working, say, thirty hours per week to be substituted for men. However, officials were amenable to more modest measures that would make hiring married women cheaper, and they agreed that the marginal area of non-insured employment could be expanded. In January 1958, adopting the essence of plans proposed by both the retailers and the TUC, the government doubled the number of hours needed to trigger insurance coverage. As a result, only employees working more than eight hours per week (and earning more than £2 per week) could be covered by national insurance.

The change primarily benefited the retailers, who had a great need for employees to work just a few hours a week to fill the rush periods. At Marks & Spencer, for instance, the 1,300 women comprising the "Saturday staff" (1,200 of whom were married) were officially designated as marginal employees. The widening of the net of "marginality" to encompass a whole new segment of workers, virtually all of whom were married women, was not supposed to work to their detriment; it was assumed that they would choose not to have national insurance regardless of how their work was categorized. But depriving these women of the choice to participate in national insurance had tremendous symbolic meaning in a culture that placed such value on the newly crafted system of social security.

In effect, national insurance policy developed in a way that paralleled the labor market's subordination of married women. Those women most marginalized in the labor market, working a few hours a week in low-paying jobs, were also the most marginalized in the national insurance scheme. The exclusions fell hard on some women who had relied on the post-war promise of social security. A Mrs. Wright, for instance, worked for the LCC as a server and supervisor in a school canteen throughout the

1950s. Though she worked only twelve hours a week, she contributed to the national insurance fund. After working for nine years at the school, the LCC informed her that she was not eligible for national insurance. Her twelve weekly hours of work, they said, came from two separate employments (as supervisor and server); consequently, she did not meet the eight-hour rule in either of her jobs. Mrs. Wright appealed to the Ministry of National Insurance, but to no avail. The full range of insurance benefits she had sought through nine years of contributing to the fund was wiped out.[60]

The banishment of Mrs. Wright, and many like her, from the safe haven of national insurance represents one major strand in the refashioning of the welfare state that occurred in the late 1940s and 1950s. Policymakers discarded one of the grounding principles of the new welfare state—that employment automatically converted workers into citizens who had well-defined rights and obligations concerning national insurance—in favor of a system that linked national insurance only to certain kinds of work. The process of delineating a sphere of marginal employment was informed by the same understandings of work and family life that underlay the overtly discriminatory practices of the interwar years. The presumed dependencies of marriage were at the center of the calculus that distinguished significant (and therefore insurable) work from the insignificant. It was no accident that the expanding realm of marginal (and therefore uninsurable) work was almost solely occupied by married women; it was not so much the number of hours they worked as the assumption that insurance was irrelevant for them that led to their exclusion. This assumption, of course, was an important structural feature of the postwar welfare state and was embodied most visibly in the provision of the 1946 National Insurance Act that made married women's participation optional. All married women's work, then, was potentially insignificant in the context of national insurance. For women in the margins, whether there by compulsion or choice, welfare state citizenship was not available.

WOMEN'S CLAIMS TO UNEMPLOYMENT BENEFIT AND THE DEMISE OF THE ANOMALIES REGULATIONS

In addition to the considerable barriers involved in securing the coverage of national insurance, married women who were insured also confronted discrimination in claiming the unemployment benefit that national insurance provided. The notion that women were not "genuine" beneficiaries was a legacy of inter-war policy on unemployment, which denied that women were workers who needed the protection of unemployment insurance. In the ongoing post-war restructuring of the welfare state, the tendency to treat women's claims for benefit with suspicion lingered. The Anomalies Regulations, used extensively in the 1930s, remained available to officials as a means to deny married women's claims for unemployment benefit. In the late 1940s and early 1950s, civil servants debated how and when the Anomalies Regulations should be invoked. Given the expected decline in the number of married women who would contribute to the national insurance fund because of the opt-out provision, top-level officials at both the Ministry of Labour and the newly-formed Ministry of National Insurance began to rethink the necessity and efficacy of the regulations. Some worried that the special investigations and additional inquiries made of married women were not worth the expense and administrative complications. Skepticism about married women's desire to work, however, was habitual among policymakers, and it persisted in discussions of unemployment administration. An inquiry into the Anomalies Regulations by the Ministry of Labour in 1947 prompted an outpouring of support for the restrictions. "If large numbers of married women remain within the scope of the [unemployment] scheme," commented one official, "it might be dangerous to abolish entirely the special restrictions on their title to benefit." Many women, he argued, came to the local unemployment offices "with the idea of 'cashing in' on their contributions rather than of securing further employment."[61]

To comply with the Anomalies Regulations, a married woman had to prove that she normally sought "to obtain her livelihood by means of insurable employment." Labour Ministry officials contended that many married women were defrauding the government by misrepresenting their intentions on government forms. They had learned the "correct answers to give" to avoid further questioning, and in effect, were procuring benefit under false pretences. No specific evidence of such misconduct was discussed in official reports; the unstated proof of the charges lay in the assumption that the vast majority of married women could not possibly intend to sustain employment. Local officers' methods of testing women's intentions in this regard varied. The more lenient ones disallowed a claim only if "positive evidence" (e.g., failure to sign the unemployment register each week, an expressed desire for part-time employment, refusal of suitable work) created the inference that the woman did not really want employment.[62] The desire for part-time rather than full-time work was not a violation of the Anomalies Regulations, but in practice, was frequently cited by insurance officers as the basis for denial of claims. In reviewing local practices in 1947, officials at the Ministry of Labour spoke approvingly of a harsher approach adopted by some local officers. These officers denied the claims of women who signed the unemployment register each week as required, but had remained unemployed for a "substantial period." The mere fact of continuing unemployment and the failure to take additional measures to find work were taken as proof that the women did not really want jobs.

The other stumbling block for married women under the Anomalies Regulations was the burden of showing that employers were likely to hire them. Although local officers were supposed to undertake formal and statistical assessments of employment opportunities for married women in their areas, they relied primarily on their "general impressions" of employer preferences, which usually boiled down to the conventional wisdom that single women were more reliable employees than married women. Although it is certainly true that some employers preferred to hire single women, even the local insurance officers acknowledged that this propensity was not ubiquitous. Hiring patterns depended on the labor market, and many employers were certainly willing to hire married women if their labor was more readily available or cheaper than that of their single counterparts. In any case, local officers in the late 1940s did not devote much attention to the nuances of an expanding economy that enlarged women's employment possibilities. Instead, they focused reflexively on the well-worn cliché that married women were not desirable employees, and promoted it as a convenient rationale for denying what they considered to be frivolous claims. One official argued that employers in the north of England believed that the "nimble fingers" of single women made them better workers than married women.[63] This approach disregarded the most direct evidence of employability: the fact that the women applying for benefits had worked for most of the preceding two years, building up enough contributions to qualify for national insurance. Still, some officials applied the Anomalies Regulations in a way that negated this logic: women who had recently been hired and had worked for sustained periods of time were denied benefits because, according to local insurance officers, they did not have a "reasonable expectation of finding work."[64]

Regional insurance officers, gathered for a conference in London in October of 1947, emphasized the utility of the Anomalies Regulations in rooting out merit-less claims. After their meeting, new policies were implemented to make full use of the Regulations. Previously, the Anomalies Regulations had only been invoked after a woman had been on the rolls for a few months. Under the new guidelines, however, all new claims for benefit by married women were to be evaluated with the Anomalies Regulations in mind. If a married woman began receiving benefits, she was to be interviewed more frequently than past policies had mandated; no longer than six months should elapse between inquiries. Special interviews would be conducted in the claims section of the local office of the Ministry of Labour. Difficult cases would be referred to the local insurance officer of the Ministry of National Insurance.[65]

In March 1948, officials of the Ministry of National Insurance elaborated on how married women's claims should be handled. Local insurance officers were instructed to consider the circumstances of each case rather than mechanically applying the rules, a mandate that might have allowed for a loosening of the restrictive bonds of the Anomalies Regulations. But the attention to the context of married women's working lives served only to provide additional justifications for denying their claims for benefit. If a woman's age, state of health, domestic responsibilities, or ability to commute appeared to compromise her ability to work, she would be disqualified. The only way for a married woman to circumvent the Anomalies Regulations was to prove that she could not possibly expect her husband to support her. Women whose husbands were incapacitated for work thus escaped the intrusive inquiries mandated by the regulations, as did women whose husbands had deserted them.[66]

In April 1952, Gilbert Williams, a senior official at the Ministry of Labour, weighed in on the long-running discussion among policy makers about the continued need for the Anomalies Regulations. While acknowledging growing sentiment that such rules were inefficient and counterproductive, Williams worried that in their absence, a flood of manipulative women who did not need or deserve unemployment benefit would overwhelm local offices. "There may well be lots of these women lurking in the shadows," he claimed, "who, as economic conditions get tighter, might be tempted to try their luck again, and so much would then depend upon what other means we have of eliminating the non-genuine."[67]

In the years just after the war, most national, regional, and local administrators viewed the Anomalies Regulations as necessary and useful. Some officials, however, voiced dissent. The prevailing orthodoxy, they argued, was out of step with other government policies concerning women's employment. The post-war Labour government had made economic growth a top priority and encouraged all those who could enter the labor market to do so, even married women. Public sector employment, which included increasing numbers of women, was growing as well. When canvassed in late 1947 about the Anomalies Regulations, a few regional controllers and local insurance officers expressed concern about their application. In particular, they objected to the common practice of denying claims based on local employers' alleged reluctance to hire married women. Pointing to government efforts to promote the employment of married women and the multitude of new factories scheduled to begin production, they argued that even if there were no immediate demand for the services of married women, their labor would soon be needed.[68] Officials also began to complain about the administrative burden and expense imposed by the Anomalies Regulations. This burden fell most heavily on the staffs of the local employment exchanges, and in March 1952, D.D. Ward, a senior civil servant at the Ministry of Labour, questioned the need for the additional paperwork and interviewing required by the regulations. "Staff economies" would be promoted, he contended, by eliminating the special evaluation of married women's claims for benefit.[69] By the mid-1950s, the drive for administrative efficiency, strengthened by the recognition that married women's employment was no longer anomalous, prevailed, and the regulations fell out of use.

The gradual willingness to abandon the Anomalies Regulations resulted in large part from the structural change in national insurance that cemented women's second-class welfare-state citizenship into the core of the unemployment scheme. By making married women's participation in national insurance optional, the 1946 National Insurance Act reduced the number of married women who could even apply for unemployment benefit. For women who were not relegated to the margins of national insurance, whose employment was labeled as "significant," welfare state policy of the 1950s gradually broke down some of the barriers to claiming insurance benefits. The Anomalies Regulations, which had crippled married women's attempts to get unemployment benefit for two decades, became obsolete. The rationale behind the Anomalies Regulations—that married women did not want and could not find employment—conflicted too blatantly with the oft-repeated governmental mantra that married women's work was essential for economic expansion. The accommodation of business interests could cut both ways, of course, as evidenced by the exclusion of women that resulted from the eight-hour rule. Still, the demise of the Anomalies Regulations significantly increased women's access to unemployment benefit.

How women fared in the post-war welfare state depended on whether or not their work was insured. For those whose work was excluded (by measures such as the eight-hour rule) and those who opted out of national insurance, employment-based benefits were unattainable. However, the women who worked enough to be included in the privileged core of the national insurance scheme and, who, if married, could afford to make the insurance contributions, had substantially better prospects in the welfare state. The mere fact that they were insured workers had symbolic benefits for their social citizenship. Moreover, if they were prepared to persevere in their fights with government bureaucracies, they had a chance of securing the material benefits, such as unemployment benefit, so fundamental to the post-war promise of social security.

EXERCISING RIGHTS TO BENEFIT: WOMEN, MEN, AND UNEMPLOYMENT

Unlike most employed women, Mary Lowe, who cleaned and sewed for a London school, was in the privileged core of the welfare state because she was covered by national insurance. In the spring of 1950, she suddenly found herself without child care and without a job. The friend who had looked after her two-year old had moved away, and Lowe was forced to leave her job at the school. Confident that she could rely on the protections afforded by national insurance, she immediately filed for unemployment benefit. The local insurance officer denied her claim, however, saying she was ineligible for benefit because she was not available for work. Lowe fought through two levels of appeals, but finally won her case. Using a rationale that would have been unthinkable twenty years earlier, the deputy commissioner who ruled in her favor argued that her child care responsibilities did not preclude employment: "I cannot believe," he wrote, "that in these days there are no part-time domestic jobs where children are allowed to be brought."[70] Because the deputy commissioner thought Lowe was able to work, she was awarded unemployment benefit. Mary Lowe's victory represented a transformation in the way upper-level policymakers thought of the possible accommodations between women's paid and unpaid work. This change in outlook, driven by the demands of economic expansion, resulted in a shift in the way unemployment benefit was used to regulate women's work and domestic lives.

Of all the benefits provided by national insurance, distribution of unemployment benefit was the most sensitive to changing social and economic influences. Ostensibly, unemployment insurance was a straightforward matter—workers paid in contributions to the national insurance fund while employed and could then collect benefits when out of work. However, an analysis of the over 1,500 appeals filed by London workers between 1949 and 1963 after unemployment benefit denials reveals a rather different picture.[71] The actual distribution of benefits involved a complicated set of rewards and punishments, inclusions and exclusions that reflected the increasingly complex relationships linking the state, the labor market, and domestic life. Scholars have long recognized that welfare state benefits have been used to regulate labor markets. In the United States, for example, benefits have been granted liberally at some times to minimize social unrest, and restrictively at other times to maintain work incentives and fill the needs of the labor market.[72] In Germany, certain groups of potential workers—pensioners and women—have periodically been lured away from employment by government benefits in order to keep unemployment rates down.[73]

Decisions on unemployment benefit appeals reveal yet other ways in which the state used the distribution of benefits to accomplish certain ends, primarily to endorse a particular integration of employment and domestic work. The terms under which the government granted or denied claims for unemployment benefit reshaped the gendered definitions of "worker" and "citizen" in light of, on one hand, a rapidly expanding economy that drew in more and more women, and on the other, longstanding, deeply rooted convictions about women's domestic obligations. The confluence of these material and ideological forces produced a welfare state that insisted on women's responsibility for work at home, but allowed space for some employed women, by virtue of their status as insured, non-marginal "workers," to share in the benefits of national insurance during periods of unemployment. This post-war inclusion of women in the unemployment benefit system stands in sharp contrast to the punitive, exclusionary practices of the 1920s and 1930s described by Jane Lewis.[74] Women who could combine paid work and domestic work were encouraged to do so in the 1950s and 1960s, and some of those who did received qualified acceptance as citizens of the welfare state. Men, on the other hand, were judged by their reliability as obedient subordinates in employment. Those who contested the terms or conditions of employment were usually penalized.

Unemployment insurance was designed to work in tandem with other government programs that made workers available to employers. As a condition of receiving unemployment benefit, claimants had to register at the local employment exchange each week and cooperate with employment officers trying to place them in jobs. Applying for benefit and signing the register, though, did not guarantee that unemployment benefit would be paid. The local insurance officer had the power either to deny benefit altogether or to impose a disqualification period of up to six weeks during which no benefit would be paid. Claimants who were denied benefit could appeal the local insurance officer's decision to a local tribunal made up of three members of the community. The local tribunals were constituted in a way that was supposed to give equal representation to different class interests. One member was to have ties to employers, one to employees, and the third was not to have overt links to either group. Michael Hill has described the typical tribunal as consisting of:

> a chairman, who may have legal training, who is chosen by a secret process which tends to throw up upper-middle-class people active in voluntary organizations, and two other people who are generally a small businessman and a minor trade union official respectively.[75]

The local tribunal held a hearing on the disputed claim, at which the claimant—usually unrepresented—could make his or her case.

If the local tribunal denied the claim, one final appeal could be made to a deputy commissioner of the Ministry of National Insurance. Eight deputy commissioners sitting in London handled all the appeals from local tribunal decisions from across the country. The deputy commissioners were appointed by royal warrant on the recommendation of the Lord Chancellor and were required to be barristers or advocates of at least ten years' standing. The deputy commissioners occasionally held oral hearings on appeals, but usually based their decisions on written submissions.[76]

Only a tiny fraction of claimants seeking unemployment benefit made their way to the top of the ladder of appeals. It is difficult to measure with precision the percentage of people in the London area who, having been denied initially, exhausted their appeal rights, but the figure is certainly under 1%.[77] Claiming unemployment benefit could be a lengthy and discouraging process. A claimant who went through all three levels of decision-making (local insurance officer, local tribunal, and deputy commissioner) might spend months dealing with the bureaucracy, only to come away empty-handed. Persistence could pay off, however, as some of the claimants' appeals were successful. Of those whose claims were initially denied by the local insurance officer, women in particular stood a much better chance of receiving benefit if they persevered through the next two levels of appeal.

Though all three levels of decision-makers worked under the auspices of the same government agency, the Ministry of National Insurance, they applied the rules governing unemployment benefit with a striking lack of uniformity. Differences in opinions on the way women's unemployment should be understood and dealt with were especially pronounced. The deputy commissioners, standing atop the three-tiered adjudicative apparatus, were more inclined than the insurance officers and local tribunals to use unemployment benefit as an affirmation of what they saw as the desirable combination of women's domestic and paid labor. Their perspective was consistent with the interests and policy objectives of other elite civil servants in the upper reaches of the Ministry of National Insurance, with whom they shared similar backgrounds, outlooks, and experiences. By the 1950s, as evidenced in the gradual abandonment of the punitive Anomalies Regulations, elite governmental opinion was moving toward a new conception of the interface between the welfare state and the labor market. The deputy commissioners perpetuated this view in their decisions, which crafted a new identity for insured women as legitimate workers and participants in a segment of the welfare state.

The insurance officers and local tribunals at the two lower levels of adjudication, on the other hand, did not exhibit the same enthusiasm for an unemployment benefit scheme that made allowances for women's domestic responsibilities. The ministry elite's inclinations concerning women's unemployment were not formalized in regulations or directives to local insurance officers. These local officers, not immersed in the shifting policy currents that influenced the deputy commissioners, worked in a bureaucratic culture that retained the distinctly punitive attitude toward women's claims for benefit that had become entrenched in the 1920s and 1930s. The local officers, much more than their upper echelon superiors, based their practices on older, but still powerful, notions of unemployment benefit that tended to penalize women.

The local tribunals, to whom aggrieved claimants could appeal unfavorable decisions made by the local insurance officers, were also removed from the practices of the deputy commissioners. They were designed to be independent bodies, citizens bringing "community values" into the process rather than agents of the government.[78] But as Michael Hill has pointed out, the composition of the tribunal—upper-middle-class professional, small businessman, and trade union official—restricted the range of "community values" brought to the process.[79] Many claimants who appeared before the local tribunals felt that the bodies did nothing but rubber stamp the decisions of the insurance officers. One claimant complained to the deputy commissioner on appeal that the chairman of the local tribunal had only taken testimony from the insurance officer. This allegation drew an angry response from the Deputy Commissioner considering the case, who ordered a new hearing before the local tribunal:

> the unceasing efforts of the Ministry to convince the public that the statutory authorities are completely independent judges will produce no results if the public are given the slightest justification for believing that it is the insurance officer, not the tribunal, who decided the appeal. [80]

At all levels, the outcome of a disputed claim depended on the answers to three questions: 1) was the claimant available for work when he or she applied for benefit?; 2) if the claimant had quit or refused a job, had there been "just cause" to do so?; and 3) if the claimant had been fired, was the termination a result of misconduct? These criteria were set out in the regulations governing unemployment benefit, and adjudicators seemed confident that their conclusions arose naturally from the proper use of the relevant legal standards. However, decisions were not the inevitable result of a mechanical application of the law to the facts. Regulations were flexible enough to allow a considerable role for discretion, and as in all legal proceedings, the assumptions and predispositions of the adjudicators shaped their decisions. Selecting and attributing meaning to facts was a complicated process, involving a wide net of judgments concerning the domestic and workplace behavior of claimants.

The threshold question of a claimant's availability for work was a deeply gendered issue that tapped into concerns about the balance between the public and private spheres. Of the three determinations adjudicators made, the availability question had the most profound impact on claimants. A ruling that a claimant was not available for work resulted in a complete denial of benefits, rather than a temporary disqualification. In applying the "availability" criterion, the local insurance officers in the various branches of the London region were alert to the possible conflicts between domestic obligations and the demands of employment. Despite protestations to the contrary from claimants, the insurance officers frequently concluded that such conflicts rendered claimants unavailable for work and therefore ineligible for benefit payments. Not surprisingly, insurance officers most often found that non-employment responsibilities infringed on the ability to work when handling women's claims for benefit, and the local tribunals followed suit. Of those claimants who filed appeals with a deputy commissioner, women were six times more likely than men to have had their availability for work questioned, first by the insurance officer and then by the local tribunal. While nearly 20% of women's appeals at the deputy commissioner level involved the issue of availability, only 3% of men's appeals did. This selective application of the availability requirement sprang from the notion that women's employment, in contrast to men's, was contingent, intermittent, and secondary to domestic work. This was often, but not always, the case, and in any event, women were increasingly able to combine paid and unpaid labor. Still, cultural assignments of identity—men were employed, women worked at home—informed the thinking of insurance officers and local tribunals and made it difficult for them to envision a systematic integration of home and work life for women. Willingly recognizing women with domestic responsibilities as workers deserving of unemployment benefit was tantamount to providing state sanction for an arrangement with which they were not at all comfortable.

As a result, women with restrictions on the hours they could work were apt to run into trouble with the local insurance officer. Under the regulations, part-time employees paid the same national insurance contribution as full-time workers and were supposed to receive the same benefit. Some local insurance officers, however, propagated the idea that limitations on working hours voided an individual's right to unemployment benefit. Deputy commissioners who discovered this practice scolded local officers for the persistence of this "common fallacy." Even as late as 1963, misinformation about benefit requirements was still coming out of some local offices. When, in the spring of that year, Jean Ridgers inquired about her right to unemployment benefit, the Croydon insurance officer told her that only full-time workers could apply. Later, after discovering from another officer that she was entitled to benefit, she filed an application. Seeking the five months of benefit payments she lost because of the first officer's misstatement, Ridgers unsuccessfully appealed to the local tribunal. It was not until a deputy commission considered her case that she was awarded the backpay of benefit.[81] Given the common misconception about part-time employment, reinforced in public consciousness by some insurance officers, many part-time workers (the vast majority of whom were women) must have unknowingly forfeited benefits to which they were entitled.

Preventing someone from filing an application for benefit was an extreme measure. A more commonly employed tactic was simply to deny the claim on the grounds that the claimant was unavailable for work. Women could not reasonably expect to find part-time positions, insurance officers and local tribunals contended, and were, in effect, unavailable for employment. Deputy commissioners who heard these claims frequently pointed out that such arguments ignored the work histories of women who, only weeks earlier, had held part-time jobs. Lily Jebinsky, for example, cared for her diabetic mother and invalid brother in a small East End flat and had worked part-time for years. When she lost her job as a tea packer in November 1950, she filed for unemployment benefit, but the insurance officer and local tribunal found that her limited availability made her unemployable. These decisions drew an impatient response from Deputy Commissioner D'Allembuerque, who heard her case and awarded her benefit. Impressed by Jebinsky's presentation of her case, he summarized her arguments with approval:

She observes, with some force, that in 8 ½ years work up to the tenth of November, 1950, she was unemployed for less than a year. (For all that time she had worked more or less for the hours to which she now restricts her availability.) She also says that during 7 ½ years she was able to satisfy the requirements of four industries and prove her skill in at least four trades. She goes on to call attention to the rearmament programme which will result in a call for more workers, and she refers to her domestic position giving rise to her responsibilities for her aged mother and invalid brother.[82]

Janetta Rees also found herself in the position of proving that there was plenty of part-time work to be had in London. She had worked full-time as a clerk, but when she filed for unemployment in early 1950, she told the King's Cross insurance officer she could work only part-time. Both the insurance officer and the local tribunal concluded that she was unlikely to find employment. The Deputy Commissioner allowed her appeal, finding it "hard to believe that part-time clerical work from 9 a.m. until 2 p.m. for six days a week is not available in London."[83]

It is important to note that the deputy commissioners' willingness to find part-timers available for work had limits. Women had to be ready to accept the kind of work the deputy commissioners thought they were likely to be offered; in other words, the poorly paid, low-status jobs so common in the service economy. If a deputy commissioner had an inkling that a woman might restrict herself to skilled work, he was much less inclined to find her available for employment. In 1950, Alma Brown, who had worked most of her life as a skilled bookbinder, made the mistake of expressing her preference to work in that trade. The deputy commissioner chastised her, saying she should be willing to accept employment in domestic service. He found her unavailable for work and ineligible for benefit.[84] Outright refusal of domestic service almost guaranteed failure on appeal. The conditions attached to unemployment benefit could be used to push women into unskilled, low-wage work, thus reinforcing the gender-based stratification of the labor market.

Still, as evidenced in most of their decisions, the deputy commissioners took a more liberal view of the boundaries of the welfare state than the insurance officers and local tribunals, revising the definition of "worker" to allow more opportunities for women to benefit from social policy. While the deputy commissioners agreed that women's domestic responsibilities sometimes limited their work opportunities, they saw the post-war labor market as a fluid entity that, out of necessity, would accommodate women's domestic schedules. They recognized that part-time work was a staple of the London economy. As a 1955 study of the East End borough of Bethnal Green showed, "part-time work is plentiful . . . both in the small local factories and in the tens of thousands of offices which have to be cleaned in the nearby City."[85] Though poorly paid, part-time cleaning, clerical, retail, and factory positions were relatively abundant, and as long as women seemed willing to take such jobs, their part-time status did not prejudice their right to unemployment benefit in the eyes of the deputy commissioners.

Of the women who appealed their claims to the deputy commissioners because they had been deemed unavailable for work due to their restricted working hours, 75% were granted full benefits on appeal. For married women, the approval rate was even higher; 80% of married women who appealed a finding of unavailability based on restricted hours won their appeals before the deputy commissioners. The proportion of claimants whose appeals turned on the issue of unavailability due to restricted hours was overwhelmingly female—almost 90% of these claimants were women. Because the women were deemed employable, they were available for work and entitled to benefit during unemployment.

These approval rates stemmed not only from the recognition that part-time work was available, but also from the value the deputy commissioners placed on women's primary roles as domestic managers and caregivers. In awarding benefit to women whose responsibilities at home curtailed their employment, deputy commissioners affirmed female domesticity as a legitimate reason for working restrictions.[86] Domestic responsibilities other than childcare also justified restrictions on availability. The insurance officer and local tribunal had denied fifty-six-year-old Margaret Mason's claim for benefit in 1952, questioning the necessity of the restrictions she imposed on her working hours. Mason was married, but no children lived at home; she claimed she needed early morning employment so she would have sufficient time for shopping and housework. The deputy commissioner found this to be a "good enough reason in the case of a married woman of her age," and he noted that jobs cleaning offices in the early morning hours in the City of London and the West End were widely available. Mason won her appeal.[87]

In their decisions, the deputy commissioners also emphasized the importance of a woman's role as a caregiver for her extended family. Evelyn Kirby, who had been a finisher for a West End firm of tailors for fifteen years, had to restrict her hours of work in order to care for her uncle, aged eighty-two, and her young niece. The insurance officer and local tribunal had concluded that she was unavailable for work, but the deputy commissioner disagreed. In approving her claim, he cited her excellent employment record and stressed the invaluable nature of the work she performed at home.[88]

A finding of unavailability carried with it the harshest penalty: total ineligibility for benefit. The issue of restricted working hours, however, could also arise in other contexts where the potential punishments were less severe, but the rationales for deciding claims were the same. In disqualification cases, adjudicators determined whether claimants who had left or refused employment did so with "just cause." Claimants who found working hours unacceptable, for example, had to prove they had good reason for their restrictions. Those who left or refused employment without "just cause" forfeited benefits for up to six weeks, and the length of the disqualification was left to the discretion of the adjudicator. Disqualification determinations sent messages about how people should behave in the labor market. Disqualifications were based on the fundamental premise of unemployment insurance: it should relieve hardship during periods of unemployment, but should not undermine the coercive forces of the labor market that compelled workers to maintain employment. Unemployment benefit was certainly not intended to weaken employers' power over workers. Consequently, unemployment policy discouraged workers from leaving jobs voluntarily and mandated penalties for those who did. Becoming a burden on the national insurance fund was not to be taken lightly.

The circumstances under which a claimant quit, lost, or refused a job received careful scrutiny, as officials weighed the claimant's reasons for losing or leaving employment against the inherent value of labor market stability and the integrity of the national insurance fund. The deputy commissioners' tendency to be forgiving of work disruptions caused by domestic demands suggests that they considered domestic propriety to be as important as labor market stability. Their decisions are replete with praise for women who spent enough time at home to be proper wives, mothers, and caregivers. With the prevalence of new patterns of women's employment, deputy commissioners felt compelled to emphasize the importance of domestic duties in order to protect the delicate balance between employment and home life. Just as it had in availability cases, the approval of domestic rectitude worked in women's favor, at least in terms of maximizing their unemployment benefit. Deputy commissioners tended to find that women were justified in quitting jobs because of domestic responsibilities or crises, usually granting full benefits in such cases. Of the women penalized by insurance officers and industrial tribunals for leaving or refusing jobs for domestic reasons, about 60% were given full benefits by deputy commissioners on appeal. These appellate victories were significant. Loss of up to six weeks of benefit, though less injurious than total ineligibility, could be a substantial hardship, especially for low-wage workers.

The deputy commissioners took great care to highlight women's primary obligation to their children. In 1950, Elizabeth McManus, who was unmarried but had a seven-year-old daughter, refused an evening job (found by the employment exchange) as a counter hand in King's Cross because she needed to be at home to feed her daughter and put her to bed. Hit with a six-week disqualification by the local insurance officer and the local tribunal, she appealed to the deputy commissioner. Evening work was unsuitable because of her "domestic circumstances," he declared, and reinstated her benefits.[89]

Child care was not the only extenuating domestic circumstance that excused leaving a job. Elizabeth Bolter, for instance, had worked as a part-time cleaning woman in the evenings, but in 1951 quit her job and filed for unemployment. She did not want to work evenings any longer because she felt it "essential to be at home in the evenings to prepare a proper hot meal which her husband and daughter could have as soon as her daughter got home [from work]."[90] The deputy commissioner found this desire to be reasonable and allowed her appeal from the unfavorable decision of the local tribunal. The sympathetic response was undoubtedly enhanced by the fact that Bolter's husband was disabled, still suffering from the effects of poison gas in World War I, but the result was not an anomaly.

The deputy commissioners considered a surprisingly wide range of domestic duties to be sufficiently important to warrant giving up employment. Violet May Fillery refused a job in 1953 as a kitchen hand at a club because it required working on Saturdays. The schedule was unacceptable to her because she wanted to cook Saturday dinner for her two sons, aged fifteen and twenty, who had to eat out during the week. Although the local insurance officer and local tribunal penalized her refusal with a six-week disqualification, the deputy commissioner who heard the case agreed with Fillery on the necessity of a home-cooked meal for her sons. He eliminated the disqualification period imposed by the insurance officer and local tribunal and awarded her the full benefit amount.[91] In another case that further expanded the sphere of domestic responsibility, a deputy commissioner sanctioned and rewarded long-distance diplomacy. Alice Sheasby, a kindergarten teacher, left her job so she could move to the town where her daughter lived, "in order to prevent, if possible, the breakup of the daughter's marriage."[92] After hearing the case, the deputy commissioner expressed his sincere hope that the marriage could be saved and eliminated the six-week disqualification levied by the local insurance officer and local tribunal.

Deputy commissioners demonstrated far less sympathy for employment interruptions that grew out of dissatisfaction with the job itself or misconduct at work. Workers who quit because of bad pay or poor conditions, as well as those who lost their jobs after complaining about such things, were usually penalized. Sarah Fish, for example, encountered considerable hostility in her appeal to the deputy commissioner. When she applied for unemployment benefit in August of 1950, she had worked in a hotel in Marylebone for only nine days. She had been fired after refusing to clean a lavatory, a task which she maintained was not one of her assigned duties. Unmoved by her indignant claim that she "did not take on the job to clean up human filth," the deputy commissioner reprimanded her sharply for her insolence and imposed the maximum disqualification period of six weeks for her misconduct.[93]

The deputy commissioners' decisions are filled with stern warnings against leaving or refusing employment unnecessarily. In a typical tirade against what he considered to be a frivolous job refusal, Deputy Commissioner George wrote in 1951,

It is necessary to point out that unemployment benefit, which is paid in part out of public funds, is <u>not</u> intended to be a substitute for wages which a claimant might earn if he would, but is compensation for wages which he cannot earn in spite of all reasonable efforts to do so. A person is not at liberty to refuse suitable employment and make himself a charge on the National Insurance Fund . . . [94]

The deputy commissioners believed cleaning work was almost always "suitable" for women, and the outright refusal of a domestic service position virtually guaranteed a disqualification from the deputy commissioners. Fifty-year-old May Edwards, who had always worked in factories, declined a position as a domestic worker in a hospital in King's Cross in 1958. Though the deputy commissioner acknowledged that factory work was Edwards' usual occupation, he insisted that:

> it cannot, in my opinion, be said that domestic work was unsuitable in her case by reason only that it is employment of a different kind from that to which she had been accustomed. There is no evidence that it was unsuitable in any other respect.[95]

He affirmed the six-week disqualification imposed by the insurance officer and the local tribunal.

The multitude of vignettes contained in these appellate decisions, though filtered through the assumptions and prejudices of the deputy commissioners, provide a window on the world of work in the 1950s and 1960s. Clearly gendered patterns emerged in the circumstances that caused workers to leave, refuse, or lose jobs. Men, for example, were far more likely than women to have left employment voluntarily, comprising 84% of the claimants who came before the deputy commissioners because they had quit their jobs. Men, it seems, had more confidence that other work could be found, and a greater sense of control over their fortunes in the labor market. Similarly, men were much more likely than women to have quit or refused work because of low pay or bad conditions. Of the claimants appealing to the deputy commissioners on this issue, 76% were men. The gendered composition of this group of claimants inverts that of the group of claimants whose employment had been interrupted because of restrictions, usually imposed by domestic responsibilities, on the hours they could work. In that group, only 18% were male.

As a group, then, men had a greater sense of entitlement to employment in general and to acceptable remuneration and working conditions in particular. This tendency is not surprising, given the strength of men's connections to the labor market and the added security lent by membership in predominantly male trade unions. The conditions attached to unemployment benefit, however, could hold the relative power of workers in check, and the deputy commissioners exercised their authority to punish and deter behavior that might upset the balance of power between employers and employees. Deputy commissioners were more often troubled by men's rejection of employment conditions than by comparable behavior by women, probably because men had more leverage in the labor market. Of the men who had left or refused jobs because of pay or conditions, only 32% were awarded full benefits by the deputy commissioner, whereas the comparable approval rate for women (45%) was significantly higher.

The deputy commissioners saved their strongest criticism for men who rejected work opportunities. John Paul, for instance, refused to take an unskilled agricultural job several miles from his home in 1961. On appeal, Deputy Commissioner Neligan affirmed the maximum disqualification from benefit and expressed his contempt in unequivocal terms: "To decline work for the reasons on which he seeks to rely can, in my opinion, only be described as deplorable."[96] The deputy commissioners adopted a similarly hard line against work stoppages by trade unions. The National Insurance Act prohibited payment of unemployment benefit to striking workers, and the deputy commissioners interpreted the provision as broadly as possible, denying benefit to any worker who, though not involved in the strike, was thrown out of work because of it. Thus, if one company laid off workers because another company could not provide supplies due to a strike at its plant, the deputy commissioners denied benefits to the workers at both companies. If the deputy commissioners could discern any connection between strike activity and the unemployment of other workers, no matter how tenuous, benefits were denied.

In late 1952, for example, William Kennedy, who worked at a Dagenham motor company, could not go to work because picketers stopped him from entering the plant. Though the local tribunal had allowed his claim, the deputy commissioner who reviewed the case found that benefit could not be paid. Kennedy was unable to work, the deputy commissioner ruled, *because of* the work stoppage and was therefore ineligible for benefit.[97] Strikes in London in the 1950s and 1960s produced scores of appeals to the deputy commissioners which were summarily denied. Such practices, of course, promoted resentment of trade unions among workers penalized in this fashion, a consequence that was surely intended by the deputy commissioners. Their rulings in this area reflected the fairly common sentiment among elite civil servants that the unions had excessive power that needed to be curbed.

Just as the deputy commissioners' decisions created a picture of the vaguely threatening, overreaching union man, they also depicted his counterpart–the earnest, trustworthy, not overly assertive male employee. In some cases, the deputy commissioners took the opportunity to hold up an example of their vision of the ideal worker—a man who richly deserved the rewards of the welfare state when he was out of work. The model worker was diligent, obedient, respectful, not associated with a union, and, above all, committed to maintaining employment. These attributes could excuse acts that, if committed by a less deserving claimant, would doom an appeal. Rather than adhering to the mantra that work should never be abandoned, the deputy commissioners in these cases relied on their general impression of the man's integrity. Frederick Miller was the perfect example of the ideal employee for whom the usual rules could be bent. A wood machinist by trade, Miller took a job in 1952, which he left after a few weeks. Deputy Commissioner George felt confident that Miller's judgment of the suitability of the job could be trusted. Miller was "a genuine steady-going workman," George noted. "He does not appear to be the kind of man to give up a situation without good cause."[98]

In the 1950s and 1960s, men and women participated in the unemployment benefit system on very different terms. Workers, usually men, who refused employment that seemed unacceptable to them endured criticism and penalties from the deputy commissioners. In contrast, the deputy commissioners rewarded "steady-going workmen." A different set of criteria applied to female workers, who were praised for reconciling work and domestic duties. The willingness of deputy commissioners to make allowances for the domestic work performed by women, particularly married women, grew out of the shared objectives of government policy makers and business leaders to increase the labor supply for the post-war economy and to safeguard women's ability to fulfill their responsibilities at home. As one deputy commissioner noted just after the National Insurance Act was implemented in 1948;

> It is well known that married women are being persuaded to go out to work, even though their circumstances may not permit them to give their full-time services to their remunerative employment.[99]

Allowing insured women who were unemployed to profit from the national insurance scheme marked a shift in the way some welfare state benefits were used to regulate women's domestic and paid work. In some areas of unemployment benefit policy, the carrot replaced the stick, as benefits rewarded good domestic and workplace behavior. This approach also institutionalized women's employment in a way that worked to the advantage, in the long run, of employers and the government. Women receiving benefit registered at the employment exchanges as available workers, and they were more likely to remain in regulated employment where contributions to the national insurance fund were made.

In the two decades following the war, women who could combine paid, insured employment and domestic work and who fought for their right to benefit found some degree of inclusion in the welfare state. Paradoxically, although deputy commissioners were fashioning a new welfare state identity for women as "workers" who deserved employment-based benefits, the new formulation retained much of the ideology that made it difficult for women to have equal footing with men in the labor market. This proved to be a mixed blessing: women profited from the material gain of benefit money and the measure of independence it may have provided and from the sense of direct citizenship in the welfare state. However, these gains carried a price: the rhetorical and symbolic enforcement of their responsibility for a wide range of unpaid work at home.

2 "Not the Normal Mode of Maintenance"

Bureaucratic Resistance to the Claims of Lone Women*

With the passage of the National Assistance Act in 1948, the British Parliament swept away the remaining vestiges of the Poor Law, which for centuries had been the last recourse for the poorest members of the population. The legislation was one of several acts that defined the modern welfare state after the Second World War—a welfare state that significantly expanded governmental responsibility for health, education, and social security. The National Assistance Act set out not only to centralize and reorganize poor relief, but also to create a new vocabulary and philosophy that would eliminate the stigma of the Poor Law system. In contrast to the relief systems in place before the war, inextricably linked in popular memory with humiliating abuses of the means test, the post-war welfare state celebrated the government's role in the realization of social rights and common citizenship. Politicians introduced welfare legislation to the public in populist terms that emphasized inclusion and destigmatization, and many Britons took the message to heart. Poor women with children, for example, turned to the state for assistance in record numbers in the two decades following passage of the National Assistance Act in 1948.

But the welcoming rhetoric of the new welfare state was at odds with the institutionalized belief that the state should not take up responsibilities that ought to remain in families. For the National Assistance Board (NAB, or Board), which took over responsibility for means-tested relief from local Poor Law authorities, the tremendous growth in the number of claims made by women who were not being provided for by men was an unanticipated and unwelcome development. The public's heightened expectations of government after the war thus came into direct conflict with the state's inclination to limit its role in social provision. It quickly became clear that in the actual implementation of the new legislation, the NAB would attempt to restrict the assistance given to women by broadly defining familial responsibility for their support. These gendered notions of dependence and obligation were deeply entrenched in the interlocking systems of the Poor Law and family law, which for centuries had regulated the duties of kinship. In both systems, a husband was required to maintain his wife (assuming she was not guilty of adultery or desertion) even after separation. In searching for ways to make women turn to individual men, rather than the state, for support, the NAB tried to enforce the long-standing liabilities of family law. Moreover, the NAB also sought to *extend* private obligations for women's maintenance in ways that conflicted with both family law and the statutory requirements of the National Assistance Act. From its inception until it was replaced by the Supplementary Benefits Commission (SBC) in 1966, the NAB tried to redirect women's claims for assistance to absent husbands, fathers of the women's children, alleged cohabitees, and, less often, other family members. NAB officials did not succeed in slowing the stream of women who made their way onto the national assistance rolls, but their begrudging extension of aid and their development of tactics to deter these claims foreshadowed the more openly hostile stance toward poor women so evident under Thatcherism.

The NAB's concerns were crystallized in a 1953 memorandum sent to all its area offices. Barely five years old, the NAB was struggling to rid itself of a responsibility with which it had never been comfortable—the task of supporting separated and divorced women and unmarried mothers. Discomfited officials at NAB headquarters had watched with dismay as the number of these "lone women" receiving assistance steadily increased, and they impressed on area officers that the trend had to be reversed. "Assistance ought not to be regarded," the circular warned, "either by us or by the public, as the normal mode of maintenance of a woman whose marriage has broken up or who has an illegitimate child."[1]

In the development of many different welfare states, governments have struggled to balance the need to ensure adequate support for children against the need to enforce patriarchal family dependencies and labor market discipline. The policies and practices elaborated in the 1950s and 1960s to channel women's requests for support away from the government echoed familiar themes in the long history of poor relief. Neither the claims of lone women on the state nor the hostility with which they were often met was new. From the sixteenth century on, local Poor Law authorities were often reluctant to support women and their children.[2]

However, there have also been other strands in policy discussions that reframed the state's responsibility to families. Between the First and Second World Wars, the notion that all married mothers provided a valuable service to the nation formed the basis of a movement led by Eleanor Rathbone to "endow motherhood" through government provision of family allowances. Under the Family Allowances Act of 1945, British mothers were paid an allowance for all children except the first in each family. But the opposition of trade union leaders, who feared that employers would use family allowances to justify wage reductions, ensured that the allowances were too small to be of much help to women. In inter-war France, by contrast, pronatalists succeeded in securing relatively generous allowances to subsidize wages to support children.[3] In the United States, family allowances were not present in any form in the social security legislation of the

1930s. Only poor women with children had recourse to the state, and they were relegated to the means-tested (and stigmatized) Aid to Dependent Children program.[4]

In post-war Britain, national assistance certainly had strong continuities with the poor relief it replaced, but the post-war period also marked a different phase in the state's provision for poor women. The advent of national assistance produced a new set of coordinated strategies to push women away from reliance on state aid. The NAB pressured women to take legal action against their husbands or the fathers of their children, tried to broaden the scope of spousal liability through litigation, deployed special investigators to collect evidence to justify termination of allowances, and, in a revival of the discarded household means test, denied assistance to some women who lived with (nonspousal) relatives who earned wages. Implementation of these strategies was possible because the NAB, unlike its Poor Law predecessors, had the resources and organization of a centralized bureaucracy. Officials acted with unprecedented urgency because of their substantiated fear that the state might become the provider of first resort for lone women. The NAB's attempts to restigmatize aid for lone women did not prevent a significant and sustained expansion in the number of women claiming assistance, but the increase might have been much larger if the NAB had not taken the course it did. In addition, the NAB's tactics did much to make women who asserted their right to aid feel undeserving and demeaned.

The scholarship on the government's attitudes toward lone women in the post-war era has neglected the first two decades of post-war welfare policy, focusing instead on the "crisis" period that began in the late 1960s. In these crisis-centered accounts, confidence and consensus about social policy began to collapse when economic malaise resulted in a growing demand for social services and a declining ability to pay for them. Scholars of social policy have described the efforts made to discourage applications for aid by lone women, measures employed from the late 1960s through the 1990s by the successor of the NAB, the SBC. These accounts concentrate on the intrusive and punitive methods of the SBC that accompanied the tremendous increase in the number of lone women on the rolls after 1965, an expansion caused by a rapidly escalating divorce rate and a sharp rise in the number of births to unmarried women.[5]

Hilary Land has suggested that the claims of lone mothers did not concern the NAB in the 1950s and early 1960s. It was really only in the late 1980s, she contends, that the government launched a frontal assault on their right to assistance, using various tactics to cut or withdraw their benefits.[6] But the defensive posture against such women was actually adopted much earlier, in a relatively neglected portion of the history of means-tested relief. In its early, formative years, the NAB assembled an arsenal of tools to beat back the onslaught of lone women seeking inclusion among the deserving needy. These strategies, and the rationales that gave them legitimacy, became fixed in the bureaucratic repertoire and were later available to bolster various attacks on the welfare state itself.

THE GROWING PROBLEM OF LONE WOMEN
AND THEIR CLAIMS ON THE STATE

The expressed, official objective of national assistance was to "meet need" in a way that minimized the embarrassment of those seeking the means-tested benefits offered by the program. In theory, a weekly national assistance allowance would be provided to those who lacked the income and resources to meet basic living expenses.[7] The broad mandate of the NAB, as set out in the enacting legislation and explained to the public, was to relieve need wherever it existed. In practice, however, the government's provision of assistance was neither universal nor uniform. The very availability of assistance and, if granted, the conditions attached to it depended on the applicant's sex, marital status, and domestic relationships. The obligation the government defined for itself, hammered out unevenly, sometimes in official regulations and sometimes in broad patterns of practice, arose from the conviction that the state would not assume responsibility for people who should turn elsewhere for support. In separating the deserving from the undeserving, officials tried to enforce a particular model of domestic economy in which women were to rely on other wage earners, usually men, for support.

The National Assistance Act prohibited married women whose husbands were in full-time work from receiving assistance.[8] The presumed reliance on husbands' wages followed the assumptions of the Poor Law, which derived from the common law requirement that a husband maintain his wife.[9] These assumptions were confounded, however, when women, often with children, lived apart from husbands who did not provide regular or sufficient support. Between 1948 and 1966, more and more of these women sought aid from the NAB. Contrary to popular stereotypes about the causes of dependence on state aid, it was separation—not out-of-wedlock births or divorce—that drove the most lone women on to national assistance. Throughout the period in question, separated women claiming assistance outnumbered unmarried mothers by more than three to one, and divorced women with children by nine to one.[10]

NAB policies, therefore, tended to focus on separated women, particularly those with children. Throughout the 1950s and 1960s, worried officials tried to find ways to compel absent spouses to support the women and children who were seen as unnecessary burdens on the national assistance fund. Their efforts, however, were largely ineffective. Women who might have been reluctant to ask for poor relief were far more willing to claim national assistance. In June 1949, 1 year after the National Assistance Act had gone into effect, about 34,000 separated wives were drawing national assistance allowances. By the end of 1965, 104,000 separated women were claiming benefit, a 200% increase in 16 years. The number of separated women on the assistance rolls climbed at a moderate pace from 1949 to 1953, remained fairly stable from 1953 to 1957, and then skyrocketed from 1957 to 1965. The statistics on unmarried mothers claiming benefit reflect a similar trajectory. Though not as numerous as separated women, the number of unmarried mothers on assistance rose by 300% between 1949 and 1965, from 9,000 to 36,000. Taken together, the number of separated women and unmarried mothers grew by 225% during these years, while the number of claimants in all other categories increased by only 63% during the same time. The number of divorced women with dependent children on assistance increased as well, though not as dramatically.[11] Though lone women represented only about 8% of all national assistance recipients in 1965, their share of the NAB's total expenditure on allowances was closer to 20%.[12] This was because most other claimants were paid only a partial national assistance allowance to "top up" national insurance benefits or pensions they were already receiving. In addition, lone women received full allowances for themselves and for any dependent children.

From the inception of national assistance in 1948, women with dependent children were generally not expected to register for employment in order to claim assistance. In the calculations of policymakers, the premium placed on maternal care outweighed the savings to public funds that might be achieved by forcing lone women into the labor market. The importance attached to mothering grew in the 1950s, as psychologists such as John Bowlby warned that lack of maternal attention caused irreparable damage in children. Bowlby's well-publicized theories influenced both public opinion and policymakers, including upper-level officials at the NAB. In 1950, the NAB's regional controllers complained that area officers should have more leeway in requiring some women to look for employment, but the chairman of the NAB, George Buchanan, refused to amend the Board's policy, reminding his subordinates that even during the war, mothers with young children had not been required to work.[13]

Notwithstanding the Board's official policies, some groups of women were pressured to work full-time. West Indian women, in particular, were expected to support themselves.[14] NAB officials observed that West Indians were anxious to return to wage-earning after giving birth, but by 1958 were having trouble placing their children in nurseries because of discrimination. This trend alarmed officials at NAB headquarters, who worried that the women "would become content to settle down on national assistance."[15] Concerns about stunted childhood development, so prevalent in the NAB's discussions of official policy, were disregarded in the Board's dealings with non-white mothers. Though less systematic, other proposals to push women into work periodically surfaced in the meetings of the regional controllers. Unmarried mothers, always the most stigmatized of the lone women claiming assistance, were usually the target of such plans.

In 1965, one of the regional controllers suggested that "the young girl with an illegitimate child who was living with her parents" should be prodded to find full-time employment.[16] Local officers occasionally urged separated women to find work as well. In London, for example, area officers sometimes pressed separated women who lived with their parents, and presumably could call on them for child care, to find part-time jobs.[17]

NAB officials thought of national assistance as a program designed for certain groups of the needy. The Board was untroubled by claims made by "the old, the sick, and the widows: [the] people who have always been accepted as having the first claim to the helping hand of the community."[18] Between 1948 and 1966, the elderly made up 70% to 80% of all national assistance recipients.[19] Absent from the list of truly legitimate claimants were women who, unable to support themselves because of child-care responsibilities, were expected to seek assistance from their husbands or the fathers of their children. These "liable relatives" did not live with their wives and children, but the NAB insisted on their legal and moral responsibility for their dependents.

Ironically, although lone women were marginalized in the NAB's hierarchy of merit, many rushed to avail themselves of national assistance when it became available in 1948. In just the first five months that the National Assistance Act was in effect, the number of separated women claiming benefit more than doubled (from 16,000 to 33,000), as did the number of unmarried mothers (from 4,000 to 9,000). The total number of claimants receiving benefit rose by only 25% in the same five-month period.[20] Throughout the 1950s and 1960s, the rate at which lone women took up benefits continued to outpace the rate at which poor people in general claimed assistance. Even more than other potential claimants, lone women apparently embraced the rhetoric surrounding national assistance—rhetoric that emphasized a new kind of public assistance that would deliver aid to anyone in need. Lone women cautiously accepted the message of destigmatization and turned to the NAB in numbers that would have been unimaginable under the Poor Law. Despite the dramatic rise in the 1950s and 1960s in the number of women claiming benefits, there were many others who were eligible for national assistance but did not apply for it. Dennis Marsden, a social scientist at the University of Essex, conducted an in-depth study of 116 "fatherless families" receiving national assistance in 1965. Marsden's interviews highlighted the demeaning and deterring nature of the application process, which kept many women away. In addition, he found that many women were not aware that they might qualify for aid.[21] Still, the willingness of large numbers of lone women to assert their rights to national assistance permanently altered the parameters of means-tested relief.

If NAB officials were worried about the claims of lone women, they did not reveal their concerns at first, not publicly at least. In its annual reports for 1948 and 1949, the Board downplayed its responsibility for supporting lone women, saying that it dealt "only with the exceptional cases." [22] The vast majority of separated women and unmarried mothers did not need the Board's help, officials speculated, and those who did would probably require assistance for only a short period. In the early years of national assistance, the NAB promoted the optimistic, but unsupported view that separated women and unmarried mothers formed a limited, temporary class of claimants who posed no significant problems for the government. This characterization later proved to have been wishful thinking, but it reveals much about policymakers' beliefs about who should and should not have depended on the state for support.

In theory, there should have been no need for separated women to require state assistance. A husband's common law duty to maintain his wife did not end upon separation. The difficulty, though, lay in enforcing this obligation. At common law, a woman could pledge her husband's credit for the purchase of necessities, but this was an impracticable remedy. In the late nineteenth and twentieth centuries, the Summary Jurisdiction (Separation and Maintenance) Acts, 1895–1949, improved women's prospects for enforcement by empowering magistrates' courts to order a husband to pay maintenance for his wife and children.[23] Unmarried mothers could also seek "affiliation" orders to force fathers to maintain illegitimate children. However, a woman had no right to maintenance for herself if she had committed adultery or if she had deserted her husband. This bar to maintenance, which followed the common law, created difficulties for NAB officials, who wanted husbands' liabilities to be as broad as possible.

Despite the availability of these remedies, many women did not seek maintenance or affiliation orders from their husbands or the fathers of their children. In his 1965 survey, Dennis Marsden identified several of the reasons for women's reluctance. Some women, he discovered, had been the victims of domestic violence and feared revealing their whereabouts. Others worried that court proceedings might give custody or visitation rights to the abusive spouse. Many women dreaded the intrusion into their personal affairs, and, with some justification, were skeptical about their chances of benefiting from the proceedings. Proving that a husband's cruelty had forced a woman to leave could be difficult. Marsden found that physicians who might be in a position to provide evidence of physical abuse were often reluctant to become involved. Even if the evidence presented to the court strongly supported a maintenance award, as in the case of desertion by the husband, a woman might be penalized due to the prejudices of court officials, who assumed that desertion usually followed some provocation by the wife.[24]

In addition, some women who secured maintenance or affiliation orders did not receive regular payments from the men against whom the orders had been obtained. The task of supporting these women, as well as those who avoided the courts, fell to the NAB. Like the Poor Law guardians, the NAB did have legal power to pursue the liable relatives of women claiming assistance. Under the Poor Law, the local authorities could enforce this liability in the courts, both by trying to recoup payments made to wives and children and by criminally prosecuting the men. The NAB had similar powers, with the caveat that criminal prosecution was only available if a man's failure to maintain had been persistent. Rather than initiating legal actions against defaulting husbands and fathers, the NAB usually encouraged women who were receiving national assistance to file their own claims. The women then signed their right to any payments made by the husbands/fathers over to the NAB. In this way, the women could receive an uninterrupted weekly allowance from the NAB without having to prove that their husbands (or the fathers of their children) had not made the required payments each week.

PURSUING HUSBANDS AND FATHERS

Despite the publicly expressed confidence that separated women and unmarried mothers would not be a significant expense to the Board, by late 1949, the NAB's ten regional controllers began to voice concern about national assistance payments made to women and children who should have been supported by men.[25] When the regional controllers convened in 1949 and 1950, they emphasized that these women represented a serious problem for the Board.[26] In the following years, the drive to keep separated women and other "fatherless families" off the national assistance rolls assumed increasing importance in NAB policy. The pursuit of liable relatives consumed much staff time. NAB discussions on the subject tended to focus on separated women for two reasons. First, the claims for assistance made by these women greatly outnumbered those made by unmarried mothers and divorced women. Second, a husband's identity and legal liability for support of his family were clear. Though an unmarried mother might name the father, establishing paternity and the accompanying legal responsibility for children was much more difficult. And in the case of both unmarried mothers and divorced women with children, the fathers were obliged to support only the children, not the women involved.

NAB officials were insistent that men be pressured, with court action if necessary, to support their dependents. Visiting officers who interviewed women in their homes soon after they filed for national assistance questioned women closely about their efforts to secure commitments of support from their spouses. If no legal proceedings had been initiated, the officer urged the woman to apply to the magistrates' court for a maintenance order. If a husband was not complying with an existing maintenance order, the officer inquired about the steps the woman had taken to have the order enforced.[27] In 1953, press reports brought public attention to the fact that, because many husbands were not supporting their estranged wives, the women were relying on the public funds of national assistance. The chairman of the NAB and the regional controllers agreed that area officers had to be more aggressive. Women, they believed, could not be trusted to go after their husbands for support. "If the wife and children are being provided for through assistance and the wife does not stand to gain from her husband's payments, she may feel quite indifferent whether he pays of defaults," one official noted. "As the loss when he defaults falls not on her but on public funds she has no financial incentive to seek enforcement." [28]

Officials at NAB headquarters therefore revamped the regulations to "give a greater sense of urgency" to the enforcement of men's obligations to their wives. Regional controllers prodded area offices to be more persistent in pressuring men to meet their responsibilities. "The husband should be tackled at the very start," one controller advised. [29] Instructions for local officers drafted in 1953 emphasized the need for a forceful tone when dealing with a husband who had missed payments:

> as soon as it is known that [he] is in default on his payments he must at once be approached in a way which will leave him in no doubt that the Board intend that he shall meet his obligations. The more quickly this is brought home to him, especially on the first lapse, the less likelihood there will be of continuing trouble. [30]

Frequently, however, the trouble did continue, which necessitated convincing the woman involved to get a maintenance order. NAB officers did all they could to encourage prompt action. Neither the National Assistance Act nor NAB regulations required women receiving national assistance to file for a maintenance or affiliation order, but it was not uncommon for NAB officers to lead women to believe otherwise. A manager of one NAB local office admitted to Dennis Marsden that some women were "bullied" into taking legal action against their wishes. [31]

In the case of enforcement of existing orders, the NAB officer prepared a letter to the clerk to initiate enforcement proceedings, went to the woman's home, and asked her to sign it. As one official commented, "as she is dependent on the Board for her maintenance it is most unlikely that she will refuse to sign." [32] The more difficult task, of course, was actually wringing money out of the men in question. From the NAB's perspective, delinquent husbands who forced their wives on to national assistance threatened the public trust. NAB officials therefore asked the court collecting officers to give priority to those cases "for the better protection of public funds." [33] Though the court collecting officers were responsible for compliance with court orders, the NAB viewed their efforts as inadequate and sought more direct involvement in pressuring men to pay. Citing its nationwide staff of visiting officers, the NAB argued that it was better equipped to track down irresponsible husbands than were the court officers. [34]

For the most part, the NAB's missionary zeal to make men take responsibility for their dependents reflected prevailing social and legal norms about the requirements of marriage. As noted above, both the common law and statutory provisions required husbands to maintain their wives. The principles of family law, though, conflicted with the imperatives of national assistance in determining the effect of a wife's marital fault. Family law had long denied women guilty of the marital offenses of desertion and adultery the right to maintenance.[35] Denying maintenance in these circumstances was intended to deter women from bad marital behavior and to punish and stigmatize women who broke marriage vows. The Poor Law had respected this method of stabilizing the institution of marriage and had not held husbands responsible for poor relief given to offending wives.[36] The National Assistance Act of 1948, however, could be read to impose absolute liability on husbands for maintenance, thus creating an obligation not conditioned on wives' innocence. It was this interpretation that NAB officials endorsed, even though it contradicted the standards of family law that defined and circumscribed men's accountability.

In the early 1950s, the NAB tested the courts' commitment to the well-established common law rule that deserting or adulterous wives had no right to maintenance from their husbands. In *National Assistance Board v. Wilkinson*,[37] the NAB argued that the terms of the National Assistant Act were unequivocal in holding *all* husbands responsible for supporting their wives, and that the NAB could therefore recover from a husband whose wife refused to live with him. The lower court ruled against the NAB, and the NAB appealed. The appellate court affirmed the lower court's decision, rejecting the idea that:

> the National Assistance Act, 1948, has entirely altered the law on this subject and that a husband is liable to an order being made against him to maintain his wife whether she be guilty of adultery or desertion.[38]

The court held that the National Assistance Act had to be read in conjunction with the common law and that the statute could not eradicate the defenses normally available to a man responding to a maintenance claim. The court refused to construe the National Assistance Act:

> in such a manner as would make a husband liable, for the first time in the history of the law, to maintain a wife who was either living in adultery or refusing to live in the home which he had provided.[39]

A husband's responsibilities *vis-à-vis* the National Assistance Act flowed from his obligations under the common law, the court found; therefore, the NAB could not broaden the scope of his liability. The ruling revealed how deeply the common law rules of marital fault structured judicial thinking.[40] And, ironically, the inclination to punish guilty wives would also become evident in the NAB's own dealings with such women.

In another area, the goals of minimizing state expenditure and adhering to common law principles were again in harmony. The NAB was able to establish clearly its right to recover from men the assistance given to their wives. Again, though, the rights of the NAB mirrored the rights of the women involved. In the 1950s, appellate courts held that separation by mutual agreement did not relieve a husband of his maintenance obligation. In *National Assistance Board v. Parkes*,[41] a wife pledged in a separation agreement not to make any claim for maintenance against her husband in the future. Later, the woman became destitute and received national assistance. The NAB sued the husband to recover the payments it had made to his wife, but the husband argued that the separation agreement barred his wife and the NAB from collecting any money from him. On appeal, Lord Denning, the renowned family law reformer, emphasized that the common law did not allow a separation agreement to serve as a bar to a maintenance obligation. An important basis for the common law rule, Denning wrote, was the potential cost to the state: "A husband cannot shift his responsibility on to the rest of the community in that way. His duty to maintain her remains, despite the agreement."[42] The court held that the separation agreement did not negate the NAB's claim against the husband.[43]

However, another appellate court decision in 1957—this one concerning a woman's right to temporary alimony payments while a divorce was pending—again set back the NAB's efforts to force men to support their wives. In *Sterne v. Sterne*,[44] the court held that a woman filing for divorce was not entitled to temporary alimony payments from her husband if she was already receiving national assistance. The availability of temporary alimony depended on the woman's need, and the court concluded that the payment of national assistance, temporarily at least, filled that need. The NAB, having financed the appeal of the case, was dismayed at the result. Although it affected a very small number of claimants, NAB officials were concerned that the holding compromised the general principle that the state should not relieve a man of his obligation to support his family. In the wake of the decision, the NAB solicitor and other officials discussed how NAB policies might be changed. Some advocated denying assistance to women in divorce proceedings so that the courts would be forced to issue temporary alimony orders. Although this proposal would have saved the NAB money, it was rejected. Rodger Winn, a solicitor for the NAB, feared that the denial of support might lead to desperate, depraved acts: "it . . . would, or might, put on some ill-balanced women a psychological stress sufficient to produce consequences of a grave and probably scandalous character."[45]

The NAB enjoyed a parliamentary victory in the family law arena in 1958. The Maintenance Orders Act introduced a new procedure for enforcement of maintenance orders (including affiliation orders for illegitimate children). If payments under a maintenance order were in arrears, the court was empowered to direct the man's employer to deduct a portion of his wages and pay that amount directly to the court.[46] Attachment of wages did insure payment of at least part of the maintenance obligation in some cases, but the system was not foolproof. The man in question first had to be located. If he could be found, the court held a hearing to determine the amount to be deducted from his paycheck. A "protected earnings rate" was established, which was the amount the man was allowed for himself and any other dependents, for instance, children of another mother. Courts tended to be generous in setting the protected earnings rate, and often there was little left to be paid under the maintenance order. Men could avoid the attachment process altogether by changing jobs and making themselves difficult to find, particularly in urban areas. In addition, employers found the process a nuisance, and some fired workers with attachment orders rather than bother with the paperwork. [47]

The concerted efforts of the NAB and the courts did result in more money being collected from men whose wives and children were receiving national assistance. In 1954, men paid just under £2 million to wives, mothers, and the Board itself. By 1964, the figure had increased to slightly over £6 million. But this increase barely made a dent in the spiraling cost of national assistance allowances paid to separated wives, unmarried mothers, and divorced women with children. In 1954, the NAB's expenditure on these women was £9.7 million. By 1964, the total stood at £32.7 million, and in 1965, it jumped to almost £43 million. Though the amount of money paid by husbands and fathers increased during this period, their share of the total cost of supporting the women and children on national assistance actually declined—from 18% in 1954 to 16% in 1965.[48]

Despite the best efforts of the NAB, then, the burden of supporting the women and children who turned to the state for aid had not been shifted back to the men who were legally responsible. As had been the case since the inception of national assistance, the cost to the government was defrayed by the irregular and/or inadequate payments made by some men, but the share of total spending represented by these contributions was small and stagnant. Moreover, the number of women claiming national assistance for themselves and their children rose steadily throughout the 1950s and then exploded in the early 1960s. The biggest increases were to be found among separated wives. Throughout the 1950s, between 70,000 and 80,000 separated women claimed national assistance each year, but in the early 1960s, the total exceeded 100,000. As the NAB came to realize, this was just the tip of the iceberg. Though the NAB paid allowances to many women who lived apart from the fathers of their children, a far greater number managed to survive without the aid of national assistance. There were no official statistics on the total number of separated women in the country, but two studies undertaken in the early 1960s attempted to estimate the number of "fatherless families" in Britain.[49] In a book that caught the attention of the NAB, *Fatherless Families*, Margaret Wynn estimated that in 1963, 250,000 married women in Britain were living with their children apart from their husbands. Not even one-third of them (73,000) received national assistance, and of the 60,000 unmarried mothers in the country, only 23,000 claimed assistance allowances.[50]

This tremendous pool of potential claimants, previously unknown to government officials, made the NAB more defensive about its operations. The NAB's insistence that it should not be a provider of first resort gained intensity when voluntary organizations criticized its policies. In the early 1960s, the National Council for the Unmarried Mother and Her Child sought legislative measures that would make it easier for separated and single women with children to get assistance. Representatives of various organizations observed that women were being "pushed from pillar to post" between NAB offices and the magistrates' courts before assistance was granted.[51] NAB officials bristled at the complaints, saying that the system operated satisfactorily and that no significant changes were necessary. The NAB's defensive posture stemmed not so much from its objection to expediting women's claims for assistance, but rather from its fear of a larger shift toward full governmental responsibility for "fatherless families." Though the bill in question made no mention of such a scheme, the NAB anticipated that the voluntary organizations most interested in such issues might push the debate in that direction.

In *Fatherless Families*, Margaret Wynn had proposed that additional government payments be made to *all* families where no father was present. The NAB wanted no part of that sort of arrangement. Such a system would amount to an abandonment of the principle, deeply rooted in family law and welfare state policy, that husbands and fathers must be held responsible for the support of wives and children. Assigning this responsibility to the state would have not only ideological significance, but great fiscal import as well. As one official noted, "large sums of Exchequer money" were at risk if women were granted assistance without question simply because of the absence of the father.[52] And the drain on public funds might not end there. What about "ordinary families" for whom national assistance was not available because a working father lived in the home? Would pressure be brought to bear to expand national assistance to cover them as well? Preoccupied by these dangers, the NAB regarded even minor changes in the system for paying separated women as the top of a steep, slippery slope of social policy that plunged toward the abyss of total familial dependence on government.

SCRUTINIZING WOMEN'S CLAIMS

The Board was well aware that its campaign to collar irresponsible husbands and fathers was not changing the broad outlines of public provision for women and children. Though the rhetoric generated for public consumption resolutely insisted that men could not escape the long arm of the NAB, the reality, acknowledged in internal communications, was quite different.

Thousands of men could, and did, leave their obligations unfulfilled. How, then, could the NAB contain the rising cost of national assistance paid to women on their own? The obvious answer, which would be elaborated in a myriad of policies, was to deny or deter more women's claims for assistance. This strategy was adopted early on, as the NAB developed a two-pronged attack on what it saw as a debilitating and expensive familial dependence on the state. In governmental policy, skepticism toward some women's claims for assistance grew up alongside the stigmatizing of men who defaulted on their obligations to their dependents.

In addition to the well-advertised campaign to make wayward men shoulder their obligations, in 1949 the NAB began examining separated women's claims for assistance more carefully. At the annual regional controller's conference that year, the consensus that "some of the women get assistance too easily" led to a more vigilant stance toward separated women that would typify NAB policy in the 1950s and 1960s. [53] To reduce "the abuse of public funds," regional controllers, whose directives shaped the practices of the local officers, began revising the way they looked at marital breakdowns. Many felt that the state provided assistance too hastily when a marriage foundered. As a result, local NAB officers became reluctant to give allowances to married women who, they believed, might salvage the marriage. Women who had left their husbands "after a quarrel" and returned to their parents, for instance, were discouraged from filing claims. [54]

Reconciliation

From the government's perspective, the reunion of an estranged couple was the most desirable outcome, and local officers who conducted the initial interview with separated women kept this possibility in mind. If a woman had recently separated from her husband, the visiting officer was to inquire about the circumstances in which the separation occurred and to determine if reconciliation was possible. [55] If a reunion could be orchestrated, no national assistance would be payable. The NAB's annual reports were periodically sprinkled with reconciliation success stories, the most surprising of which involved a forty-nine-year-old laborer who deserted his wife and three children in 1945. Because he persistently failed to make maintenance payments, the Board prosecuted him three times, each case resulting in a two-month prison term. With the timely help of an officer from the NAB, he and his wife reconciled shortly after his last stint in prison, thus allowing the Board to report with satisfaction in 1953 that he was employed and living with his family. [56] NAB officers could save themselves time and the Board money if couples could be persuaded, temporarily at least, to forget their differences. Consequently, putting a man back in his marital home was the overriding imperative in this variant of marriage counseling. A man who had deserted his wife and children and gone to Australia, for example, later returned to find his wife on national assistance and not inclined to reconcile. The Board's officers were happy to help in "smoothing over [the] difficulties," which resulted in a patched up marriage and a family removed from the assistance rolls.[57]

The NAB's interest in reconciliation generated a variety of methods designed to promote reunions, and the line between encouraging reconciliation and coercing it was often blurred in agency policy and practice. Among the tools available to local officers was the ability to deny assistance to a separated woman altogether, a power that could rather quickly compel the woman to return to (or take back) her husband. Anticipating objections to such heavy-handed tactics, NAB officials reassured Parliament and the public that it did not have a "general policy" to withhold benefits to force reunions. In its annual published report to Parliament for 1953, the Board paid lip service to the notion that attempts to starve women into reconciliation would be inconsistent with the agency's mission. The report expressed disapproval of proposals to "withhold assistance if there seems any prospect of forcing a reunion by this means."[58] These statements, however, represented only the veneer of NAB policy. Despite officials' apparent distaste for forced reconciliations, the NAB stopped short of prohibiting the practice altogether and left considerable room for its use by local officers.

The NAB's interest in repairing broken marriages coincided with a growing enthusiasm for marital reconciliation in other government projects outside the context of social security. Coordinated efforts to prevent marital breakup first appeared in social policy just after the war. In 1947, Parliament appointed a special committee to determine what kind of machinery should be used to reconcile separated couples. After months of investigation and discussion, the committee resoundingly endorsed reconciliation as an important policy objective, saying that:

> the preservation of the marriage tie is of the highest importance in the interests of society. The unity of the family is so important that, when parties are estranged reconciliation should be attempted in every case where there is a prospect of success.[59]

Impressed by voluntary organizations' strategies to reconcile estranged spouses, the committee suggested three ways to prevent divorce: (1) educating children, teenagers, and young people considering marriage about marital responsibilities; (2) encouraging spouses to seek marriage guidance at the first sign of discord; and (3) providing counseling to encourage reconciliation after breakups occurred. The committee strongly recommended that marriage guidance and reconciliation services be funded as a form of social service, and a second committee immediately met to finalize plans for funding and administration. State grants were made to facilitate the development of the "new social work," as it was called, with the proviso that the government would supervise marriage guidance programs and control counselor training. The bulk of funding went to the National Marriage Guidance Council, a voluntary organization in the business of preventing and reversing breakups. Marriage guidance work enjoyed strong public and political support throughout the 1950s, including the enthusiastic endorsement of the Royal Commission on Marriage and Divorce in 1956.[60]

Marital repair work was also a staple in the magistrates' court. When a separated woman sought maintenance from the court, she first saw the probation officer, who did his or her best to effect a reconciliation. Probation officers teamed up with local government welfare officers and clergymen to persuade women to return to their husbands.[61] The court system, church workers, and voluntary organizations concerned with the plight of separated women agreed that reconciliation attempts were essential. Even individuals who were critical of NAB policies concerning separated women agreed that reconciliation was usually the best solution to the problems they faced. Margaret Wynn, who pressed for reforms in NAB policy that would increase benefits for separated women, also vigorously advocated reconciliation work. "The protection of the family as the basic social unit of our society must remain a primary end of social policy," she wrote. "Administrative measures for coping with broken families should take second place to measures for promoting reconciliation where this is possible."[62]

Women's Culpability

The NAB's discussion of the pros and cons of forced reconciliation focused in particular on women who might have been at fault in the breakup of the marriage. The Board endorsed the position that a married woman had a "right to live apart from her husband" only if she had been blameless in the breakup.[63] Board officials were clearly disdainful of women who had not established this "right," but they denied making marital innocence a condition of receiving benefits. This framing of the issue obscured the fact that while local officers were not *required* to deny benefits to culpable separated women, they were *allowed* to do so. Rather than clearly instructing local officers not to consider the cause of the separation when women applied for national assistance, upper-level NAB officials left the parameters of decision-making to the local officers, who were "to use their common sense on the situation as they find it."[64] The NAB made clear that in some circumstances, refusing the claims of separated women who had acted foolishly was appropriate: "Plainly assistance ought not to be granted without question," a report noted. "The officer must be cautious about what he grants if the cause of the separation appears to be trifling."[65] The Board's disavowal of the unsavory practice of starving women into reconciliation was thus qualified so as to amount to merely a criticism of abuses of discretion. Though the Board had rhetorically distanced itself from forced reconciliation, in practice it continued to manipulate benefits to coerce some women to look elsewhere for material support. If a "commonsense" assessment by the local officer suggested that the cause of the breakup was trivial, the Board sanctioned the withholding of national assistance.

Local officers, then, were given the latitude to inject moral criteria into their decisions about the claims of separated women. In addition to considering the need for assistance, the local officer could consider the cause of the breakup. Had the woman acted justifiably in threatening the sacred and sustaining bonds of marriage? Denying the claims of women who were considered blameworthy undercut the basic premise of national assistance, which was to meet the needs of those who had no other means of support. Perhaps more than separated women who were "victims" of their husbands' misconduct, women who were thought to have broken the marriage were often completely dependent on the NAB for support. As discussed on p. 55, under the laws governing men's obligation to maintain their wives, women who were at fault in the separation had no claim on their husbands for support.[66] Therefore, the women who were legally prevented from compelling husbands to support them might also be denied assistance from the NAB because of their moral culpability. The Board had said that "a woman cannot be left to starve because her marriage is broken," a compassionate statement of policy suggesting that the Board would relieve want regardless of its cause.[67] In practice, however, this simple criterion of relief was compromised, as the need for assistance could be conflated with the worthiness of the applicant. In effect, national assistance practice mirrored the common law's punitive treatment of culpable wives who sought maintenance from their husbands.

Fraud

NAB officials also began searching more carefully for women who might be abusing or defrauding the system. In the early 1950s, local officers were instructed to be alert to the possibility that women who claimed they had been deserted were actually being supported by and sometimes living with their husbands.[68] Officers were advised to look for evidence of collusion between the spouses, particularly any unwillingness on the part of the woman to obtain a maintenance order. A circular distributed to all area offices in 1953 recommended that the legitimacy of a claim be tested by pressing the woman to take immediate action:

> If the woman shows any reluctance to co-operate in tracing the man, taking proceedings against him, etc., there can usually be no objection to bringing strong pressure to bear on her.[69]

Officials might lead a woman to believe that obtaining a maintenance order was a condition of receiving assistance (this was not the case) or threaten an intrusive special investigation. These tactics were sometimes effective in inducing women to abandon their claims: "In some cases," the circular noted, "the woman will prefer to make herself independent of assistance, and this will often be the most desirable solution." [70] Women, of course, had many reasons for not wanting to initiate proceedings against their estranged spouses, few of which involved fraud. The practices and culture of the NAB, though, became increasingly permeated by the fear that women were trying to cheat the government.

Cohabitation

This general climate of suspicion was also fostered by the NAB's hostility toward another group of women thought to be undeserving of assistance—those living with or having sex with men to whom they were not married. The Board generally denied assistance to women cohabiting with men, a policy loosely based on the assumption that such women were supported by their male companions. Married women who lived with wage-earning spouses were not eligible for national assistance; therefore, the Board maintained, "it would not be right to treat [cohabiting women] more favorably" by granting their claims.[71] The strict obligations and dependencies that the NAB demanded of spouses were thus imposed on other relationships that resembled marriages. There was a disjuncture, however, between the Board's stated rationale for the policy and its application. NAB officers denied women benefits because of their relationships with men, but did not determine whether or not the men involved were acting as breadwinners. There was no attempt to ascertain what support, if any, the men actually provided and no assurance that the support given was adequate to meet even basic needs. The amount of support and the woman's degree of control over it were left entirely to the discretion of the man with whom she lived. The NAB would not provide national assistance if a woman's suspected cohabitee was working, regardless of her impoverishment. In sum, once the NAB concluded a woman was cohabiting, it did not concern itself with the particulars of the relationship: to the state, a marital or quasi-marital relationship was a black box that rendered the material and power relationships within irrelevant, a realm in which public provision had no place. The steadfast refusal to delve into the specifics of deprivation—the shortfall in rent payments, the lack of proper clothing—was out of step with the Board's usual emphasis on measuring need with precision. In cohabitation cases, investigative scrutiny focused not on the quantification of assets, income, and expenses, but on proving the existence of a sexual relationship.

The specific language of the National Assistance Act prohibited only *married* women who lived with wage-earning husbands from claiming assistance, but the NAB applied the prohibition to *any* woman residing with a man. This sleight of hand conflated marriage and cohabitation, but conveniently glossed over the fact that only marriage gave women the legal right to claim support. A man living with a woman was under no obligation to support her unless the two were married. NAB officials were well aware of this legal reality, but did not let it affect their policymaking. Upper-level NAB officials debated this general issue and concluded that national assistance would not be paid to a cohabiting woman. Realizing that the harsh consequences of such a policy needed to be obscured, officials at NAB headquarters instructed officers dealing with such cases to say only that the woman must seek support from the man with whom she was cohabiting, "without going into the fact that the man has no legal liability." [72] The NAB was effective in perpetuating the myth that men were legally obliged to support the women and children with whom they lived. The NAB's policies and practices in this area resulted from careful political calculations about public opinion. High-ranking officials acknowledged privately that the NAB's treatment of cohabiting women was not explicitly supported by the National Assistance Act, but they felt it was a safe bet that "public opinion would support the Board's attitude towards cohabitation."[73] NAB policies were later codified, to some extent, in the law: in the Social Security Act of 1966, under which national assistance became supplementary benefit, "two persons cohabiting as man and wife" were to be treated as spouses for the purpose of assessing need for benefit.[74]

Denying assistance because of cohabitation was a fluid rationale that came to be applied to situations bearing little resemblance to marriages. In practice, the mere existence of a sexual relationship, rather than cohabitation, was sufficient to justify a denial of national assistance. NAB officers operated on the assumption that any relationship between a man and a woman was likely sexual, and they believed that many women were concealing their relationships with men in order to claim assistance. NAB officers thus took on the role of investigators. Women who took in male lodgers were subject to intensive scrutiny by NAB officers, who looked for evidence of a sexual relationship, which would, in turn, lead to a denial of benefits.

Officers were also suspicious of women who claimed they were living alone but appeared to be in relationships with men. Preconceptions about race meant that suspicion fell more heavily on some groups than on others. West Indian women, a memorandum from NAB headquarters stated, did not understand the value of marriage and "constitute[d] a problem" for the NAB. Officers were instructed to keep a close eye on West Indian immigrants (particularly unmarried mothers) living in overcrowded housing where it was difficult to know "whether the women are solely dependent on their own resources or whether they have joined up with coloured men in work." [75] In this context, cohabitation was inferred merely from the close living quarters and the alleged moral laxity of the West Indians.

The NAB's definition of cohabitation was expansive, often collapsing any distinction between an ongoing relationship and the existence of a common household. The NAB often employed special investigation units to uncover evidence of cohabitation, as in the case of Jane Larson, who lived in northern London.[76] Larson, who had two dependent children, was in the midst of divorce proceedings, and her husband had alleged in his divorce complaint that Martin Patterson broke up the marriage. Patterson lived with his mother, but the special investigator contended that he spent most of his days and nights off duty with Jane Larson. The local NAB officer concluded that they were "to all intends [sic] and purposes living together and that Patterson returns occasionally to his mother's house to confuse the issue." [77] To complicate matters further, Patterson maintained his "legal wife" from whom he had separated. Still, the NAB found that Jane Larson should look to him for support, and her application for national assistance was denied. There is no record of what became of Jane Larson and her two children, but it is unlikely that Martin Patterson, earning only £13 a week and under a court order to support his wife, was willing and able to provide reasonable material support.

Jane Larson's case demonstrates the development of a relatively new method for investigating claimants. The NAB officers who interviewed claimants routinely looked for evidence of cohabitation, but they did not always have time to perform thorough investigations. For this reason, selected officers were assigned to special investigative duty. These special investigators spent all of their time looking into cases of possible fraud or abuse. They focused on two types of claimants: the man with unreported earnings and, as in the case of Jane Larson, "the woman who claimed she was living on her own when she was actually living with and being maintained by a man." [78] The special investigative unit had first been formed in 1953, but was not much used or discussed until 1957. At that time, the unit had only twenty-eight men, but by the end of 1959, the cadre of special investigators had grown to sixty. Investigators worked on false desertion cases, but devoted more time to allegations of cohabitation. [79]

At first, the investigations usually led to either the NAB's withdrawal of the allowance or the woman's abandonment of the claim. But as the number of separated women claiming benefit mushroomed in the early 1960s, the scope and character of the special investigations changed. Forty more special investigators were added, bringing the total to 100, and for the first time, criminal prosecution for fraud became a significant objective in the investigations. In 1963, fifty-eight women were tried on fraud charges. In 1964, 98 women were prosecuted, and in 1965, the total leaped to 525. [80] The overall effect of the special investigations was even greater than the number of prosecutions indicates. The NAB proudly reported that "in very many more cases" allowances were withdrawn from women, in spite of the lack of sufficient evidence for prosecution. Very few women appealed these denials. In many other cases, the threat of a special investigation resulted in a withdrawal of a claim for assistance.[81]

The stepped-up special investigations of the late 1950s and early 1960s were public symbols of the NAB's resolve to punish women who lived on public funds when male financial support was thought to be available to them. However, many of the women turned away by the NAB had no claim, legal or otherwise, on the earnings of the men the NAB saw as providers. The NAB's indifference to this fact suggests its policies concerning cohabitation served multiple, unstated functions. The punitive nature of the NAB's practices expressed official disapproval of sexual relationships outside marriage. The conditions attached to benefits were used as a means of regulating the sexuality of a suspect class of lone women, who, if they chose to have relationships with men, could not also count on material support from the government. Moreover, by defining cohabitation very broadly and likening it to marriage, the NAB attempted to widen the sphere of marital responsibility and dependence. There was no corresponding expansion, however, of men's liabilities in this regard in family law.

Extended Families

The NAB's enforcement of female dependence was not confined to marital or quasi-marital relationships. In households of extended families, NAB officers regularly denied assistance to unemployed women who, they assumed, performed domestic labor for wage-earning relatives. NAB policymakers drew an analogy between the household economy and the broader labor market. In this market model, women provided services in the home in exchange for food, lodging, and other support. In considering national assistance applications from unmarried (or separated) women living with relatives, NAB officers assumed an income equivalent to the market value of the housekeeping and personal care services the women supplied. Attributing this income to women meant that they were denied national assistance altogether or received severely reduced allowances. NAB guidelines on this subject advised officers how to explain such decisions to the women seeking assistance:

> It can, if necessary, be explained to the applicant, or on appeal to the Tribunal, that a man in employment who requires domestic assistance in his home will ordinarily expect to have to pay for it (if the mother has died, the position is, of course, that the daughter has taken her place and should not expect to get assistance which her mother could not get). [82]

Although women in these situations probably received some degree of in-kind support from relatives, the NAB made no inquiry to see if it actually rose to the level of the assumed income. Again, like the cohabiting women discussed in the previous section, these women could not compel the wage earners in the house to support them. As a practical matter, they were at the mercy of their relatives and were deprived of the small measure of autonomy conferred by a national assistance grant. Similarly situated men, on the other hand, were not penalized by the NAB. The NAB's strict presumptions about the gendered division of labor in a household economy shielded men from the harsh results that fell on their female counterparts. Officials assumed that unemployed men who lived with relatives were not responsible for household labor and therefore did not have income from other members of the house. Their national assistance allowances were not reduced or eliminated.

In the 1950s, London was full of extended family households. War-time bombing and a campaign to eliminate substandard housing created an intractable housing shortage after the war. The situation of Gloria Barnes, who lived with her father and sister in Kingston, was common. In the summer of 1958, after years of employment, she began giving full-time care to her ailing father. Unable to work, her father received national assistance. In October 1958, Gloria Barnes filed for national assistance as well, presenting a doctor's certificate that she was required at home to give constant attention to her father. She received a reduced national assistance grant, however, because her sister was employed. The NAB reasoned that the sister benefited from Barnes' housework and therefore had to be contributing to her maintenance.[83]

Embedded in social policy was the understanding that women could always be called on to be caregivers and housekeepers. The state would not interfere with this arrangement by providing full benefits to destitute women, who were left no choice but to be at the beck and call of family members. Though E. M. Cranford was sixty-nine years old herself, she cooked and cleaned for the brother-in-law, with whom she lived in a rural area south of London. Laying the groundwork for a reduced national assistance allowance, the NAB officer described her as:

> an example of the 'spinster aunt' who is always available to look after her various relations when they are in difficulties and who seeks nothing in return but her maintenance and enough money to replenish a meagre wardrobe and purchase the little necessary extras.[84]

The state of happy penury depicted by the NAB officer was apparently an illusion, however, as Cranford sought national assistance in July of 1959. The Board awarded her only a reduced allowance, arguing that her brother-in-law should be expected to provide board and lodging in exchange for her services.

One of the most despised aspects of the government's relief efforts of the 1930s had been the household means test. Need was assessed on a household, rather than individual basis. The result was that the government would not give assistance to an unemployed individual if he or she could depend on the wages of someone else for subsistence. The system was universally condemned as demeaning, usually because of the humiliation suffered by male breadwinners, and the National Assistance Act of 1948 had been intended to erase the demoralizing dependencies that were created. Of course, the dependence of a wife on a husband was considered to be normal and appropriate, so by the terms of the act, married women were forced to rely on their husbands' wages. However, the household means test, which had been repudiated so adamantly in post-war social policy, continued to be imposed on women even outside of marriage.

According to the standard narrative of twentieth-century social policy, the early years of the post-war welfare state in Britain were an uneventful period, requiring no major legislative interventions and dominated by the political consensus that the state should be the primary guarantor of social security. But the administrative records of those who actually implemented the national assistance scheme reveal a different picture of the government's conception of its responsibility. What is striking about the welfare state that was actually being built—as opposed to the depictions of it by politicians—was administrators' discomfort with the very concept that the government should ensure material support to all citizens.

In the 1950s and early 1960s, the NAB fought to keep the state from becoming the primary source of support for poor women who had some connection to a wage earner. In various contexts, the NAB cast about to find an individual who might take over the state's role of provider. Drawing on the legacies of the poor law and family law, officials discouraged women from turning to the government and pressured men to assume financial responsibility for their estranged wives and children. Long-standing gendered principles of dependence and obligation were re-institutionalized in the post-war welfare state, articulated and enforced differently, but still carrying essentially the same ideologies that had long grounded the state's view of families. In the grand scheme of post-war welfare policy, the NAB's efforts were not successful. Women embraced the post-war welfare state's possibilities of inclusion, and the number of women seeking assistance, particularly those with children, continued to climb. Still, the intent of post-war social policy, and for many individual women the effect, was to reinforce and increase women's subordination to partners and family members and circumscribe their rights in the welfare state.

3 Reform and Deterrence
The National Assistance Board's Strategies for Unemployed Men

In the 1950s and 1960s, the specter of unsupported families living off the public purse was a source of perpetual anxiety for officials at all levels of the British National Assistance Board (NAB, or Board). The NAB devoted considerable time and attention to the increasingly arduous task of encouraging and coercing lone women to turn to men, rather than the state, for economic support. The premise of this approach, of course, was that men were willing and able to sustain their families by wage-earning. What good were policies encouraging women's dependence if men themselves had no qualms about seeking public assistance? To deter men from claiming national assistance, which had replaced poor relief in 1948, the NAB developed complicated machinery to reinforce a norm of masculinity centered on male breadwinning and autonomy. Well-publicized programs to correct and reform unemployed men on the national assistance rolls became part and parcel of the NAB's program, as important as its payment of cash allowances. Despite the oft-repeated public renunciations of the punitive and stigmatizing features of the old Poor Law, the NAB's strategies to shore up masculinity owed much to the disciplinary aspects of poor relief that had, in theory, been discarded once and for all after the Second World War. The rationales of the workhouse persisted in NAB policy, as did the use of communal sanctions to reprimand the morally deficient. But in its project to reform and discipline unemployed men, the NAB could also draw on the assets of the modern bureaucracy, including specialization within its own ranks and medical and vocational expertise from other agencies. In the 1950s and 1960s, the practices of both the old and new worlds of welfare converged; the result was a mixture of disparate methods that ultimately functioned more effectively in dissuading men from seeking assistance than in reforming them.

In the literature on the British post-war welfare state, scholars generally focus on the last quarter of the twentieth century, rather than the 1950s and early 1960s, when discussing significant governmental scrutiny and criticism of unemployed men receiving public assistance. Alan Deacon argues that when unemployment rates rose dramatically in the late 1960s and 1970s, widespread press coverage of alleged fraud and abuse inflamed public hostility toward the unemployed. The resulting "scroungerphobia," he contends, prompted officials to introduce several measures to detect and deter malingering.[1] Chris Jones and Tony Novak detail the backlash against the unemployed under Thatcherism, which included benefit reductions, stigmatization, and efforts to monitor the behavior and appearance of claimants.[2] The literature pays scant attention to the NAB's views of unemployed men before the late 1960s, characterizing the period as one of "quiet obscurity,"[3] during which officials did not concern themselves with malingering or scrounging.[4] However, an examination of the NAB's policies and practices in its early years belies this picture of complacency. Instead, the evidence indicates that officials, who were intensely concerned about unemployed men claiming assistance, developed elaborate mechanisms for moving them off the rolls. By the early 1950s, the drive to cut the number of unemployed applicants had begun; an undertaking that gradually pulled together various threads of the modern bureaucratic state.

Various narratives emerged in the NAB's explanations of its mission, narratives that featured the state as a benevolent, guiding hand enabling a transition from idleness to productivity, or alternately, as a stern taskmaster refusing to subsidize laziness. These straightforward morality tales imposed order and meaning on a far more complicated social and administrative reality. The causes of prolonged male unemployment—often involving mental and physical disability—were complex, and the NAB's tools were often ill-suited for the task of getting men into sustainable work. Yet, the simplified representations produced by the NAB—for its own self-definition, for the edification of its claimants, and for broader public consumption—played a large role in forming prevailing cultural beliefs about what welfare was and what it should be. In NAB narratives, men's reliance on assistance signaled a failure of masculinity. Proper manhood, fostered by NAB programs, would result in self-sufficiency and obviate the need for state support. In practice, however, the deterrent effect of the government's methods for instilling manliness overshadowed their rehabilitative achievements. In the 1950s and 1960s, thousands of men left the national assistance rolls to avoid the various sorts of reform dispensed by the NAB. To NAB officials, this outcome was just as acceptable as successful rehabilitation; in the end, the measure of appropriate masculinity was abstinence from national assistance.

National assistance, like the Poor Law it succeeded in 1948, was a means-tested program. Only those with income and resources below certain levels were eligible for allowances. Many recipients of national assistance also received national insurance benefit—either old-age pensions, unemployment benefit, or sickness benefit. They were entitled to national insurance benefit by virtue of their payroll contributions to the National Insurance Fund, but national insurance alone was not sufficient for subsistence. For many people, national assistance "topped up" their national insurance payment. An unemployed man, therefore, might receive unemployment benefit and an assistance allowance. But unemployment benefit could only be paid for six months; once this was exhausted, he was entirely dependent on national assistance. Also, for men who did not have stable work histories, unemployment benefit through national insurance was not available since they had not made enough contributions to the National Insurance Fund. They, too, were completely reliant on national assistance.

THE EMERGENCE OF MALE UNEMPLOYMENT AS A PRIORITY AT THE NAB

The NAB's various plans to deal with the male shirker unfolded only gradually during the 1950s. Under the terms of the National Assistance Act of 1948, most men under sixty-five who filed for national assistance were obliged to register for work at the local employment exchange and check in at the exchange twice a week. Initially, this requirement was thought to be a sufficient check on any scrounging tendencies of male applicants; thus, in the first couple of years of the NAB's existence, the problem of work-shy men did not figure prominently in internal discussions or in reports generated for the public. Instead, the Board preferred to highlight the role it played in relieving the poverty of those who clearly deserved help—the old, the sick, and the severely disabled.

A good barometer of the Board's priorities could be found in the work of the local Advisory Committees, charged with the task of advising the Board's officers on difficult issues of policy and on particularly troublesome individual cases. The Advisory Committees were designed to incorporate community opinions and standards into the distribution of national assistance at the local level. In London, for example, planners broke the region up into seven areas, each of which had its own Advisory Committee. Each Advisory Committee consisted of subcommittees drawn from the different towns and boroughs in the Advisory Committee's jurisdiction. Held every two months, meetings of the Advisory Subcommittees provided members with the chance to participate directly in the practice of welfare distribution. Each Subcommittee had four or five members, usually including at least one town councilor or alderman. The subcommittee members were unpaid, and many members had been involved in the voluntary social services. Half were nominees of the NAB, a quarter were nominees of the local authorities, and a quarter were "industrial" nominees—half employers and half employees. The vast majority were business or governmental elites who welcomed the appointments as an opportunity for honorable public service. Terms of service were two years, but the same people were often reappointed year after year.

In the Advisory Subcommittee meetings, members considered cases referred to them by the local NAB office because they had been difficult for NAB officials to resolve. Only a tiny fraction of the total caseload was referred to the Subcommittees, which dealt with seven to ten cases per meeting. Subcommittee members discussed each case with the local NAB officer and often interviewed the applicant as well. In the London region in the late 1940s, the types of cases taken on by the Advisory Subcommittees varied widely. Notably, concern about male unemployment did not dominate their agendas as it would just a few years later. Although about one-third of the cases sent to Subcommittees in the London region involved "lengthy unemployment,"[5] neither the Subcommittees nor the NAB chose to emphasize this part of the Board's work. In defining the contribution of the Advisory Subcommittees and its own larger mission, the NAB gravitated toward other reference points that focused on the Board's capacity for compassion and resourcefulness in responding to the needs of the poor. Reporting the success stories of the London region's Advisory Subcommittees in 1949, the Regional Controller detailed ten cases that were to serve as examples of the Subcommittees' efforts. Typical of the recipients of the Subcommittees' good works were a seventy-five-year-old man suffering from seizures whom the Subcommittee persuaded to enter a home for the elderly; a couple with tuberculosis whose move into a larger flat was made possible by the influence of a Subcommittee member; and an elderly woman who, through the good offices of Subcommittee members, began to receive hot meals from the Women's Voluntary Services and home visits from the British Red Cross Society.[6]

But it did not take long for the sentiment and self-congratulations of these stories to be eclipsed by more pressing moral imperatives. By the early 1950s, the presence of men who seemed capable of work on the national assistance rolls began to elicit indignant criticism. Press reports, editorials, and letters to the editor questioned the wisdom of supporting able-bodied men and their families. Complaints about the "abuse of public assistance," while not an overwhelming presence in the media, were voiced frequently enough to focus NAB officials' attention on men who might be taking advantage of the system.[7] A "special correspondent" for the *London Times* in 1953 charged that men "can and do throw themselves out of work" in order to collect national assistance. Moreover, the correspondent alleged, national assistance enabled criminal activity.

> A great many thieves and shop-lifters are recipients of National Assistance. They supplement this income by stealing and, in so far as they are able to commit crimes because of idleness, it will be seen that the assistance given with the object of relieving destitution is, in fact, helping the recipients to break the law.[8]

B. E. Astbury, General Secretary of the Family Welfare Association (formerly the Charity Organization Society) argued that such behavior had rarely occurred under the watch of the Poor Law relieving officer, whose close supervision of recipients of relief minimized shirking and other abuses.[9] Other readers echoed this nostalgia for the Poor Law, reciting the virtues of the local relieving officer who had intimate knowledge of the community's residents and almost total discretion in deciding whether applicants should get relief. "Under the old system," wrote F. E. S. Hatfield of Essex, "the relieving officer was the channel through which payments were made. He lived in the district and he knew all his 'clients.' Any abuse soon reached his ears at the local."[10]

By the late 1950s, officials at NAB headquarters were acutely sensitive to public perceptions of abuse of national assistance. In order to "forestall adverse criticism," in 1958, headquarters issued new instructions to all its area offices to be more aggressive with suspected scroungers.[11] But negative publicity continued. To the Board's chagrin, a minor criminal case in Chesterfield drew extensive press coverage in 1960 because the convicted man had been receiving national assistance. Prosecuted for stealing coal, Jack Cooper and his wife had been receiving about £12 per week from the NAB, and the local and national media held him up as a symbol of abuse of the welfare system. The case was the subject of a Parliamentary Question in November 1960, and both the NAB and the Ministry of Labour launched what they called a campaign against "Idle Jacks."[12]

NAB officials were ambivalent about the complaints against them; they shared their critics' disgust for scroungers, but resented what they saw as exaggerated and unfair coverage of the issue. The chairman of the NAB, Sir Geoffrey Hutchinson, complained that the public had been misled by inaccurate reporting and by the omission of "the full facts of the case which unfortunately newspapermen did not always trouble to get."[13] The Board found itself in the uncomfortable position of having to defend its provision of allowances to unemployed men publicly, while simultaneously trying to devise ways to remove them from the rolls. Upper-level NAB officials were clearly anxious to stave off any allegation that the state was underwriting the idleness of British men, for such a charge had sufficient ideological power to undermine the Board's credibility. To protect its legitimacy, the Board began taking steps to deter working-age men from applying for assistance and to create the impression that it was doing everything possible to transform shirkers into productive workers. Fear of negative public and political opinion was an abiding concern at the NAB, as negative depictions of unemployed men on the rolls continued to surface in the media periodically throughout the 1950s and early 1960s. In 1965, the last year of the NAB's existence (the following year it was replaced by the Supplementary Benefit Commission), officials at headquarters still worried about public misperceptions of the provision of assistance to unemployed men:

Where these men have poor work records, the general public—influenced by hearing about occasional flagrant cases of willful idleness—tend to see the issue as one of workshys or layabouts sponging on the Welfare State.[14]

NAB officials feared that in the popular imagination, national assistance provided a haven for shirkers, a misconception that threatened the integrity of the welfare state itself. Moving unemployed men off the rolls thus remained a top priority at the NAB.

In 1951, the NAB conducted a detailed survey in an attempt to determine the number of unemployed men on assistance and the reasons for their unemployment. In all of England, Scotland, and Wales, 5,500 men receiving national assistance were thought to be capable of securing employment. This group made up only about 10% of all the men classified as "unemployed" on the assistance rolls.[15] The other 90% had mental or physical disabilities that seriously impaired their employment prospects. In its 1952 Annual Report, the NAB put the proportion of work-shy men on assistance in perspective: the average area office (serving a population of about 140,000) would provide assistance to about 5,000 people (for themselves and their dependents); of those, only about 20 were thought to be work-shy. The NAB used these statistics to defend itself against allegations of improvidence, but officials realized that violation of the male breadwinner ideal, however slight, could not be tolerated in the national assistance scheme. "[Workshy men]," the NAB report noted, "though they may be numerically insignificant, are an unnecessary burden on the State, causing great offence to industrious members of the community."[16] It was not the number of alleged scroungers or the cost, but violation of principle that drove policy.

NAB officials became increasingly preoccupied with schemes to move unemployed men off the rolls, often taking little care to differentiate between the lazy and the disabled. Married men with children presented the greatest challenge. Although it was within the power of the NAB to withdraw the allowance of a man who refused offers of work, the allowance for his wife and children could not be withheld. NAB officials feared that if the man's portion of the allowance was terminated, he would live off the money intended for his dependents, resulting in their impoverishment and probably greater expense to the Board in the long run in the form of emergency grants for the household. In addition to the financial cost, the government's support of men with families raised ideological issues as well. Officials worried about the creation of what would later be labeled a "culture of dependency." At a Regional Controllers' meeting in 1951, the Chairman of the NAB urged staffers to give preference to men with children when trying to make job placements. He stressed that, "it was demoralizing to children to be brought up in a household which had grown to rely entirely upon the State as its means of support."[17] There was a certain amount of nostalgia among high-level NAB officials for the unpleasantness of poor relief, which had prevented all but the most desperate and pathetic from living for long periods off state aid. In the NAB Annual Report for 1952, Board members lamented the passing of the workhouse, which had served as an effective tool for forcing the scrounger into employment: "At one time such a man could have been told that the only form of relief open to him and his dependents was the workhouse, but this is no longer possible. . . . "[18]

RE-ESTABLISHMENT CENTERS

The workhouse may not have been available, but NAB officials busied themselves developing other deterrents more in tune with the modern sensibilities that recoiled from the cruelties of the Victorian Poor Law. In June 1951, the Board opened its first Re-Establishment Center at Clent, near Birmingham. The Re-Establishment Center, which provided residential accommodation for about forty men, aimed to:

> build up the physical strength and vigour of men who have neglected themselves; to accustom to regular occupation and to doing a fair day's work men who have had no regular occupation for some time; and to get to understand the man and win his confidence and to stimulate his pride in himself and his interest in things about him.[19]

Officials were careful to note that the Re-Establishment Center would *not* teach a man a trade or provide any vocational training. Instead, the Center would build character and instill the regular habits necessary to maintain employment.[20]

The NAB quickly acquired property to begin its rehabilitation project. Located outside a small village, "the healthy site in the countryside" was thought to be an ideal environment for setting irresponsible men on the path to self-sufficiency.[21] The site had formerly been used by the government to house agricultural workers, and because the building and grounds were Crown property, the cost of launching the project was minimal. The building had one large room with cots for sleeping, a kitchen and dining area, a room for reading and listening to the radio, and a workshop. To build discipline, the men were expected to put in a full day's work. They maintained the Center by cleaning, painting, making minor repairs, and tending the vegetable and flower gardens. They also did simple woodwork, made mats, chopped wood, and dismantled obsolete telephone exchange equipment. Only a small staff was required to supervise and feed the men: a warden, an assistant warden, a full-time cook, and a part-time cook.

The men sent to the Re-Establishment Center were released when "they appeared ready to be put in employment." Stays at the Center ranged from a few weeks to a few months. While living at the Center, men did not receive a national assistance allowance. Officials estimated that the cost of running the Center would not be much more than the cost of the allowances that would have been paid if the men had been at home. Some of the residents of the Center had been ordered to attend by an Appeals Tribunal, but they were greatly outnumbered by men the NAB referred to as "volunteers." Publicly, the NAB maintained that the local officers and Advisory Subcommittees merely "persuaded" the men to go to the Center, but it is unlikely that the men felt they had any real choice in the matter. Candidates for the Re-Establishment Center were made to understand that they should not expect continuing support from the NAB if they were not cooperative. The NAB could take the formal steps to have a "section 10" order issued by an Appeals Tribunal, which resulted in immediate termination of national assistance if the man did not report to the Center, but in practice, the same message was conveyed by the informal pressure applied by local officers and Advisory Subcommittees. Violation of a formal order to attend the Center could later be used very effectively as evidence against a man if officials decided to institute criminal proceedings against him for failure to maintain himself and/or his dependents.

Despite the Board's advertisements of the Re-Establishment Center as a rejuvenating, bucolic retreat, most men wanted no part of it. In 1952, only 20% of the men directed to attend the Center under a section 10 order actually showed up.[22] They probably regarded it as being uncomfortably similar to the workhouse it was supposed to replace; re-establishment, like the workhouse, required working without pay and leaving home. The Re-Establishment Center therefore had a tremendous deterrent effect, and many men who were instructed to report there simply abandoned their claims for national assistance allowances. In this sense, the Re-Establishment Center functioned exactly as the workhouse had: when working at the Center was the only form of state aid available, many men chose to fend for themselves. This came as no surprise to NAB officials, who saw deterrence as rehabilitation's most important function. "The success of Clent [Re-Establishment Center]," the NAB 1952 annual report stated,

> is not to be measured by the number of 'conscripts' who go to the Centre and profit from its regimen so much as by the number who refuse to attend with the result that they cease to be a charge on public funds.[23]

NAB officers also maintained that for those men who did attend, the Re-Establishment Center was succeeding in its ostensible role as an institution of reform. In 1956, the Board proudly reported that the residents had demonstrated their newly adopted values of teamwork and respect for authority in an unexpected but satisfying way. A new resident, on his first day at the Center, announced that he would do no work and invited others to follow his example. The attempted revolt failed, as the other men kept working and the insurgent was quickly removed. To ensure that similar behavior from others would not follow, the NAB brought criminal charges against the man, and the prosecution and subsequent conviction received considerable attention from the press. The warden gave an interview for a BBC television program, and on the day of his planned appearance, the NAB reported, some of the men at the Center

> rallied round with offers of help. Two of them volunteered to wash down his car, one took his shoes away to clean, one pressed his suit, while another offered him some sedative tablets with the assurance that they were not habit-forming. This esprit de corps displayed by a group of men whom most people would regard as lacking in a sense of social responsibility is an encouraging indication of what can be done in a small self-contained community under firm but sympathetic leadership.[24]

NAB officials assumed that the men's obedience in the face of possible rebellion and their kindness toward the warden resulted from their rehabilitation at the Center. The NAB did not acknowledge the possibility that the men were capable of obedience and kindness before they arrived or that their motives may have been different than the Board understood them to be. Self-preservation and the hope for more favorable treatment from the warden and staff may have provided as strong an impetus as the "esprit de corps" taught at the Center, but such considerations, of course, would have undermined the straightforward narrative of reform in which the Board was so heavily invested.

The Board produced this anecdote as proof of successful rehabilitation, perhaps because evidence more relevant to the stated purpose of the Re-Establishment Center—achieving self-sufficiency in the labor market—was in short supply. By the end of 1953, the 250 men who had completed a stint at the Center fell into three categories: those who had found and maintained employment; those who had left the assistance rolls (but were not known to be employed); and those who remained on the assistance rolls, unemployed. Only 23% of the men had gotten work and were believed to be still employed in December 1953. The Board, however, inflated its success rate to 40% by including not only men in employment, but also men who left the rolls but were not known to have employment.[25] The results of re-establishment work only grew more dismal during the 1950s. Of the men who left the Center between August 1956 and August 1957, only 15% had sustained employment through December 1957.

Despite the NAB's enthusiasm for the virtues of fresh air, hard work, and clean living, the Re-Establishment Center's remedies for lengthy unemployment did little to address its underlying causes. As the NAB's own survey in 1951 had shown, much of the failure to stay in work could be attributed to mental and/or physical disability. Another NAB survey conducted in 1956 concluded that the vast majority of the "hard core of the unemployed" were unskilled men with some form of disability that made finding work difficult or impossible.[26] The men who populated the Re-Establishment Center typified the "hard core of the unemployed," and for many of them, disability was an important factor in their failure to conform to the industrious ideal promoted so zealously by the NAB. NAB officials were aware that many of the candidates for reform struggled to perform work tasks, even in the sheltered environment of the Re-Establishment Center. The staff reported that many of the residents "are limited by mental and physical handicaps in the quantity and quality of work which they can do, and it would be wrong to expect too much of them."[27] The staff had few complaints about the men's attitudes, pointing out that nearly all of them "cooperate to the best of their ability in the arrangements made for them."[28]

When NAB officials felt compelled to explain why so few of the Center's graduates could find and hold jobs, they cited the prevalence of mental and physical incapacity. The re-establishment program, they suggested, could not be blamed for the handicaps of its students. In 1953, for example, the NAB reported that two-thirds of the men who went back on national assistance after they left the Re-Establishment Center were incapable of work because of a variety of problems ranging from tuberculosis to schizophrenia.[29] The effect of disability on the employment opportunities of the Center's recruits was probably even more far-reaching than the NAB recognized. The NAB claimed as "successes" the men who disappeared after their completion of the re-establishment program, not because they found employment, but because they left the assistance rolls. It seems likely, however, that many of them had the same difficulties maintaining steady employment as their counterparts who continued to receive state aid.

The Re-Establishment Center rested on two premises: first, that lengthy unemployment resulted from a deficient work ethic and an absence of regular habits; and second, that the necessary values and discipline could be instilled. But by the NAB's own account, a large proportion of the men sent to be reformed had handicaps that could not be remedied by the training offered at the Center. In addition, to the extent that the men's unemployment stemmed from a willful refusal to exert themselves, the prescribed character-building exercises had only minimal effect. Why, then, did the NAB continue to promote a program that accomplished so little? As officials candidly acknowledged, the deterrent effect of the Re-Establishment Center was invaluable. Many men who were threatened with rehabilitation left the assistance rolls, at least temporarily, as did many men who completed the rehabilitation course. Moreover, the idea of re-establishment served as a savvy public relations strategy to answer charges that the NAB was doing nothing to stop scroungers from abusing public funds. Finally, the NAB had a hefty ideological investment in this particular kind of reform as social policy. Despite the contradictions in the objectives and methods of re-establishment, NAB officers believed that a generous dose of the masculine virtues could only help men receiving state aid. As one NAB official put it:

The tonic effects of the healthy environment, with good and regular meals and an orderly routine may well have given the man a little more self-respect, and in several instances the stay at the Center, though achieving no immediate success, pointed the way to possible further remedial action.[30]

The various messages conveyed by the re-establishment project were important to the NAB, and in February 1959, a second Re-Establishment Center, modeled after the one in Clent, was opened at West Hill in Durham. The West Hill Re-Establishment Center would serve the northern counties and Scotland, while the Clent facility would draw recruits from the southern counties and Wales. Re-establishment had become available to virtually all of Britain.

Two and a half years later, the NAB began another re-establishment project that would become its most admired innovation. Brady House, in the working-class district of Stepney in the East End of London, opened its doors in November 1961. The tonic effects of the countryside were traded for an urban environment, which officials hoped would offer more employment opportunities for the men after their release. Unlike the two other Re-Establishment Centers, Brady House was non-residential; participants lived in London and returned home each night. It was "designed for the married man with a bad record of unemployment who has some excuse for not leaving home to go to a residential Center."[31] The "will to work," the centerpiece of re-establishment, was fostered in an immediate context of familial relationships and responsibility. Regular work in the day complemented regular domestic routines in the evening. By designing Brady House specifically for married men with families, the NAB underscored the necessity for men to understand and fulfill their obligations to their dependents. Providing public financial support for entire families, after all, was an expensive proposition for the government. Brady House made its appearance at a time when NAB officers were increasingly worried about another problem faced by the Board—the rapidly escalating number of women with children claiming assistance because their estranged husbands did not support them. NAB officials hoped men would learn that defaulting on their familial obligations was unacceptable. For the NAB's constituency of applicants, Brady House was a means to integrate the work ethic with the moral duty to support a family. Perhaps the men on whom the NAB could exert influence would be steeled against any inclination they might later have to abandon their dependents.

Like the other Re-Establishment Centers, Brady House doubled as both a site of indoctrination in male breadwinner ideology and an effective deterrent to further claims for assistance. In a confidential memorandum circulated in early 1962, officials at NAB headquarters made clear that the value of Brady House lay in its deterrence:

The mere existence of the London Centre is more likely to make an important contribution to removing unemployed men from the Board's books and saving public funds than whatever is achieved for those men who attend there.[32]

In the first two months of Brady House's existence, managers in the NAB offices in the London area reported that forty men, with allowances totaling £200 per week, had abandoned their claims after being told they would be expected to attend. Upper-level NAB officials also encouraged local officers to secure orders from Appeals Tribunals for men to report to Brady House, which, if violated, could then provide grounds for criminal prosecution:

> In this way Brady House should be the means of invoking the ultimate sanction of prosecution against the man whose workshyness cannot otherwise be established because he is able to make himself unacceptable to any employer.[33]

The Brady House regimen of reform varied little from the formula of the first two Re-Establishment Centers. The men reported at 8:30 in the morning, and spent the rest of the day cleaning, painting, doing simple carpentry, and working in the kitchen. The warden allowed two tea breaks and a lunch hour, and the men returned home at 4:30 in the afternoon. The staff gave the men haircuts for neatness and uniformity. W. J. Botwright, the warden, prepared brochures about Brady House for local employers and actively promoted re-establishment work. Emphasizing the premium placed on cooperation rather than compulsion, the Warden insisted that Brady House bore "no resemblance to the old 'Workhouse.'"[34] He sought to improve the men's timekeeping, stamina, reliability, attitudes, appearance, dexterity, and health. Botwright was a proficient publicist for Brady House, and his skills helped win a good deal of favorable press coverage. In July 1963, *The Economist* published a positive editorial on the facility. Enamored of both its deterrent and rehabilitative functions, the editors marveled that so much money could be saved by getting tough with men who had no business on national assistance. Brady House was characterized as "a remarkable experiment" and held up as a shining example of welfare policy.[35]

The results of the Brady House program, measured by the employment status of the men who completed it, were less than remarkable. Less than a quarter of the men who passed through Brady House's doors in the first ten months of its operation (November 1961–August 1962) were working at the end of 1962. Like the other Re-Establishment Centers, Brady House dealt with some of the most intractable unemployment cases, which meant that a large proportion of the men were unskilled and disabled. Even the most well-intentioned attempts to inculcate the "will to work" could not provide the tools these men needed to hold employment. These realities went unmentioned by *The Economist* and other newspaper reports. Even more significantly, the Centers' poor results failed to alter the NAB's policies. The governmental and public support for re-establishment continued, and in 1963, the NAB made plans to open a facility like Brady House in Manchester. By the mid-1960s, a thousand men passed through the Re-Establishment Centers each year.[36]

ADVISORY SUBCOMMITTEES

At the same time the Re-Establishment Centers were growing in popularity, the work and the priorities of the local Advisory Subcommittees were shifting to reflect the NAB's preoccupation with the work-shy male. In the first years of national assistance, the Subcommittees, which advised local officers on difficult cases, spent most of their time on the dilemmas of the old and sick. In 1949, one-third of the cases referred to the Subcommittees in Surrey, just outside London, involved lengthy unemployment, but by the late 1950s and early 1960s, the proportion had shot to 90%. Local NAB officers selected the cases sent to the Subcommittees and therefore determined the focus of the work done there, but the Subcommittee members embraced their new roles as vocational counselors and disciplinarians. In their meetings every other month, the four or five members of the Subcommittee would discuss troublesome cases with the local NAB officer and would usually interview the individuals involved. Receiving an "invitation" to appear before the subcommittee sent dread into the heart of even the most assured recipient of national assistance. Subcommittee members invariably probed into occupational and personal matters, asking about past work, efforts to find a job, living arrangements, and relationships.

The subcommittees produced their own narratives about what transpired during and after their meetings. Two basic types of stories about the long-term unemployed emerged: 1) the heartwarming success story featuring the helpful advice and/or beneficent intervention of an influential subcommittee member; and 2) the more common cautionary tale highlighting the moral deficiency and recalcitrance of the man and the stern reprimands of subcommittee members. The stories of kind assistance usually depended on the local influence and connections of Subcommittee members, but occasionally simple tips on appearance or presentation skills sufficed. One Surrey Subcommittee reported that a man who had been unemployed for eight months had found work after being advised to "clean himself up a bit" before approaching prospective employers.[37] Subcommittee members could also involve themselves more directly in job searches, persuading local employers to find work for men who had been difficult to place in employment. The local authority, in particular, usually agreed to give special consideration to men the Subcommittees recommended.

Subcommittees bestowed their patronage on claimants considered worthy of it, those who impressed the members with their diligence in looking for employment or their responsibility in handling difficult circumstances. In 1960, for example, one of the Surrey Advisory Subcommittees interviewed an unemployed Pakistani man who had lived in England intermittently since 1939. Though qualified as a barrister, he had been unable to find employment in his profession; his only work in the preceding years had been as a laborer. Pleased with the evidence he presented of his persistent job search, the Subcommittee arranged for him to be hired by the local Education Authority as a supply teacher.[38]

Sympathy for a claimant's domestic situation and respect for his fortitude could also result in special efforts made on his behalf, as in the case of a forty-year-old self-employed painter who appeared before one of the Surrey Advisory Subcommittees in late 1963. The man's work options were limited because his wife, who had been hospitalized several times for a nervous disorder, needed to be able to contact him throughout the day. After verifying that the wife's ailments were as severe as claimed and that the husband was appropriately humiliated about his unemployment, the Subcommittee responded with compassion. The members "were impressed by his integrity and were completely satisfied that he was far from happy with the current state of affairs."[39] Two of the Subcommittee's members were also borough council members, and they convinced the Housing Department to put the man on the maintenance staff of the housing estate on which he lived. The Subcommittee's report delighted in this "very happy solution," which provided the man "employment with a degree of security that he and his family have never enjoyed before."[40]

String-pulling of this kind, however, was not an unlimited commodity. There were only so many jobs that could be finagled into existence by the connections of Subcommittee members. But rather than acknowledge this reality, the Subcommittees rationalized their distribution of favors by setting up a dichotomy based on implied merit. In their narratives, the Subcommittees emphasized the virtues of those they gave special help, while denigrating other claimants. The stories of the deserving few were necessarily accompanied by harsh reprimands of the undeserving majority. Thus, the more dominant trope in the annals of the Advisory Subcommittees was the cautionary tale, in which threats of punishment replaced offers of help. Though the Subcommittees' representations clearly distinguished the deserving from the undeserving, the circumstances of men praised by the committee often closely resembled those of men labeled as degenerates.

Like the unemployed painter with the ailing wife discussed previously, many of the men who appeared before the Subcommittees had some limitation on the kinds of jobs they could take. The same report that related the story of the painter also detailed a far more common scenario in Subcommittee proceedings. A married man with two young children, who had previously maintained a good work record, came before the committee in

1963 because of lengthy unemployment. Registered as a disabled person with the Employment Exchange, the man had an artificial leg, and the Subcommittee recognized that "his work prospects were clearly limited." He and his family lived on a war disability pension, family allowance, and a national assistance grant. When registering for work at the Employment Exchange, he had made a poor impression on the staff, who informed the Subcommittee that he "was now settled in his idle ways."[41] In the Subcommittee meeting, the members took him to task for his lack of ambition. "[We] made it clear," they said, "that his idle habits would not be tolerated."[42] Apparently, the warning had the desired effect, the Subcommittee reported; the man found work two weeks later. The report did not indicate what kind of employment he obtained or whether he kept the job; for the subcommittee, the only significant fact was his departure, temporarily at least, from the national assistance rolls.

Stories of this kind filled the reports of the Advisory Subcommittees. Local elites' repeated browbeating of unemployed men served a peculiar function in NAB policy. The persistent, insoluble dilemma for the NAB was the problem presented by the unemployed man with children. If the man's benefits were summarily terminated, the NAB feared that he might act as a parasite on the remainder of the allowance intended for his family. In NAB policy, this state of affairs epitomized the lowest depths of moral depravity and the loss of masculinity. Such a man had not only failed as a breadwinner, but had lost his status, *vis-à-vis* the state, as head of the household. In addition, the smaller allowance penalized the children for whom the NAB had become sole provider. Officials were reluctant to create this situation by terminating the man's share of the assistance allowance. Though they expressed concern for the children who would be affected, NAB officials had other worries as well. Normal relationships of power within families would be destabilized if a father were forced to sponge off those he should have been supporting. Emasculation of this sort, officials reasoned, further reduced the odds of restoring masculine pride and self-sufficiency. Moreover, the family would probably require emergency grants periodically, thus wiping out the savings achieved by reducing the regular allowance. Officials were much happier if the entire family abandoned the claim for assistance altogether, in which case the NAB no longer concerned itself with the family's standard of living.

The local Advisory Subcommittees were therefore enlisted to put the fear of God into the alleged shirkers, to make them *believe* they would be cut off if they did not find employment, even though this was not really the case. Upper-level officials at NAB headquarters felt that constant pressure could wear down male claimants, who would get work or at least leave the assistance rolls. In general, subcommittee members shared the conviction that a hard line should be taken with unemployed men and were often inclined to be even harsher than policymakers wanted them to be. In particular, they became impatient when NAB officers rejected their recommendations to terminate the allowances of men they thought were work-shy. In a speech to an Advisory Committee meeting in the south of London in 1959, Sir Geoffrey Hutchinson, Chairman of the NAB, reminded committee members that full or partial withdrawals of families' national assistance allowances placed the Board in a difficult position.

> Advisory Committee members sometimes think that the Board's officers are too ready to keep people on assistance: a wife and young dependent family, however, cannot be left to sink, as they would sink, into complete destitution, if the allowance were withdrawn.[43]

Instead, Hutchinson encouraged committee members to use their interviews with claimants as coercive instruments. Repetition of stern warnings was crucial, Hutchinson contended, and he tried to reassure the Advisory Committee members that their efforts were not in vain:

> With the help of the Sub-Committees quite a lot can be done with a man who should be making the effort to support his family. Keep on bringing him before the Advisory Committee and stop him from settling down permanently on assistance. If these men appear before you perhaps month after month, meeting after meeting, and nothing much seems to happen, I do hope you will not feel you are wasting your time, because the mere fact of the interview is in itself, I am quite sure, an important factor in preventing the result which is the most distressing result of all, when a man sits back and says the National Assistance Board will keep him going for the rest of his life because of the wife and kids. He must not be allowed to get into that frame of mind.[44]

The subcommittees enthusiastically obliged, always eager to provide moral instruction to men who allowed their families to depend on state aid. In the eyes of the Subcommittees, such men lacked the power and respect that belonged to breadwinners, and members chastised them for their impaired masculinity. Shame became a familiar tool in the hands of the Subcommittee members, who tried to revive a sense of male responsibility through humiliation and disdain. The Subcommittees' preoccupation with moral failure produced skepticism about other causes of unemployment. If the man really wanted to work, members reasoned, virtually any obstacle to employment could be overcome. In keeping with their insistence on male breadwinning, the Subcommittees never suggested that a wife should find a job to support the family if there were children in the home, even if the husband's physical or mental limitations severely restricted his employment possibilities. A man with five children who came before one of the Surrey subcommittees in 1961 quickly discovered that no excuses would be accepted for unemployment. He had worked very little in the preceding three years because of a back injury, finding either that he could not handle the work required or that employ-ers refused to hire him. The Subcommittee reproached him sharply, "pointing out his moral obligations to his family" and advising him "that he should set an example to his children so that they would look up to him instead of having a father who was always unemployed."[45] The man found a job a week later, but as usually happened in such cases, the Subcommittee did not follow up to determine if the man was able to keep the job for a significant length of time. Whether the claimant sustained employment was irrelevant—what really mattered was the short-term effect of the Subcommittees' scolding. Given the fact that their warnings were essentially toothless, the Subcommittees and NAB staff considered any return to work, no matter how brief, as a victory.

SPECIAL INVESTIGATORS

Despite the Subcommittees' triumphs, which took center stage in their reports, the members realized that they often failed to move men and their families off the national assistance rolls. They were frustrated by the Board's reluctance to terminate men's allowances, and in the late 1950s, they began to ask for more help from the Board's area offices in dealing with "voluntary unemployment." The vast majority of cases that the Subcommittees dealt with involved male unemployment; they naturally assumed that the scope of the problem was greater than it was. At the Surrey Advisory Committee meeting in October 1958, members railed against what seemed to them to be a contagion of idleness among men on assistance. A. A. Bell, one of the more vocal committee mem-bers, contended that "voluntary unemployment and failure to maintain [dependents] was like a disease which spread rapidly in a community," and he suggested that the NAB appoint special officers to investigate such cases.[46] NAB officials at headquarters had already been mulling over the benefits of further specialization within the ranks of the local officers. If designated officers focused their efforts on unemployed men, the argu-ment ran, perhaps the men would leave the rolls before their cases came before the Advisory Subcommittees.

In 1961 the NAB launched an experimental program that allowed ten officers to concentrate full-time on men with records of lengthy unem-ployment. NAB officials had come to believe that intensive and persistent efforts were required to bring the unemployed man "to a proper sense of his responsibilities and to change his attitude to work."[47] Officers who had other duties—aiding those "in need through no fault of their own"—were unable to provide the special attention demanded by difficult unemploy-ment cases. The special officers, by contrast, could employ methods that would have been unfeasible for the regular staff. Officials at NAB head-quarters found the results of their experiment "distinctly encouraging."

It was found that an officer who had sufficient time to conduct long and often repeated interviews with the man concerned, to arrange for him to receive offers of employment through the Ministry of Labour (which co-operated very closely in the experiment), to make sure that he went after the jobs offered and to question him closely about the results of his applications (confirming his story with the employer where this seemed desirable) was often able to bring about quicker and more decisive results than an officer who had normal Area Office duties to carry out at the same time.[48]

Surveillance and intimidation thus became bureaucratic mainstays in policing undesirable applicants. The tactics of the special officers, later dubbed "unemployment review officers," were designed to impress men "with the seriousness of their situation and the determination of the Board to do something about it."[49] But like the posturing of the Advisory Subcommittees, this threat was primarily an elaborate bluff on the part of the NAB. Despite stern warnings to the contrary, the Board had no intention of terminating the allowances of men with families. As NAB officers had frequently explained to the advisory committees, punishing men by terminating their allowances was unacceptable because they might live off the assistance intended for their families. It was thus all the more important to make the grasp of the unemployment review officers seem as inescapable as possible; to apply such intense pressure that men would voluntarily abandon their claims, either because they believed their allowances would soon be terminated or because they felt the conditions attached to assistance—the scrutiny and criticism—were intolerable.

The work of the unemployment review officers also frightened those who merely heard about their methods. The NAB lauded the resulting "hidden" savings to public funds produced by voluntary abandonment of claims: "The knowledge that a specialist is operating in an area itself results in some men ceasing to draw their allowances."[50] In the first 7 months of the experiment, the 10 unemployment review officers had, directly or indirectly, been responsible for over 1,000 men leaving the rolls. These dramatic returns on the investment in specialization convinced the NAB to increase the number of officers. In 1962, fifty unemployment review officers made their way to the Board's ten administrative regions to handle cases of long-term unemployment, and they did not disappoint their superiors at headquarters.[51] The NAB reckoned that because of their efforts, 6,800 men had left the rolls for at least part of the year during 1962. Ten unemployment review officers went to London, and in the summer of 1963, 65% of the 693 men they interviewed ceased receiving assistance. Nationally, the Board estimated that the activities of the specialists saved half a million pounds a year in public funds. Although the Board claimed that about half of the men interviewed obtained work, there was no follow-up to determine how long they lasted in the jobs.[52]

The Board's officials were particularly pleased that the methods of the special officers had not drawn political criticism, and the program was aggressively pushed forward. In 1965, special officers across the country saw 17,500 men.[53] The Board implied that men abandoned assistance because, having found employment, they no longer needed it. But the impressive statistics cited by the NAB failed to reveal how many men actually maintained employment. The unemployment review officers' objective was to make men "independent of assistance," which did not necessarily mean placing them in sustainable work. In this project they succeeded.

MEDICAL EXAMINATIONS

The NAB's interest in specialization and expertise also found expression in another experiment initiated in the late 1950s, an ambitious project that drew on the resources of several different arms of the post-war welfare state. In cooperation with the Ministry of Health and the Ministry of Labour, the NAB arranged for medical examinations of the long-term unemployed (in this case, those who had not worked for at least six months). Local officers referred men who might have had physical or mental disabilities to the Regional Medical Service, where physicians examined them to assess their limitations. After each examination, the physician discussed the case with officers of the Ministry of Labour and the NAB; sometimes the claimant attended the meeting as well. According to the NAB's annual report for 1961, these case conferences helped

> lay officers to understand any physical or mental limitations affecting the person's capacity for work, and to consider what line offered the best possibility of his making use of that capacity.[54]

The program started on a trial basis in two regions in England (North Midland and Northwestern) and in Scotland in 1960. The following year, the NAB extended medical examinations to the whole country and made them part of "the normal procedure for helping such men to overcome their personal problems and to get back into work."[55]

The NAB presented the medical examination process as the perfect marriage of scientific knowledge and bureaucratic efficiency. Backed by the unassailable certainties of medical science, a physician, after a thirty-minute examination, could determine whether or not a man actually had any physical or mental problems, and if so, their severity. NAB officers and Ministry of Labour officers could then come up with strategies to find men lasting employment that would accommodate legitimate, verifiable impairments. Unemployed men would be rejuvenated "by the fact that their handicaps and problems were receiving special attention."[56] But despite the Board's emphasis on gaining understanding of men's disabilities so that the appropriate help could be offered, very little in the way of special vocational assistance ever materialized. The results of the 1,014 examinations conducted in 1960 illustrate the lack of concrete vocational aid given to the vast majority of the men selected for evaluation. The examinations were perhaps most helpful to the 71 men (7% of those examined) who, according to the physicians, were incapable of any work and were therefore no longer required to register at the Employment Exchange in order to receive assistance. Fewer benefits accrued, however, to those men who were found to be partially disabled in some way. The physicians concluded that about two-thirds of the men examined had significant physical and/or mental handicaps, but only 17% of them were placed on the disabled register at the Employment Exchange. The disabled register was a list of men with acknowledged restrictions on their ability to work; officers from the Ministry of Labour tried to place the listed men in work that suited their capacities. Inclusion in the register was probably the most valuable vocational assistance available to the disabled. It is not clear why only 17% of those who might have benefited from the special services provided to those on the disabled register were selected for it. The only other opportunity offered in the way of concrete assistance or training was a stint at one of the Ministry of Labour's Industrial Rehabilitation Units, which supplied training for specific trades, but only 51 men (5% of those examined) were accepted into the program.[57]

Therefore, out of the 1,014 men examined in 1960, only 164 (16%) received any help that could realistically improve their chances of getting sustainable work. The consequences for unemployed men examined in following years were substantially the same. Judged on these grounds, the medical examination program fell far short of its goals. But by other standards, medical examinations proved to be strikingly successful. Like the other projects orchestrated by the NAB in the 1950s and 1960s, medical examinations functioned primarily as devices of deterrence and intimidation. The NAB gauged the program's effectiveness by the number of men who abandoned their claims because of it. In many cases, threats of medical examinations were sufficient to induce men to leave the rolls. In 1960, for example, local NAB officers summoned over 1,500 men to inform them of the compulsory examinations. Almost 500 (one-third) of them gave up their allowances rather than submit to the exam.[58]

As for the men who did acquiesce, the examinations and the ensuing case conferences convinced many to stop drawing assistance. Of the 1,014 men examined in 1960, 375 (37%) left the rolls almost immediately after the examinations.[59] The "special attention" that prompted claimants to forego assistance allowances was likely akin to the attention given by Advisory Subcommittees and unemployment review officers. In the case conferences that followed the medical examinations, the physician and the government officers may have acknowledged some degree of disability, but the discussions must have emphasized the necessity of buckling down and finding some kind of work. When medical examinations were first tested, the NAB recognized that the case conferences could be particularly valuable for intimidation purposes, and for pushing men off the rolls who "had been inclined to shelter behind a minor disability."[60] The case conferences carried the usual admonitions to find employment, but with the additional leverage of medical authority. Rather than providing the basis for the specially tailored vocational assistance and therapy that had been promised, the specialized knowledge employed in the medical examinations merely legitimated the pressure tactics that typified the NAB's dealings with the long-term unemployed.

The NAB counted on the fact that many claimants would abandon their claims in anger or resignation. The cumulative effect of the various forms of pressure could lead men off the rolls, even if they had no prospects of work. A fifty-three-year-old Surrey man, for example, attracted the attention of an Advisory Subcommittee because of his family's intermittent presence on the assistance rolls. The man claimed to have a pulmonary ailment that restricted his work capacity, and he had been called before the subcommittee several times. Dissatisfied with "his attitude to work," the Advisory Subcommittee decided that he should be sent to an unemployment review officer and to the Regional Medical Service for a medical examination. When the Subcommittee informed the man of its plans, he replied, "If you are worrying about the miserable allowance you are giving me, you can keep it, I shall refuse to accept it."[61]

CRIMINAL PROSECUTIONS

Interrogations and examinations of various sorts discouraged many men from claiming a "miserable allowance," but the NAB had at its disposal an even greater sanction. The National Assistance Act allowed the NAB to file criminal charges against any man who made himself a charge on the national assistance fund by persistently failing to maintain himself and his dependents. A conviction could lead to a three-month prison term. The Board used prosecution sparingly, in part because "Parliament clearly intended that criminal proceedings should be reserved for serious cases in which other remedies were unsuitable or had been tried and failed."[62] Courts were reluctant to imprison men for lacking what the NAB called "the will to work" unless the Board produced strong evidence against the accused offenders. NAB officers quickly learned that they could secure a conviction only if the man had refused offers of work on several occasions. Building a case against a claimant took time, and NAB officials complained that:

> even in conditions of good employment there are not everywhere suitable vacancies all the time, and it can happen that a man makes himself so unattractive to employers that it becomes difficult to put his intentions to the test.[63]

Collecting evidence for a prosecution was a labor-intensive process, and officials were doubly galled that, in addition to the labor cost, the Board incurred the expense of the offender's assistance allowance until a conviction could be secured. Upper-level officials made half-hearted efforts to promote the remedial effects of imprisonment, as in their description of the case of an "emotionally unstable and aggressive" London man who eagerly sought out work after his release from prison.[64] For the most part, however, officials acknowledged that criminal prosecutions were neither administratively efficient nor effective in transforming men into steady wage-earners. Between 1948 and 1965, the number of prosecutions each year never exceeded 180.

Still, as in other facets of the Board's work, officials were ever mindful of the deterrent effect of the relatively small number of prosecutions. "Probably the threat of prosecution," the NAB's report for 1953 noted, "has had more effect on turning men's minds towards work than the penalties which have been imposed in the cases which actually get to Court."[65] Eight years later, the Board reiterated the importance of making examples of at least a few of the scroungers: "Successful prosecutions, which are usually reported in local newspapers, also serve as a deterrent to others who might be tempted to follow the same course of idleness at the public expense."[66] In 1961, the NAB prosecuted twice as many men as it had the year before.[67] Though still small in absolute terms, the relative increase in the number of prosecutions reflected the focus on deterrence that dominated NAB policies in the 1960s.

* * *

By the time that the Supplementary Benefits Commission took over the tasks of the NAB in 1966, a myriad of practices to deal with unemployed men had been institutionalized: there were Re-Establishment Centers to rehabilitate, Advisory Subcommittees to shame, unemployment review officers to investigate, physicians to confer scientific imprimatur, and prosecutors to imprison. It is not surprising that many men facing the full range of bureaucratic surveillance and penalties would think twice about pursuing their claims for assistance. The NAB devised its system to induce men with dependent children to abandon their claims *voluntarily*. In this way, NAB officials could assure themselves and the public that the Board was not refusing assistance to families in need of it. The notion that men willingly left the rolls maintained the fiction that the post-war welfare state was based on consensus rather than coercion. Moreover, the NAB could hold itself out as an agent of modern rehabilitation and reform, not merely supplying cash as the Poor Law authorities had, but conditioning men to assume their appropriate masculine roles. The fact that rehabilitation produced only marginal vocational benefits for the men involved was largely irrelevant. The edifice of reform, combined with more substantial deterrent results, insured the perpetuation of the NAB's policies for the unemployed.

4   Paradoxes of Imperialism
Immigration, Welfare, and Citizenship

In a world in which restrictions on personal movement and immigration have increased we still take pride in the fact that a man can say
Civis Britannicus sum [I am a British citizen] whatever his colour may
be, and we take pride in the fact that he wants and can come to the
Mother Country.[1]

> —Henry Hopkinson, Minister of State for Colonial Affairs,
> November 1954

... the public are concerned about the possible abuse of our social
services by coloured immigrants from the Colonies ... We cannot
keep them out—or send them home again—and no doubt our standards of life—even on Assistance—are attractive to them.[2]

> —Osbert Peake, Minister of National Insurance, July 1952

Both the desire and the inability to "keep them [immigrants] out" grew out
of one of the central contradictions of imperialism. Part of the ideological
justification for empire was the insistence that colonization would produce
substantial benefits for colonial subjects, including the unrestricted ability
to enter and live in the United Kingdom. Found in both imperial tradition
and law, this right to move freely across national boundaries could also be
exercised by citizens of former colonies that had joined the Commonwealth
after achieving independence. But imperialist ideology also assumed that
Britons were racially and culturally superior to their non-white subjects in
foreign lands, and a range of negative attitudes about Asians, Africans, and
West Indians (collectively described as "coloured") pervaded British society. Consequently, when large numbers of immigrants from the colonies
and "new" Commonwealth (e.g., India and Pakistan) began to arrive in
England after the Second World War, they were viewed with suspicion.

In the 1950s and 1960s, suspicion rapidly turned to widespread antag-
onism, as white Britons discovered that colonial and Commonwealth
immigrants had the same rights of citizenship as natives. Many whites
were especially dismayed that, legally, these immigrants could make the
same claims on the welfare state as anyone else. The nation was entering
a new era of social security, having rationalized and extended its welfare

state just after the war, and the rejuvenated welfare state—the pride of politicians and the public alike—was seen as the embodiment of a highly developed concept of citizenship. In the 1950s and 1960s, it was welfare state citizenship—as much as any other kind—that white Britons were reluctant to extend to Asian and black British subjects. The availability of social security to newcomers, as well as the common but unfounded belief that they abused it, hardened anti-immigrant sentiment. As a result, unprecedented legal restrictions on immigration became politically inevitable, materializing in the 1962 Commonwealth Immigration Act and subsequent legislation that made entering the country increasingly difficult for colonial and Commonwealth subjects. In this chapter, I argue that the popular belief that immigrants came to Britain to receive welfare state benefits not only fueled the drive for restrictive immigration policies, but also made welfare administrators excessively vigilant against abuses by "coloured" residents.

As is well documented by scholars who have studied twentieth-century immigration policy, considerations of race determined which immigrants were seen as desirable and which were not.[3] During the 1950s and 1960s, black and Asian immigrants, as a group, became an object of public policy as a distinct and problematic class, whereas white immigrants from Ireland, Europe, and the "old" Commonwealth (i.e., Canada, Australia, New Zealand, and South Africa), though far more numerous, warranted no special attention from administrators. In various ways in the post-war period, many white Britons searched for conceptions of national identity and citizenship that excluded non-white immigrants.[4] The welfare state became an important site in which racial differences led to hierarchies of social citizenship.

This backlash against full citizenship for non-white immigrants was clearly visible at the National Assistance Board (NAB, or Board), which provided cash payments to those who lacked the income and resources to meet basic expenses. In keeping with legal requirements, upper-level officials at the Board repeatedly reminded local officers that immigration, *per se*, was not a reason to deny or reduce an assistance allowance. At the same time, though, some of these same officials either initiated or condoned a variety of practices that, in effect, discriminated against black and Asian applicants. Despite public assertions from the NAB that "the Board met need without regard to race, creed or colour," its methods of administering the assistance program eroded black and Asian citizens' social security. The Board's practices were based on a composite identity of "coloured immigrants" that made modifying their welfare state citizenship seem natural, reasonable, and necessary. It was an identity derived not so much from the NAB's experience in administering assistance, but from a set of assumptions about racial and cultural difference that prevailed in public discussions and were deployed in efforts to restrict the influx of non-whites. The pronouncements and rhetoric of members of

Parliament (MPs), their constituents, community leaders, and local government authorities reflected and fueled anti-immigrant sentiment and seeped into the ideological fabric of the Board's work.

A constructed identity of the "coloured immigrant" become instrumental in shaping the way the welfare state perceived and dealt with immigrants. A handful of themes, repeated over and over in public discussions, both sketched out a profile of the undesirable immigrant and reconfigured several social problems with immigrants at their center. Overcrowded housing, unwarranted unemployment, miscegenation, cohabitation, and illegitimacy began to be seen as consequences of unrestricted non-white immigration. The immigrant's identity was in turn embedded in these social ills—an identity that precluded harmonious integration into the community. Of course, the real barriers to social integration were in large part a function of discrimination and prejudice, but rather than blaming white natives, government action focused on newcomers. In its own elaboration of this process, the NAB embraced the substance, if not the tone, of some of the anti-immigration rhetoric, but also consistently rebutted the more outrageous charges that immigrants systematically abused welfare programs. In its distribution of assistance, NAB practice was characterized by three features: 1) no special measures would be implemented to mitigate the social effects of discrimination; 2) in some cases, these same social effects would be reinforced by limiting immigrants' access to assistance; and 3) the Board would use its power to discourage behavior that deviated from prescribed moral norms.

MIGRATION PATTERNS

In the 1950s and 1960s, objections to unrestricted immigration from the colonies and "new" Commonwealth were ostensibly based on Britain's inability to accommodate a massive influx of permanent settlers. However, it was not immigration in general that was seen as a problem, but rather non-white immigration in particular. The government encouraged immigration from Ireland, Europe, and the "old" Commonwealth as a means of remedying labor shortages, and in the fifteen years following World War II, whites made up the vast majority of migrants to Britain. Between 1947 and 1949 alone, government programs drew in 180,000 European workers. Throughout the 1950s, about 40,000 European and 50,000 Irish immigrants arrived annually. About two-thirds of the immigrants who came to Britain between 1956 and 1960 were white.[5]

Blacks and South Asians, on the other hand, were seen as undesirable and were the intended targets in various administrative and legal efforts to restrict settlement in the United Kingdom—efforts that culminated in the 1962 Commonwealth Immigration Act, which, for the first time, limited the legal right of British subjects to enter the country. Before the Act,

Table 4.1 Estimates of Number of Immigrants from Ireland, Europe, and Old Commonwealth

	1956	1957	1958	1959	1960	Totals
Ireland	57,304	58,672	47,869	51,139	57,798	272,782
Europe	40,723	52,784	39,394	39,296	44,734	216,931
Australia	5,923	4,546	4,306	4,795	5,956	25,526
New Zealand	2,097	1,652	1,594	1,808	2,278	9,429
Canada	2,469	2,070	2,273	2,276	2,833	11,921
South Africa	3,250	3,008	3,199	2,986	4,006	16,449
Totals	111,766	122,732	98,635	102,300	117,605	553,038

Adapted from Ian R. G. Spencer, *British Immigration Policy Since 1939: The Making of Multi-Racial Britain*, London: Routledge, 1997, p. 91.

the British government prevailed on the West Indies, India, Pakistan, and African countries (with varying degrees of success) to restrict emigration in ways that would preserve Commonwealth and colonial goodwill, as well as Britain's reputation of racial tolerance. Throughout the 1950s, British policymakers searched for ways to curtail non-white immigration and encourage white immigration, without appearing to do so on racial grounds. The Commonwealth Immigration Act, though racially neutral on its face, was intended and designed primarily to limit settlement from India, Pakistan, the West Indies, and Africa.[6] There were small-scale programs run by both public and private employers (e.g., London Transport and J. Lyons) to bring West Indians to the United Kingdom. However, the overwhelming disposition of government action was toward restriction.[7]

Though the number of black and Asian British residents increased dramatically between 1939 and 1965, they still represented only a small fraction of the total population. In 1939, estimates of the "coloured" population in the United Kingdom stood at 7,000. By 1953, the figure had risen to 36,000 (15,000 from West Africa, 8,600 from the Caribbean, and 9,300 from India and Pakistan). In 1954, the estimated 40,000 black and Asian residents comprised less than one-tenth of 1% of the British population. In July 1962, when the Commonwealth Immigration Act went into effect, 500,000 blacks and Asians lived in Britain, still representing only 1% of the total population.[8]

Immigration patterns changed over time. The first immigrants to attract government attention were West Africans, many of who were thought to be stowaways. In the late 1940s, organized parties of West Indians began to come to the United Kingdom, with the most publicized group arriving on the Empire Windrush in June 1948. The passage of the 1952 McCarren-Walter

Table 4.2 Estimates of Number of Immigrants from Colonies and New Commonwealth

	1955	1956	1957	1958	1959	1960	1961	1962 (first half)
West Indies	27,550	29,800	23,000	15,020	16,390	49,670	66,290	31,800
India	5,800	5,600	6,620	6,200	2,930	5,920	23,750	19,050
Pakistan	1,850	2,050	5,170	4,690	1,860	2,500	25,080	25,090
Africa	2,200	2,660	2,830	1,380	1,880	-240	18,110	8,940
Totals	37,400	46,850	42,400	29,900	21,600	57,700	136,400	94,890

Adapted from R. B. Davison, *Black British: Immigrants to England*, London: Oxford University Press (for the Institute of Race Relations), 1966, p. 3.

Act severely restricted West Indian immigration to the United States, thus spurring increased migration from the West Indies to the United Kingdom.[9] Through the mid-1950s, the government was most concerned about black settlers in the country. In the late 1950s and early 1960s, immigration from India and Pakistan surged; consequently, South Asians, too, became a visible and unwelcome presence. From 1960 through 1962, immigration from the Caribbean, the Indian subcontinent, and Africa soared, spurred by the government's plans to enact legislation to curb Commonwealth settlement in the United Kingdom. This "beat-the-ban rush" included immigrants from the West Indies, India, Pakistan, and Africa who feared that the impending legislation would shut them out of Britain completely.

For the most part, politicians and government officials lumped all Asians and blacks together as "coloured" immigrants. This broad classification, of course, obscured a multitude of regional, ethnic, religious, cultural, and linguistic differences. Indian migrants included Hindus, Muslims, and Sikhs. Pakistanis came from both East and West Pakistan, and many only spoke Urdu. West Africans emigrated from Nigeria and Gold Coast. West Indians came not only from Jamaica, but from Barbados and St. Helens. In dealing with non-white settlers as objects of public policy, however, officials focused on perceived racial difference as the common denominator that precluded assimilation. Thus, policy discussions in the 1950s and 1960s usually did not differentiate among "coloured" residents. More specific national stereotypes were occasionally invoked, but these generalizations—both positive and negative—were surprisingly variable and inconsistent.

West Africans were perhaps the most persistently maligned. In 1952, an NAB officer in Birmingham characterized them as difficult to train, stupid, and troublesome. They were, he said, "big strong men who cannot get a job because they are a really bad lot given to fighting at the least provocation and I suspect drug taking."[10] A decade later, a Brixton NAB officer wrote, "West Africans do seem to have a chip on their shoulder, and are more difficult to deal with."[11] West Indians were viewed more favorably in some ways. In 1962, the Brixton NAB manager commented:

> All West Indians, (especially Jamaicans) appear to be thrifty. They save for their fare home, for a rainy day, and for anything they want badly. They can be very determined in this, and are probably helped by communal living and feeding.[12]

On the other hand, he deplored their attitude toward employment:

> The West Indian particularly, has, at home, an easy relationship with his employer, but when he is in employment in the U.K., he adopts such an easy going attitude, that he is soon in disfavour with his particular foreman—he is generally a poor time keeper—and cases of voluntary unemployment are numerous—often attributable to a row with the foreman or employer himself. These characters are quick to take offence at any supervisory criticism, thinking they are picked out because of their colour, rather than to a failure to follow the common rules of a good employee.[13]

The Slough area manager, however, had no complaints about West Indians' work ethic, commenting that they were good workers and seldom out of a job.[14]

Indians and Pakistanis were often grouped together in official discussions, described as "very poor types" with little knowledge of English, suitable only for menial work.[15] On the other hand, one official described them as "very polite and grateful for help given."[16] The Birmingham NAB officer said Indians were "generally looked upon as slow plodders and fairly satisfactory on the poorer paid work."[17] Pakistanis were variously described as "intelligent and willing to learn" and "a good lot, well disciplined and respectable."[18]

ANTI-IMMIGRANT SENTIMENT

The local authorities in London were among the most outspoken opponents of unrestricted immigration, particularly in Lambeth, Kensington, Paddington, and Stepney, where many immigrants settled. In the early phases of immigration, when there were still relatively few West Indians and Africans in London, the London County Council (LCC) and borough councils were already considering ways to disperse the black men who were living in council-owned lodging. About forty black men lived in the council's lodging house in Deptford (Carrington House), and another fifteen resided at the Camberwell Reception Center (funded by the NAB) for "persons without a settled way of living." In July 1949, the LCC's Consultative Committee for the Homeless Poor, chaired by the chief officer of the Welfare Department (which ran Camberwell and Carrington House), met to discuss an outbreak of violence between West African residents of Carrington House and white passersby.

The violence at Carrington House prompted an outpouring of complaints about the problems caused by black immigrants. The representative of the Metropolitan Police at the meeting contended that the West Africans had provoked the whites in the incident at Deptford. Others agreed that black immigrants were troublemakers. The warden from Camberwell asserted that the fifteen men residing in his institution were:

> not very amenable to the small amount of discipline imposed in the center and they band together to flaunt it. . . . trouble arises from any chance remark on colour, a blow is struck here and there.[19]

P. N. Shone advised the Chairman of the Committee that there was a fundamental difference between working-class whites and blacks: "Many of the coloured working class are uncouth, emotional, childish and with deplorable personal habits," he said. "Many of them do not possess that innate sense of decency which you will nearly always find in the roughest working man in this country."[20] Naturally, Shone said, English workers were put off by the "overbearing and almost insolent attitude" typical of the blacks.

In the early 1950s, anxiety about immigrants steadily intensified, as the number of newcomers, particularly from the Caribbean, grew. MPs made frequent inquiries to the NAB about "coloured" applicants for aid. In July 1952, Prime Minister Churchill asked the NAB to prepare a report on "coloured" immigrants and national assistance. Referring to a special inquiry made in 1950, the Board reported that of the approximately 37,000 recipients of assistance payments during 1 week in June 1950, only 572 of them (1.5%) were "coloured persons." The report noted that those who applied for assistance were "certain to attract attention, however, on account of their colour alone."[21]

Articles decrying perceived abuses of national assistance appeared regularly in local and national newspapers. "Coloured work-shys find paradise in Britain," read one headline in December 1952, "and we have to keep paying them." The article alleged that "thousands of coloured men" from the West Indies and West Africa were living on national assistance rather than working. "The National Assistance Board say that many of them do not intend to work if they can help it. They regard Britain as a paradise of something for nothing."[22] The Board denied that any of their officers had made such statements and pointed out that the figures given in the article were inaccurate.[23] However, this cycle of inflammatory reports followed by ineffective rebuttals from the NAB would be repeated many times over the next decade.

The NAB also received many letters about immigration from the public, either directly or via their MPs. A London solicitor and former member of the Croydon Public Assistance Committee, which administered the Poor Law before national assistance replaced it, complained in early 1954 about black residents of Brixton and the Board's role in allowing them to overwhelm "the white population of the districts which they infest." "The policy of your Board," he wrote, "is largely responsible for introducing into this country a Negro element which is neither respectable, responsible or desirable." He went on to allege that the NAB underwrote exorbitant rents for large numbers of black men who were involved in prostitution, and suggested that "a simple, potent remedy would be the revival of the Victorian Workhouse. Six weeks of assistance, then repatriation or the Workhouse. The news would soon spread to Nigeria."[24] NAB headquarters immediately forwarded the allegations to the area officer for Brixton, who responded that only about thirty blacks were on the books, and that "on the whole these applicants are not so much of the workshy type as casual workers in and out of work." He added that the rent allowances were not particularly high, and that there had been very few cases of applicants living on earnings from prostitution.[25]

At every opportunity, upper-level NAB officers tried to disabuse MPs and the public of the idea that colonial and Commonwealth immigrants were overrunning and abusing the national assistance program, but their denials had little impact on the emotionally charged debates over non-white immigration. In the range of criticism of uncontrolled immigration—from overtly racist attacks to ostensibly rational objections on fiscal grounds—the availability of national assistance figured prominently. A postcard sent by a constituent to his MP illustrates how social security was becoming a racialized marker of citizenship. J. L. Corney's stint on a ship's crew had brought him to West Africa, and four African dancers appeared on the front of the postcard. "Seeing this coast, with its polyglot population," Corney wrote, "am more than ever certain we must Keep Britain White. Here is a quartet which may decide at any moment, being 'British Subjects', that National Assistance in the Mother Country is their birthright."[26] These fears were not confined to the radicalism of open and virulent racism. In late 1954, the Battersea Ratepayers' Association expressed a similar grievance more temperately, insisting that its members were not motivated by racial prejudice. The Association had passed a resolution demanding that immigration be restricted on the grounds that immigrants placed an unacceptable burden on taxpayers by claiming national assistance.[27]

Misconceptions about immigrants' use of national assistance abounded. The NAB received many complaints that immigrants received more assistance than natives, that they received it automatically upon arrival, that they received it without having to register for work, and that pensions for the elderly were reduced to pay for the additional costs incurred because of immigration. None of this was true. One officer scribbled on a letter of complaint in frustration, "I wish that I could trace the origin of these stories!"[28] Scores of letters went out from NAB headquarters to other government departments, MPs, and the public reiterating that assistance was provided in the same way and in the same amount regardless of immigration status. All recipients had to meet the same standard of need, Board officers pointed out, and all who were capable of employment had to register weekly for work at the Employment Exchange. The most difficult myth to debunk was that large numbers of blacks and Asians were on assistance, despite the Board's repetition of the fact that the vast majority did not seek aid and that most of those who did were only on the rolls for a short period. In a 1961 Gallup survey, respondents were asked to identify the one or two main reasons for opposition to "coloured immigration." Topping the list was: "they have to be supported by our welfare services," chosen by 46% of respondents. Six years later, the same response was selected by an even higher proportion of those surveyed—49%.[29] The durability of misconceptions perplexed high-ranking NAB officials, who kept a close watch on the number of applications from "coloured immigrants." From the mid-1950s on, NAB responses to inquiries on the subject included boilerplate language along the following lines:

> As regards British subjects from the Commonwealth, there is no factual basis for the idea that large numbers of them seek assistance immediately following their arrival in this country, or that they throw any substantial burden on assistance funds. Our experience is that, generally speaking, Commonwealth immigrants are keen to work and to earn the comparatively high wages they can get in this country. The vast majority of them are working and are of course paying taxes and insurance contributions in the same way as other citizens.[30]

NAB POLICY AND PRACTICE

In spite of these reassurances that black and Asian applicants posed no serious problem, the Board treated "coloured immigrants" as a separate class requiring additional monitoring and different conditions of assistance. For the most part, this differential treatment did not come from formal rules, but from the room for interpretation and discretion present in virtually any regulatory scheme. Despite public statements to the contrary, NAB officers kept close track of blacks and Asians who sought aid, requiring them to provide more information than was required of whites. In addition to the standard form used for all applicants in the NAB's northern region, for example, the initial report on a "coloured applicant" included information about his physique, his command of English, his passport number, how he had financed his journey to the United Kingdom, and how he had maintained himself since arrival.[31]

The external pressures of anti-immigration rhetoric undoubtedly caused the Board to be hypervigilant against abuse, and even to limit blacks' and Asians' access to assistance. But opposition to immigration could be found within the NAB as well. Some of the Board's officers, particularly at the local level, strongly disapproved of uncontrolled immigration themselves and urged their superiors to lobby for immigration restrictions. This usually took the form of misrepresenting the "typical" immigrant on assistance, often with pathos. The manager of the Shoreditch NAB office in East London sent to headquarters in 1961 a report on a case that he described as "a good example of the immigration problem." The case involved a sixty-five-year-old recipient of national assistance from St. Kitts, who had paid £336 for his fare to the United Kingdom and had only £6 on arrival. He had left his wife and three children behind. Because he was old, sick, and unskilled, his chances of employment were slim. "It is a reasonable conjecture," the manager concluded, "that the raising of the fare has left his family in penury and the applicant can anticipate nothing more than a bare existence in an alien land."[32] Though poignant, the case was hardly typical of immigrants on assistance or in general, most of whom were willing and able to work and lived in supportive immigrant communities.

The manager of the Paddington office also endorsed restrictions on immigration from the colonies and the Commonwealth, pointing to the burden placed on public funds by those with physical or mental impairments. In February 1960, he outlined the case of a thirty-two-year-old man on assistance who had recently arrived from Jamaica. Because of a mental disability, he was completely dependent on his aunt and uncle. The manager realized that the man could not be denied assistance, but he argued that such immigrants should not be allowed into the country:

> It seems strange, to say the least, that a person should be allowed to come into the country when suffering with such a handicap that he will never be able to care for himself. . . . What does matter, in my opinion, is that mentally deficient people of the Colonies should not be allowed into the country for fear of increasing the large number already here.[33]

Repatriation

One of the most fundamental rights of citizenship was the right not to be involuntarily repatriated. Unlike aliens, who could be sent back home at the discretion of the government, colonial and Commonwealth subjects had a legal right to stay in the country as long as they liked.[34] With respect to national assistance, this meant that an alien could be deported if he failed to support himself, while a colonial or Commonwealth immigrant could not. Although the Board could not initiate repatriation without consent, its officers could certainly encourage or pressure a colonial or Commonwealth assistance applicant to agree to leave. If an immigrant appeared to be intractably work-shy or likely to be a long-term drain on public funds, NAB "getting rid of him" was seen as the best option. As J. E. Bullard, an official at NAB headquarters, explained in 1952, "Colonials, being British subjects, cannot be deported, but if we think that it is likely to be a good bargain for us we do sometimes ascertain whether they are willing to go back to the Colony if we pay the passage."[35] At the request of the NAB, about 50 colonials returned to their native countries in this way in 1951, at a cost of £2,000 to the British government. The group included "not only people who seemed to us to be idle, but people who were sick and would, we thought, be happier where they came from."[36]

Throughout the 1950s, the rate of NAB-sponsored repatriation increased modestly, and by the early 1960s, about 100 black and Asian residents, some with dependents, were repatriated at the Board's request annually. The issue arose again at the Cabinet level as a means of reducing the number of non-white immigrants. In 1964, the Home Office considered the possibility of proposing legislation that would allow the involuntary deportation of immigrants who remained on national assistance for long periods. Reluctant to take on the burden of making deportation decisions, the NAB resisted the proposal, which also appeared to violate the European Convention of Social and Medical Assistance.[37] In the end, the proposal was abandoned, not least because of the anticipated political and diplomatic fallout. The Home Office, though, still saw room for greater use of the existing rules for voluntary repatriation, and pressed the NAB to use its power in this area more aggressively. In August 1964, the NAB "agreed to *seek out* cases where it would be appropriate, from the point of view of saving public money, to repatriate; and to do what they could to accelerate the process of considering such cases."[38] The new Labour government that came into power in October 1964 instructed the NAB to proceed with this policy. As the NAB had warned, the push to repatriate more assistance recipients did not achieve dramatic results: in 1965, only about 100 Commonwealth immigrants and their families were repatriated. This was due in part to the multitude of demands on local officers, who could not devote as much time to repatriation as the Home Office would like.[39] However, the lackluster results were also a function of the determination of most immigrants to remain in Britain, regardless of pressure from the NAB.

Guarantees of Maintenance from Relatives

In response to British demands to reduce emigration from the Commonwealth, some countries attached conditions to the issuance of passports, which were necessary for citizens to leave their home countries and travel to Britain. The Indian government required passport applicants to give evidence of a firm offer of employment or a guarantee of maintenance from someone already living in Britain. These requirements were intended to ensure that immigrants would not become a charge on public funds.[40] Guarantees of maintenance were not required by British immigration authorities, however, and therefore had no legal force in Britain. Neither the immigrant nor the British government could compel the guarantor, usually a relative, to provide financial or other support. As a legal matter, the guarantees were meaningless once the immigrants had entered Britain, but many Indian settlers were probably unaware of this.

The guarantees of support secured to obtain a passport should have been irrelevant in the consideration of a person's application for national assistance, but some NAB officers denied assistance on the grounds that the applicant should look to the guarantor, rather than the British government, for aid. The issue arose most often in the cases of Indian women who settled in Britain. A Mrs. Saul, for example, came to England from India in 1961 with four dependent children and four non-dependent children. She filed for national assistance, which the local office refused. The case was sent to NAB headquarters for confirmation that the proper decision had been made. Although there was no evidence that a guarantee of support had been made, two reviewing officers at headquarters concluded that assistance should not be paid and that if Saul persisted, she should be told that she would have to get proof from the Indian High Commission that no guarantee of maintenance had been provided. H. S. Jones, one of the reviewing officers, commented:

> "I think we may assume that there was a guarantee that these people would not become a charge on public funds here and act as you suggest. . . . We should watch for similar cases, which should be reported to us, and if necessary issue some general instructions.[41]

If taken to its logical conclusion, the position taken in Saul's case—automatic denial if there was even a *possibility* that a guarantee of maintenance had been made—would have made any Indian who did not come to Britain with a job offer ineligible for assistance.

Other reviewing officers at headquarters did not take such a draconian approach, but it appears that at the local level, guarantees of support were widely seen as a reason to deny claims, as in the case of Mrs. Mula Devi. Devi moved to Birmingham from India at age 94. In May 1963, she applied for assistance. Her grandson, with whom she lived in Birmingham, acknowledged that when she had sought a passport in India, he had agreed to maintain her; however, he told the NAB that his circumstances had changed and he was no longer able to support her. Devi was denied assistance pending the receipt of guidance from headquarters. M. A. Brougham, who reviewed the case in London, instructed the local office to pay Devi, saying:

As the guarantee given by the applicant's grandson cannot be enforced (it may have been given solely to enable her to obtain a passport) and since Mrs. Devi could hardly be asked to leave this country simply because her grandson claims that he cannot maintain her, assistance will have to be paid as necessary.[42]

Though this directive, and others like it, resulted in many Indian applicants finally receiving national assistance, the delays in payment could easily have been prevented if the NAB had issued clear instructions on this point. More serious deprivations were caused by denials actually approved by headquarters (as in the Saul case) and by local officers who refused to pay claims and did not follow up with headquarters. In an uncharacteristic acknowledgment of prejudice and discrimination by NAB officers, the Regional Controller for Birmingham commented, "There are undoubtedly still some officers whom it hurts to give coloured applicants anything that can be withheld with some vestige of covering authority from above."[43] Considerable hardship was caused by officials who felt that "coloured" applicants' inclination to look to the state for aid should be curbed at every opportunity.

Housing

Britain's acute housing shortage in the 1950s was one of the most pressing social and political issues of the decade. The loss of properties in the war, combined with slum clearance, meant that private and council housing was in short supply. Although central and local governments were building at a frantic pace, thousands of people in the London area found themselves on long waiting lists for council housing. In January 1952, J. Waring Sainsbury, the Kensington Town Clerk, alleged that "coloured" immigrants were displacing native Londoners and lengthening wait times for new housing.[44] Such contentions effectively focused a vague discomfort with blacks and Asians into a specific and emotional grievance against them. The notion that blacks were partly responsible for the housing situation was not confined to officials in London's local government, but they certainly gave the claim a legitimacy that seemed to justify its repetition in newspaper reports and other public discussions. The view that immigrants threatened whites' access to housing became firmly lodged in popular opinion. In a Gallup poll taken in September 1958, in the immediate aftermath of the Notting Hill and Nottingham riots, only one-third of those surveyed thought that "coloured people should be admitted to council housing lists on the same conditions as people born in Britain."[45]

As discussed previously, non-white immigration was only part of total immigration to the country and to London. Nowhere in public or political discussion was any attempt made to quantify the proportion of blacks and Asians in the yearly increase in London's population. Though thousands of Irish, European, and old Commonwealth immigrants, as well as migrants from other parts of the United Kingdom, streamed to London each year, only the "coloured" pressure on the housing stock was questioned. Notwithstanding the pointed omission of other immigrants and migrants in discussions of the housing problem, the narrative of black culpability came to form the crux of the rarely questioned view, widely held by the 1950s, that uncontrolled non-white immigration posed a problem that required government intervention. Black and Asian landlords, the narrative ran, bought up old, large houses in certain districts (primarily Brixton, North Kensington, Stepney, and Paddington) and let out rooms at exorbitant rates to other immigrants. In order to pay the inflated rents, entire families or groups of up to ten people lived in single rooms, creating a "deplorable" public health situation.[46] White tenants left in disgust and made a beeline for the council housing office to ask for alternative accommodation.

While it is true that black and Asian immigrants often lived in overcrowded, substandard housing, local government officials spread incomplete and misleading information about the causes and consequences of such living conditions, thereby fuelling racist fires. In November 1954, *The London Times* reported the government's conclusion that the overcrowding of immigrants in substandard houses was not the result of a color bar in the housing market.[47] In fact, most white landlords refused to rent to non-white tenants. The NAB officer for North Bristol noted in 1950 that, "landlords and landladies do not like coloured men." Lodging houses run by voluntary organizations were similarly reluctant, which he found understandable:

> These places will not accommodate coloured men, they cause too much trouble with their bragging, gambling, fighting and insolence. They may be quiet for the first two days of residence but soon afterwards they offend the other residents and have to be put out. While the Salvation Army here might give a coloured man shelter for a night if he had no other place to go, they would have to get rid of him early in view of the protestations of the other residents. Finally there are very few women of a certain class in Bristol and these would not consider giving lodgings to a poor coloured man.[48]

Because they had so few housing options, blacks were forced to pay higher rents than whites. As a result, blacks—sometimes individually, sometimes in groups—did buy old properties. Though there were certainly notorious landlords, both black and white, who charged very high rents for substandard property, many black landlords had paid high prices for the property (they, too, were discriminated against in the housing market), and therefore charged high rents to recoup their expense. In any event, those bearing the burden of the overcrowding and high rents were the immigrants themselves.

The belief that whites were pushed out of rooms and onto council housing lists once blacks moved in was expressed in government circles and in newspaper reports. R. J. Allerton, of the LCC's Housing Department, for example, sent a memorandum to the LCC Clerk of Council in March 1955 that linked immigration to an exacerbation of the housing crisis:

> in a number of cases, the immigrants are acquiring possession of old properties and, it is said, by their habits and manners are making conditions of other families living on the premises very difficult, with the result that they feel compelled to seek other accommodation, and apply to the council for help in this connection.[49]

But Allerton acknowledged that "it is not known to what extent this happens," and he could not supply specific examples or give any indication of the number of white families who had actually been re-housed by either the LCC or the metropolitan boroughs.[50] In 1959, when the pressure for restricted entry had grown much stronger, Allerton repeated his description of the problem, but said only that he believed that "in a number of instances" whites had applied for re-housing because immigrants had made conditions "very difficult for them."[51] It is certainly plausible that white tenants sometimes resented their black neighbors, but there is little substantiation for the claim that black and Asian immigration, in itself, significantly exacerbated the housing problem dealt with by local authorities.

Another resentment that had settled in the public mind was the belief that immigrants were being given priority on the housing waiting lists. Local government officials knew this was not the case, but did little to disabuse the public of this notion. As a housing department representative told others at an LCC meeting on the "Coloured Problem," "Any applicant newly arrived in London would, of course, be far down the waiting list and inevitably it would be a long time before they could be offered accommodation."[52] In 1950, the LCC Housing Committee had rejected a request from voluntary organizations to improve the living conditions of non-white British subjects in East London. Throughout the 1950s, the committee took the position that no special provisions would be made for non-white immigrants. If eligible, black and Asian applicants would be added to the housing lists on the same terms as other Londoners; in other words, newcomers were last in the queue.[53] The situation was the same in the individual boroughs. In a 1955 meeting, a representative of the Paddington borough council confirmed that, "coloured immigrants had no housing priority under the points scheme as they were not old residents of the borough."[54]

Under the "points system" for council housing waiting lists, those living in overcrowded conditions had some advantage over those in better circumstances. In a March 1956 report, however, the LCC's Director of Housing pointed out that, because they were newcomers, immigrants in overcrowded housing gained no significant advantage in the housing queue:

> So far as the prospects of obtaining an offer of accommodation are concerned, the graduated scale of points which are given for time on the waiting list tends to discount any early advantage over other applicants which might be gained through the overcrowded conditions, and it should be borne in mind that there are many indigenous London families on the list who are living in overcrowded conditions.[55]

There was another way in which immigrants living in very poor conditions might have been aided. Under public health regulations, the local authorities were required to end tenancies with severe overcrowding, and, in theory, the local authorities were obliged to house the evicted tenants. Neither the boroughs nor the LCC, however, enforced these regulations because they did not want to re-house the colored immigrants. Doing so, contended borough officials, would "be regarded by the public within the borough as giving quite unfair consideration and priority to the claims and difficulties of [colonial immigrants]."[56] In sum, black and Asian immigrants received no special help for their housing problems from local authorities. This continued through the 1960s. As Sheila Patterson reported, "subtle gradations of allocation employed by all local authorities"[57] favored white applicants.

Although there was scant support for the suggestion that non-white immigrants, in particular, were worsening the housing shortage, this sort of misinformation and the hostility it generated persisted in public and political discourse and became an insidious influence in the work of the NAB. Part of the assistance allowance provided by the NAB to the poor was for lodging, which typically covered the tenant's actual rent. The idea that the NAB was footing the bill for exorbitant rents for black and Asian immigrants increasingly rankled local authorities and the public as resentment of immigrants grew during the 1950s. As a result, NAB practice shifted: the Board's officers were less and less willing to pay rents that they felt were too high. Though the general rule—reasonable rents would by covered by the NAB—remained the same throughout the 1950s, the tone and emphasis of the application of the rule to non-white immigrants changed. In a 1950 meeting of the LCC's Consultative Committee on the Homeless Poor, representatives from the NAB discussed the rent element of assistance allowances for black recipients. A representative from NAB headquarters said that even if a rent seemed unreasonably high for the quality of accommodation, it would be allowed if no alternative accommodation was available.[58] In other words, the determination of reasonableness depended on the relevant housing market, and non-white applicants' options were often quite limited. By the mid-1950s, however, the Board's articulation of its policies had changed. The local authorities had become much more vociferous in their complaints about black immigrants, and in response, the Board became less flexible.

In March 1954, J. E. Bullard, an official from NAB headquarters, advised the Birmingham Regional Controller that officers had to be very cautious when dealing with "coloured" applicants and landlords.

> I am inclined to think that the only way to deal with coloured tenants paying rent to coloured landlords is to fix arbitrary limits of (say) 15s. for a single person and 20s. for a family, and not go beyond them unless there is some uncommonly strong reason for special treatment.[59]

When questioned by London local authorities in October 1954 about payment of high rents to black applicants, an NAB representative stressed that unreasonable rents would not be covered. He reassured the group that the claims of white and non-white applicants would be handled in the same way: no special treatment would be given to blacks.[60] In fact, the NAB was institutionalizing a system of rent allowances that treated blacks and Asians far less favorably than whites. In a 1958 report to NAB headquarters, the Regional Controller for London confirmed that area officers had changed the way they determined the allowance paid to an applicant living with other individuals in a room or house. No longer would such applicants be paid the maximum rent allowed under local standards (which basically capped the amount allowable for rent). Instead, if an applicant appeared to be living "communally," he would not be given an allowance for rent, but would be given the fixed allowance for a "non-householder's" share of rent. The Regional Controller described a case to illustrate the new practice. In a house in Stepney, twenty-nine Pakistanis shared a house, but each paid rent separately. Instead of paying each applicant the maximum rent allowance of almost £1 per week, the area officer allowed only the non-householder amount of 2 shillings, 6 pence per week.[61]

Of course, the effect on applicants for national assistance was dramatic; instead of receiving an allowance that might cover a large part (but probably not all) of the rent, the individual would receive a small fraction of the rent. In July 1959, this practice was formalized in instructions sent to all officers in the London region. In addition, the instructions restricted rent allowances for "coloured" applicants not living communally to 15 shillings per week.[62] The Regional Controller for London defended the race-based rent restrictions, claiming that it was "an accepted practice for the coloured landlords to waive full payment of rent during periods of sickness or unemployment."[63] But he did not indicate how often applicants actually were relieved of their rent obligation. The NAB's rent restrictions certainly resulted in considerable hardship to those affected by them. Appeals against restricted rent allowances were rare, but as the regional controller speculated, this may have been "due to ignorance of the appeals procedure, or . . . to fear of being thought difficult." He added, "I don't think we can assume that silence in these cases means contentment."[64]

Employment

The labor market was another site in which racial hierarchies intersected with the welfare state's regulatory role. NAB officers, always interested in minimizing the number of claims that grew out of unemployment, were particularly wary of non-white, jobless applicants. Proponents of immigration restrictions conjured up visions of unwelcome newcomers living on the dole, even though unemployment among the immigrants was actually quite low in the first half of the 1950s. In this early phase of post-war immigration, most of the non-white arrivals were from the West Indies and Africa. Large-scale Indian and Pakistani immigration had not yet begun. In September 1951, in response to concerns raised by the Lambeth Borough Council, the Colonial Office reported that fears of black unemployment and national assistance dependence were unfounded. The average number of unemployed colonials registered for employment in Lambeth during the preceding few months had not exceeded twenty. Nor was there any evidence to show that immigrants were flocking to apply for national assistance. Only twelve people were receiving continuing allowances, and only twelve more were receiving temporary assistance because of sickness.[65] Still, local authorities in both Lambeth and Kensington exploited popular fears by repeating anecdotal accounts of unemployment and by warning that when the economy slowed in the future, as it surely would, masses of blacks would be idle. Despite the hand-wringing about unemployed blacks and Asians, immigrants were absorbed remarkably well into the economy, particularly in the early 1950s. Some were unemployed briefly after arrival, during which time they claimed national assistance, but generally they found jobs fairly quickly.

In June 1953, the National Assistance Board and the Ministry of Labour conducted a national count of the number of "coloured, able-bodied males" registered as unemployed, as well as the number receiving national assistance.[66] While 3,366 black and Asian men were on the unemployment rolls at the labor exchanges, only 1,870 of these men were receiving national assistance.[67] Those who did not receive national assistance either relied on friends or family or had resources that made them ineligible for aid. National assistance payments made to "able-bodied coloured recipients" represented about 2% of the total amount paid by the NAB annually to all "able-bodied recipients." Of the total number of black and Asian able-bodied recipients of national assistance, 37% were

West African, 23% were West Indian, and 17% were Indian or Pakistani. NAB officials estimated that the total "coloured" population in the country was 40,000, about half of whom lived in London.[68]

Between June 1953 and July 1955, about 25,000 West Indians moved to Britain, but the number of "coloured" national assistance recipients actually declined significantly. The NAB controller for the inner London region, for example, reported that there were only 280 "coloured" recipients in November 1954, as compared to 650 in June 1953. The mayor of Lambeth told the *Daily Mirror* in March 1955 that very few of the 2,000 West Indians who had come into the Borough of Lambeth in the preceding year had applied for assistance, and that those who did usually received only 1 week's allowance. In Manchester and Liverpool, the number of blacks and Asians on the assistance rolls dropped from 601 in June 1953 to 370 in March 1955.[69] Nationally, the number of blacks and Asians registered as unemployed at the Employment Exchanges in July 1955 was 2,853 (down 15% from 2 years earlier). And only 546 of those registered as unemployed were receiving national assistance.[70]

The relatively low rates of unemployment in the first half of the 1950s is somewhat surprising given the pervasive discrimination by both employers and other employees.[71] Moreover, this prejudice was sometimes tacitly or explicitly condoned by officials from the NAB, the Ministry of Labour, and the local government. An aversion to integrated workplaces became apparent very early in the post-war period, when few immigrants had come to the United Kingdom. In 1950, the NAB area officer for northern Bristol made clear that Jamaican stowaways (or any other "coloured" immigrants) were unwelcome. Employers, he said, would not consider hiring blacks because they were inferior workers, particularly in inclement weather. White workers also objected to the presence of blacks:

> Our own people in Bristol will not work beside coloured men. For example attempts have been made in the past to employ them in the small shipyard here but although the employers were willing to give an occasional coloured man a job, the workpeople refused to go on working while the coloured man was there.[72]

Similar opinions were expressed in London in the early 1950s. Dr. A. Plummer of the LCC's education department felt that vocational training courses would benefit black immigrants, but he worried about integrated classes. Apparently sharing the discomfort with racial co-mingling he attributed to the public at large, he warned that admission of blacks to the evening institutes would have to be strictly limited: "It would be important to send only a few [coloured men] to each institute, because otherwise it might tend to spoil the institutes for the majority of the white members,"[73] he cautioned. Workplaces employing both black men and white women were seen as particularly inflammatory. J. Waring

Sainsbury, Kensington's anti-immigration Town Clerk, claimed in 1952 that the

> sporadic employment [of blacks] is believed in many instances to be due to employers finding difficulties arising amongst their other employees where coloured people are engaged, especially where there are white girls also employed in the same works.[74]

In Birmingham, too, some employers were unwilling to hire either blacks or Asians, while others "were dismissing coloured people on the slightest pretext," particularly in the wake of the economic slowdown in the spring of 1952.[75]

In 1953, the NAB's Yorkshire Advisory Committee complained to headquarters that "the influx of coloured men into the locality was a matter for grave concern," but also made the improbable claim that any difficulties they encountered were "in no way related to any question of discrimination."[76] The committee was of the unanimous opinion that the NAB should pressure other departments to strictly limit blacks' entry to the United Kingdom. NAB headquarters accordingly passed on the following recommendation to the Colonial Office: "strong steps should be taken ... to regulate and control the influx of [coloured immigrants], in their own interests, apart from the question of them becoming a non-productive charge on public funds."[77]

In the mid-1950s, Indian and Pakistani immigration increased significantly, and resistance from fellow employees to South Asian workers began to appear, not to mention outright discrimination from some employers. Pakistanis in Bradford and Sheffield attracted attention in 1958 because a recession in the wool industry led to the stoppage of wool-combing night shifts, on which many of them worked.[78] Local NAB officers were acutely sensitive to the "anxiety among the public in Bradford and Sheffield about the influx of coloured persons into those cities."[79] In May 1958, white workers at a Haslingdon cotton mill went on strike because of the employment of three Pakistanis. The men said they would accept two Pakistani employees, but no more. Underlying the action was the union's fear that Pakistanis would undercut wages. A union member told the local newspaper that Pakistanis had indicated they would accept £4 a week for work that normally commanded £6.[80] Intermingled with the concern about wages was the pervasive resentment of immigrants being supported by the state. George Bourke, president of the Haslingdon Trades Council and the Card-Room Workers Union, complained, "The really sore point is that these people are on the means test and are drawing a darn sight more than our own people are getting."[81] Those Pakistanis on national assistance drew no more than anyone else, but Bourke's comment typified the misconceptions that shaped reaction to immigrants.

The economic downturn, particularly in woolens in Yorkshire, meant that the number of unemployed immigrants rose. In March 1958, about 4,000 unemployed Pakistanis and Indians were drawing assistance nationally.[82] A parliamentary question from the outspoken anti-immigration MP Cyril Osborne prompted the NAB to collect detailed statistics on the number of Pakistanis on assistance in April 1958.[83] Articles about out-of-work Pakistanis appeared frequently in the local and national press, with public assistance an abiding background presence. In April 1958, the *Daily Express* ran a story on Suab Ali, one of about 1,000 unemployed Pakistanis in Bradford. Ali had borrowed £138 for the airfare to Britain, which he expected to pay back from his wages. His wife and two children had remained in their small village in East Pakistan. Unable to find work when he reached Yorkshire, he received £2 10 shillings a week in national assistance, of which 30 shillings (60%) went for the rent on a small room he shared with four other Pakistani men. Ali told the *Express* that he could not return home because he would never be able to repay his debt from the £3 per month he had earned in his banana stall. But the *Express* article focused on the purported role of the welfare state in keeping immigrants such as Ali in Britain when they might otherwise return home. "Most want to stay anyway," the article asserted. "For there are no State benefits for the workless and hungry in Pakistan."[84]

Unemployment among immigrants peaked for the 1950s in November 1958, when the total number of blacks and Asians on national assistance was 8,226. Over the next 2 years, this number declined, and in November 1960, only 4,500 "coloured" residents received national assistance because of unemployment.[85] In the early 1960s, however, immigration rates rose dramatically, producing renewed anxieties about immigration, unemployment, and public assistance. In 1960, about 50,000 West Indian immigrants came to Britain, triple the number who had arrived in 1959. In 1961, the number of annual arrivals reached 66,000. And in 1961, Indian and Pakistani immigration—which had been declining since 1957—increased sharply as well. In 1960, 6,000 Indians had moved to the United Kingdom, but in 1961, 24,000 immigrated (a 300% increase). Pakistani immigration grew tenfold, from 2,500 in 1960 to 25,000 in 1961. (see Table 4.2, supra).

The dramatic increase in the number of immigrants led to high rates of short-term unemployment in some areas, and the relatively high percentage of Asians and blacks on the unemployment and national assistance lists (especially in Bradford, Brixton, and Birmingham) was used effectively by hardline anti-immigration MPs, such as Cyril Osborne and Norman Pannell, to push for restricted entry. In parts of Birmingham and Bradford, where many Pakistanis were unemployed because of the recession in woolens, "coloured" national assistance recipients represented 75% of unemployed assistance applicants in 1962.[86] In London and the Midlands, blacks and Asians made up about 20% of the total number of

Table 4.3 Number of Blacks and Asians on National Assistance
Due to Unemployment

Date	Number of Blacks and Asians on National Assistance Because of Unemployment
June 1953	1,870
July 1955	546
November 1958	8,226
November 1960	4,500
May 1962	22,500
May 1964	5,500

Source: TNA: PRO, HO 376/133.

unemployed in early 1962. Newspaper reports about the problem proliferated.[87] Nationally, the number of "coloured" immigrants on national
assistance peaked at 22,500 in May 1962, and then began to decline
rapidly. Six months later, in November 1962, there were about 15,000
unemployed blacks and Asians receiving national assistance, representing
10% of the total number of unemployed on the national assistance rolls.
In May 1964, only 5,500 unemployed blacks and Asians were on assistance—one-fourth of the national total 2 years earlier—and they represented less than 4% of the total number of unemployed workers.[88]

NAB and Ministry of Labour officials agreed that blacks and Asians
were not work-shy, and some acknowledged that their unemployment was
due in part to a color bar. The manager of the Brixton NAB, for example,
reported in November 1962 that out of thirty-seven businesses surveyed,
thirty-two said they would not hire blacks. And the Employment Exchange
had no vacancies for blacks either. The manager commented that:

> Despite this many West Indians do find work by their own efforts. I
> have heard them give details of regular, daily search for work, starting
> very early each morning, and going the rounds of building sites, and
> factories over a considerable area. Some find work as far out as Alder-
> shot, and they are in many Surrey factories. We are aware of some who
> own mini-buses, and they shuttle-service their acquaintances morning
> and evening to jobs around London.[89]

For West Indians, Indians, and Pakistanis, the main employers in London were British Railways, London Transport, J. Lyons & Co. (caterers
and food suppliers), and several contract laundries. Each of these organizations set a quota of "coloured" employees. By 1962, the quota had
been filled, and they would hire no more blacks or Asians.[90] But as the

NAB emphasized in a report to the Commonwealth Immigrants Advisory Council, immigrants neither shrank from difficult job searches, nor took advantage of public assistance:

> What is indeed surprising on the face of it is that so many immigrants have managed to get jobs, even in areas where almost all employers are reported to be reluctant to engage coloured workers. This, however, is consistent with the Board's general experience of the immigrants' attitudes to work. It has sometimes been suggested in the popular Press and elsewhere that large numbers of able-bodied coloured people come to this country specifically to take advantage of the Welfare State in general and of national assistance in particular. This is not borne out by reports received from officers of the Board up and down the country.[91]

Still, anxiety about unemployed immigrants lingered in policy discussions. In 1964, the Home Office looked to the NAB for support of a proposal to deport immigrants who were unemployed for lengthy periods. NAB headquarters declined, saying that "the question of unemployed immigrants on assistance is not one that seriously troubles the Board" and pointing out that the number of unemployed immigrants had dropped by two-thirds over the preceding year.[92]

Exaggerated fears about non-white unemployment and the resulting burden on state funds—actual or potential—intensified the feeling that immigrants should do whatever was necessary to stay in work. It was in this connection that the NAB could play an important role, not in punishing the scrounger (another important function of the Board), but in refusing to underwrite immigrants' reluctance to take or stay in undesirable jobs. The most common features of the work experience for immigrants were downgrading of skills and low wages. Many skilled immigrants did not secure jobs commensurate with their qualifications.[93] NAB officials acknowledged that the immigrants were not work-shy. In 1958, London's regional controller commented that "it is the unanimous opinion of the Area Officers that nearly all the coloured immigrants are keen to obtain work and to keep it once they have started and that this is particularly true of the West Indians."[94] However, on occasion, some immigrants (particularly Indians and Pakistanis, according to the London regional controller) were too "selective" in their job searches, holding out for jobs that matched their skills and experience. Officials at all levels of the NAB watched carefully for immigrants who seemed to be reluctant to take unskilled, low-wage jobs. In addition, NAB officials were particularly concerned to reassure local authorities in London that every effort was being made to keep immigrants off the unemployment and assistance rolls. In October 1954, Mr. Kingdom from NAB headquarters told London officials that "it was known that some [coloured people] came here with fixed ideas about the kind of work they would undertake and it was sometimes difficult to persuade them to accept other jobs."[95] He added that "it had been necessary to prosecute one or two who lived on national assistance and refused to do any work other than that they wanted to do."[96] If the NAB did in fact prosecute these people, it would have been an extraordinary remedy. Only a few individuals were prosecuted for this reason in the early 1950s, and prosecution was usually reserved for only the most intractable and lengthy cases of willful unemployment. Use of this sanction demonstrates just how important it was to send a message to the immigrant community and to impress upon local authorities that their concerns were being taken seriously. This practice not only kept immigrants off national assistance, but also reinforced the racial stratification of the labor market.

There were ways other than criminal prosecution, of course, to ensure that black and Asian immigrants took jobs they did not want. Difficult cases were referred to local Advisory Subcommittees, who interviewed the recipient of national assistance and pressured him or her to do what was necessary to leave the assistance rolls. In a typical example of this process, a forty-year-old Pakistani man was brought before an Advisory Subcommittee in Surrey in 1964. The man, who had come to London in 1960, was joined by his wife and seven children in 1961. In Pakistan he had worked as an electrical inspector, but was having difficulty finding work in his field in the London area. The Advisory Subcommittee "explained that it would not be possible for him to obtain the same sort of work he had had in Pakistan and persuaded him to change his registered employment even though it [was] considered a lower standard."[97] The man clearly understood that to defy the committee and to insist on other work would jeopardize his national assistance allowance. White recipients were also pressured to find jobs by Advisory Subcommittees, but they were not pushed into undesirable work as systematically as nonwhite immigrants.

The NAB also used its influence to encourage unmarried immigrants with young children, particularly West Indian women, to return to work, a departure from its general policy in this area (see Chapter 2, this volume). Although white women with dependent children were generally not expected to register for employment in order to claim assistance, West Indian women were often pressured to work full-time.[98] Concerns about black women claiming assistance increased in the early 1960s, as West Indian immigration spiked in the "beat-the-ban" rush. Exaggerated reports of hordes of single women arriving from the Caribbean—either already pregnant or becoming so shortly after arrival—spurred inquiries about the scope of the problem in London. In 1961, J. W. Grove, representing the London district of the Transport & General Workers' Union, wrote to the NAB Chairman suggesting that the immigration of "coloured women" posed an urgent problem for the Board. Many of them, he alleged, were pregnant on arrival in the United Kingdom, which placed an additional burden on the National Assistance Board for a long time which the relatives and putative fathers in the home country were able to pass on to the British tax payer without us having the chance to sue them through the Courts.[99]

A Nottingham Advisory Committee to the NAB made allegations along similar lines, saying that "a disturbingly large number" of unmarried black women with children applied for assistance.[100]

As was so often the case, public perceptions of immigrants were distorted by fear and prejudice. The number of such women on national assistance was actually quite small; only twenty filed applications during a two-month period in 1961 in Brixton, Paddington, and Kensington (the three London districts with the highest concentration of black residents).[101] Even so, in order to prevent more women from seeking assistance, the NAB worked with the London Council of Social Services to make more day nurseries and child-minders available in Kensington and Paddington, where there were sometimes child-care shortages. Most child care for working black women, though, was handled within West Indian communities without the assistance of the NAB. As one official observed, "In general, women with children are prepared to go to work, and can often arrange with other women for the care of the children—one advantage, perhaps, of the overcrowding and communal living arrangements."[102]

THE ENGLISH WAY OF LIFE: MORAL AND SOCIAL PROBLEMS

In addition to concerns about housing and employment, government officials, particularly those at the local level, were preoccupied by a wide range of moral and social problems they saw in black and Asian immigration. Complaints about unrestricted non-white immigration exposed the fear that large numbers of immigrants could not be assimilated into English society and culture, and that concentrations of blacks and Asians would be unacceptable to the native-born. Irish, European, and white Commonwealth immigrants did not present comparable problems, and the government encouraged immigrants from these areas to come to Britain. The difference in attitude toward white immigrants can be seen in the NAB's view of Polish immigrants. After the Second World War, Britain was obliged to accept several thousand Polish refugees who lived in resettlement centers run by the NAB. The Board housed, fed, and provided other assistance to the refugees as they were gradually moved into jobs and housing across England, a process which lasted nearly a decade. The state's funding of the Poles was viewed as a preliminary step in the process of assimilation. Officials at the NAB felt confident that assimilation was possible because as Europeans, Poles were sufficiently similar to the English to allow smooth social integration. In public accounts, the NAB promoted an image of the Poles as quickly becoming self-sufficient and eagerly absorbing English culture and institutions. A description of an NAB hostel for Poles emphasized a high standard of domesticity and a commendable reverence for the monarchy.

> The Pole, like the Englishman, is by nature a home-maker. Few things impress the visitor to a Polish hostel so much as the skill and labour devoted by the residents to creating an air of domestic comfort in the Nissen and Tarran huts which are often all that can be offered by way of accommodation. The national talent for decoration, which gets its full scope in the elaborate ornamentation of the altars in the hostel chapels, appears in the home mainly in the gathered white curtains at the windows, the embroidered linens with which the housewife conceals the bareness of the walls, and the lace pillows and gaily-coloured quilts on the beds: Most of the pictures in the huts are devotional, but the Englishman also notes with pleasure, as a manifestation of goodwill many coloured photographs of the Royal Family. The standard of cleanliness is impressive, and much time is spent by the women on laundry work. Innumerable rows of drying linen are one of the characteristic features of the view in a hostel.[103]

Publicly, NAB officials said nothing about the possibilities of black and Asian assimilation. What is most striking about their internal descriptions, however, is just how foreign they perceived "coloured immigrants" to be. Cultural and social distance, in the eyes of some of the Board's senior officers, precluded any real possibility of the immigrants joining British social life. In contrast to the Poles, black immigrants seemed a world apart. A high-ranking NAB official illustrated the perceived problem in 1958:

> The differences in custom are, of course, a barrier to social integration, and this applies to the attitude to marriage, living, and feeding conditions in particular. Ipswich [area office] gives a vivid picture of some of these differences: "Furnishings are scanty. They invariably share a common kitchen, oil stoves are favoured for heating purposes in their rooms. They have a queer custom of keeping their curtains closely drawn and having the electric light on during daylight hours. Jamaicans as a class live very frugally and even when in work tend to buy the cheapest food. Some of them are really extraordinary as they buy vegetables which are on the turn and also use Kit-E-Kat as sandwich paste!"[104]

By far the most disturbing among the moral problems thought to result from immigration was the possibility of romantic and/or sexual relationships between blacks and whites, particularly between black men and white women. Anxiety about interracial relationships had surfaced in the 1920s and 1930s in British seaports, and again during the Second World War with the presence of black soldiers in the country.[105] After the war, even with relatively few black and Asian immigrants in London, the local authorities stressed this problem when pleading their case for immigration restriction to the Colonial and Home Offices.[106] They linked relationships between black men and white women to a host of undesirable consequences. In an inflammatory memorandum of early 1952, the Town Clerk of Kensington, J. W. Sainsbury, painted an alarming picture of interracial relationships. He maintained that the cohabitation of white women and black men hastened the departure of white tenants even more than the presence of black tenants generally. He alleged that "considerable numbers of coloured men" lived off the "immoral earnings" of the white prostitutes with whom they lived. He concluded that "the standard of honesty and ethical conduct generally of certain sections of immigrants is deplorably low."[107] Though no concrete evidence was offered to support the claim that large numbers of black men were profiting from associations with white prostitutes, the image lingered in government discussions. At the LCC Welfare Department's conference on the "Colour Problem" in February 1955, the Chief Officer of the Welfare Department asserted that "the association between coloured men and white women was increasing. . . . In Paddington and Brixton girls living with coloured men were said to be encouraged by these men to become prostitutes."[108]

These stereotypes and variations on them, though never substantiated or quantified, were woven into the NAB's assessment of the problems presented by immigration. In 1958, the Regional Controller for London wrote to headquarters that an undercurrent of resentment among whites was evident in areas where "the white girls desert their boy friends for coloured men."[109] The next year, he asked headquarters to approve support for a program being set up by Dr. Barnardo's Homes that aimed to rehabilitate young white women who had been associating with black men, particularly women who had illegitimate children as a result. In order to instill a sense of responsibility and to minimize the risk of similar conduct in the future, the girls were provided with furnished accommodations and were required to clean and care for one of the children's cottages in the home. NAB headquarters responded enthusiastically to the possibilities of the program. The Board agreed that a national assistance allowance should be paid to the girls, including a reasonable rent allowance of 30 shillings. An official at NAB headquarters commented that "this [program] seems to be a brave attempt to deal with this problem."[110] In the 1960s, the NAB continued to voice concern about interracial relationships. In late 1962, an NAB office manager in South London complained about "the association of white girls with coloured men, these girls are in the main promiscuous and a very poor type. The presence in the household of a number of illegitimate children apparently causes no embarrassment."[111]

Illegitimate births to black women also provided fodder for those complaining about immigrants, and a considerable degree of exaggeration typified descriptions of the problem. In 1952, local authorities in Lambeth advised the Colonial Office of a problem with illegitimate births to Jamaican women living in London:

> The girls have gone into lodgings, usually kept by other Jamaicans, and have immediately been taken up by men of their own race, who rarely undertake responsibility for the children when born. Some of the girls subsequently work and support their children, but most, if not all, become a charge for a time at least, on the National Assistance Board.[112]

The information was passed on to NAB officials, who sought specific information about the prevalence of such cases. To their surprise, they found only two cases in which unmarried black women had applied for assistance from the NAB in all of Lambeth, one involving a pregnant woman and another involving a woman with an infant. Neither had been receiving assistance for more than a few months. Though there were two mother-and-baby homes in Brixton, neither had any unmarried black mothers.[113] Similar misconceptions—which NAB headquarters periodically tried to correct—persisted into the 1960s. In a 1962 report to the Commonwealth Immigrants Advisory Council, the NAB wrote:

> In some localities concern has been expressed about the numbers of single women entering the country, principally from the West Indies who are already pregnant on arrival or who soon become so. As far as the Board can judge, the numbers are not in fact large enough to justify acute concern.[114]

The NAB was perpetually worried about having to support women and children, whether natives or immigrants, and officials spent a great deal of time and effort in the 1950s and 1960s devising ways to make husbands and fathers shoulder their support obligations. Women who lived with or had sexual relationships with men to whom they were not married posed special problems for the Board's officers. The Board generally denied assistance to women cohabiting with men, a policy loosely based on the assumption that these women were supported by their male companions (see Chapter 2, this volume). NAB officers were even more alert to the possibility of cohabitation when black women applied for benefits. They believed that blacks had a "different standard of sexual morality" concerning marriage and were therefore more likely to cohabit than whites.[115] In addition, officials felt that the crowded conditions in which immigrants lived enabled women to conceal their relationships with men who were actually (or should have been) supporting their dependents.

In 1958, the London Regional Controller said that:

> the different outlook on marriage and cohabitation is one of the greatest sources of worry to Area Officers as it is often impossible to verify whether women applicants are really living alone or whether they are cohabiting and, on the other hand, whether or not the men are living with women who are at work.[116]

Officers were instructed to keep a close eye on West Indian immigrants (particularly unmarried mothers) living in overcrowded housing where it was difficult to know "whether the women are solely dependent on their own resources or whether they have joined up with coloured men in work."[117] To root out cohabitees, the Regional Controller recommended that special attention be paid to "areas where whole streets are known to be owned and occupied by coloured people."[118] In 1960, the Chief Constable of Derby alleged that many unmarried West Indian women with children were defrauding the NAB:

> I have learned that these women are satisfied to remain single because they know that they can obtain financial assistance from the National Assistance Board as well as maintenance from the father of the child. If however, they were to marry, the money from the National Assistance Board would cease. It has also been said that, whenever these women become aware of the presence of the National Assistance Board Representatives in their area, they take good care to remove any property from their bedrooms which would tend to suggest that they are living with a man.[119]

NAB headquarters immediately questioned the regional controller, who replied that the Chief Constable was mistaken—only about twenty West Indians received national assistance in Derby, most of whom would have been unemployed men. The regional controller had already instructed his area managers to be aware of possible cohabitation, but he visited the Derby office again and reminded the manager to make surprise visits to the homes of West Indian women if there were any possibility of cohabitation. He also advised them to ask the police to notify them if they had any useful information. Despite this heightened vigilance, NAB headquarters directed the regional controller to "make the fullest possible use of Special Investigators in suspicious cases" and to arrange several unnotified visits where cohabitation was suspected.[120] The added vigilance in "coloured areas" did lead to the withdrawal of assistance from claimants who were thought to be cohabiting. Because the NAB targeted black residential areas in its efforts to detect cohabitation, black women were more likely to have their assistance withdrawn than white women in comparable circumstances.

* * *

In various ways, the NAB made claiming assistance more difficult for non-white immigrants than for white natives. Implicitly, the Board was responding to J. Waring Sainsbury, the outspoken Kensington Town Clerk, who had essentially blamed the welfare state for the problems of immigration in 1952: "The attractions of social security," he complained, "and the social services provided by the Welfare State are resulting in persons from abroad flocking in ever increasing numbers to this country."[121] Then, as now, the importance of the welfare state in drawing immigrants to the country was overstated. But the conviction that social security is a magnet for immigrants, then and now, has produced reconstructions of welfare state citizenship designed to disadvantage "undesirable" newcomers.

5 "Dirt, Degradation, and Disorder"
Housing the Homeless in London

In the late 1940s, London local government was confronted with a social problem that had not been coherently addressed in the package of welfare state legislation enacted after the war. The post-war housing shortage dramatically increased the number of homeless families and individuals in London, and providing temporary accommodation for them posed new and unwelcome difficulties for the London County Council (LCC) and the National Assistance Board (NAB, or Board). The LCC's and NAB's responsibility for temporary accommodation in London lasted only until 1965, when major organizational changes took effect in both local and central government.[1] But the approach to homelessness adopted by the LCC and NAB, typified by retrenchment, set the tone for social policy in this area into the 1970s.

Both the NAB and the LCC were deeply resistant to formulating any comprehensive or integrated response to homelessness, preferring instead to adhere narrowly to separate legislative mandates that required the provision of temporary accommodation to particular groups in particular circumstances. The result was a bifurcated approach that created one system for homeless families and another for individuals without children. In both systems, gender structured the policies and practices that regulated access to both temporary and permanent housing. Particular notions of women's roles and responsibilities shaped efforts to categorize homeless families, reform them, and define the precise role local government would play in the provision of temporary accommodation. A highly idealized model of family life based on women's domesticity formed the centerpiece of rehabilitation efforts designed to make families suitable for permanent housing. Officials, however, were willing to sacrifice family unity if splitting up families would move them out of temporary accommodation more quickly, just as they were willing to encourage women without male breadwinners to become wage-earners, even if doing so compromised their domestic work and mothering. The NAB and LCC were even less willing to provide accommodation to vagrant men, and throughout the 1950s and 1960s, policies for housing men without families became increasingly restrictive.

The homelessness of families had not been a pressing social problem before or during the Second World War. To the extent homelessness existed, it had been handled by the Poor Law authorities. The destitute homeless had been provided "indoor relief"—which usually meant separate accommodation for men, women, and children in Poor Law institutions. The housing situation in London after the war, however, rapidly deteriorated. Bombs had destroyed about 116,000 houses in the greater London area, and another 288,000 needed substantial repairs. When the war ended, evacuees and demobilized service personnel began to flow back into London, and overcrowding became a persistent problem. In addition, housing construction had virtually ceased during the war, and after the war, migration from other parts of the country into London and the southeast accelerated.[2] In June 1949, the LCC alone had over 128,000 applications for housing. In addition, the metropolitan borough councils had a waiting list of 131,500 families. The combined efforts of the LCC and the borough councils could house only 1,000 families per month.[3] Housing became one of the major political issues of the post-war period, drawing pledges from both parties that the mass construction of new houses would be a top priority. Predictably, those at the bottom of the socio-economic ladder felt the housing crunch more than others, and the families in London's temporary accommodation facilities typically had very low incomes. Most of the parents were young—under thirty years of age—and about one-third were lone women with children. Most had lived in insecure and inadequately furnished accommodations before becoming homeless.[4]

Homelessness was not mentioned in any of the welfare state legislation of the 1940s. The National Assistance Act of 1948, though, required local authorities to provide temporary accommodation for people in urgent need resulting from unforeseeable circumstances.[5] Temporary accommodation was originally intended to help victims of fire, flood, or similar catastrophe. Though the short-term accommodation required by the National Assistance Act (commonly known as "Part III" accommodation) was not intended to redress a housing shortage, in London it became necessary to use temporary accommodation for just that purpose.[6] Responsibility for temporary accommodation fell to a reluctant LCC Welfare Department, which, as a Report on Homelessness concluded in 1961, was "not properly organized, staffed or equipped to deal with what is in the main a housing problem."[7]

DECENT FAMILIES AND PROBLEM FAMILIES

The Welfare Department's primary responsibility was managing the large welfare homes in London that housed the elderly in need of permanent accommodation (another type of Part III accommodation). After the war, because no other facilities were available, many of the homeless families seeking help from the Welfare Department were squeezed into these large institutions. The resulting overcrowding forced Welfare Department officials to devise strategies to relieve the pressure on the overburdened facilities. To manage the ever-increasing number of homeless families looking for temporary accommodation, the Welfare Department divided homeless families into two groups: 1) "decent" families of wage-earning men, considered to be victims of the housing shortage; and 2) "problem families," loosely identified by the overall disorder of their domestic lives. These classifications determined both the quality of temporary accommodation offered and the likelihood of obtaining permanent housing. Decent families were moved as quickly as possible through the temporary accommodation system and into council housing, whereas problem families lingered in temporary accommodation (usually the large welfare homes) because they were considered unfit for permanent housing. Because of the severity of the housing shortage, though, even many decent families could not be housed. And, of course, the categories themselves were not fixed—decent families could turn into problem families in the eyes of the authorities, often because of long stays in temporary accommodations.

Discussions about problem families began in the 1940s and continued through the 1960s. In a wide variety of contexts, governments and voluntary organizations employed the notion for diverse, sometimes conflicting, purposes: to explain family poverty in an era of prosperity, to remedy social dysfunction of various sorts, and to separate hereditary causes from social ones. Although the term *problem family* was ubiquitous in social work, the definition of the term was remarkably fluid, and the explanations of the causes of the phenomenon were as vague and divergent as the definitions. What was clear was that problem families, like the "underclass" of the 1970s, represented the residuum of society, a group that in one way or another either offended the sensibilities of the respectable or evoked the sympathies of those concerned about poverty. As John Macnicol has argued, the various definitions of problem families "implied social incompetence without being able to offer any precise quantitative measure of it, and did so in language that verges on the surreal or the tautological."[8] This was certainly the case in the context of temporary accommodation in London. Problem families were sometimes defined as the "long-stay" cases—those who did not move quickly out of the accommodation provided. In many cases, however, they were not allowed to move through the system precisely because they had already been labeled as dysfunctional.[9]

In the 1940s and 1950s, research and study of problem families strongly influenced social work in both voluntary and government circles. The Eugenics Society was deeply involved in this project, undertaking surveys to measure the scope of the problem and concluding that problem families formed a class of genetically deficient individuals. The eugenicists worked in close cooperation with several local medical officers of health, who had published articles describing the problem families they had seen in the poorest inner-city districts in the war. The other important players in this policy arena were the members of the Family Service Units, formerly the Pacifist Service Units, who had established themselves in the voluntary sector during the war by working with "difficult" families displaced by bombing. Unlike the eugenicists, however, members of the Family Service Units thought the deficiencies they saw in families were remediable, and they emphasized rehabilitation and reform for those who lacked the knowledge and skills to function acceptably in society. The common thread in the various discussions of problem families was household squalor and women's domestic incompetence.[10]

While the Welfare Department ran the temporary accommodation provided by the LCC, access to the scarce supply of permanent council housing was controlled by the LCC's Housing Department. The Housing Department and the Welfare Department agreed that problem families would not make acceptable tenants in long-term housing. Non-problem families were deemed to be suitable tenants and put on a fast track to permanent accommodations. Most were assigned to halfway houses and rest centers—which offered the highest standard of temporary accommodation—and were usually accepted relatively quickly by the Housing Department for permanent housing. The Welfare Department described the typical family in the halfway houses as "the lorry driver with wife and four children under four years."[11] In contrast, problem families were placed in the LCC's large welfare homes (Part III accommodation), the least desirable form of temporary accommodation offered by the LCC. Because of a shortage of halfway houses and rest centers, some "honest, decent families" ended up in the large welfare homes, but the wardens moved them out as quickly as possible.[12]

Families sent to the rest centers occupied one or more rooms, depending on the number and ages of the children. All furniture, bedding, crockery, and cutlery were supplied by the LCC, and apart from communal cooking arrangements, families lived separately. Residents paid a weekly rate for their accommodations.[13] Those sent to the large welfare homes also signed agreements to pay weekly fees for their lodging, but conditions were much worse in these locations than in the rest centers.[14] By the early 1950s, welfare authorities split up families destined for the large homes, only admitting women and children and directing men to find other accommodation in private lodging houses or hostels. The eight welfare homes scattered throughout London were old Poor Law institutions, and the structure of the buildings dictated communal sleeping (segregated by age and sex), communal feeding, and communal laundry. The most serious problem was the overcrowding. The institutions had already been filled to near capacity with the elderly, and packing in additional residents made conditions almost intolerable. Edward Bligh, Chief Officer of the Welfare Department, commented that "the best one can wish for these temporary residents is that for their own sakes their stay may be short and that a departure to a home of their own may come as quickly as possible."[15] However, Bligh also believed that some of the occupants of the welfare homes, like the undeserving poor of earlier times, deserved what they got. He found them "similar to those who were in and out of the poor law institutions, where they were rightly not given the concession of living together as families, or what are commonly known as problem families."[16]

The introduction of the "problem families" taxonomy into the LCC's allocation of housing produced a set of priorities and practices only tangentially related to the task at hand, which, ostensibly, was to supply both temporary and permanent lodging for as many families as possible, as expeditiously as possible. Designating some applicants as problem families did, however, provide a convenient way to distinguish the deserving from the undeserving and to legitimize such distinctions. According to the Welfare Department, problem families could not compete in the tight market for permanent housing. An assessment of the ability and/or inclination to pay the rent, however, was not the only or even the primary factor in separating good tenants from bad ones. Officials at both the Welfare and Housing Departments stated repeatedly that families with poor rent payment histories or past evictions would not be treated as problem families if they were otherwise acceptable. As the Chief Officer of the Welfare Department said:

> Where there was a reasonable record of employment by the head of the family and evidence that the parents are genuinely seeking to set up a home of their own and that they are willing to cooperate in efforts to help them, they are not regarded as problem families, even though they may have been evicted for nonpayment of rent.[17]

Rather, it was a "lack of sense of family responsibility," or "a history of bad behaviour or a failure to control children" that caused some homeless families to be stigmatized.[18]

In other contexts, an assessment of families' rent payment prospects was determinative in deciding who would be acceptable tenants. Officials from the Housing Department consistently stated that the primary cause of unsatisfactory tenancy was nonpayment of rent.[19] The family responsibility sought by local officials was more ideological, however, and was heavily invested with the nineteenth-century legacy that placed women's domestic skills at the core of working-class respectability. Underscoring the importance of a well-ordered home life, both the Housing and Welfare Departments emphasized that bad payers whose domestic habits were proper would not be penalized in their bids for housing. The elaborate constructions of what it meant to be a "good tenant" had little to do with the actual demands of council housing, which focused almost exclusively on rent payment. Instead, a romanticized vision of domestic life was the standard by which homeless families were ranked in the queue for permanent housing. This disjuncture highlights the importance of gendered notions of family propriety in welfare officials' dealings with the recipients of state aid, as well as the power of the "problem family" discourse to order governmental priorities.

Although the Welfare and Housing Departments employed the concept of "problem families" as an instrument to regulate access to housing, it took on larger proportions as a lens through which the undeserving poor were viewed. In 1950, the Chief Officer of the Welfare Department described problem families as a social menace, and the LCC's Welfare Committee on Homeless Families embraced this notion, expressing the desire

> to consider not only their present limited task of the temporary accom-
> modation of a comparatively small section of problem families, but
> also what contribution they can make . . . towards the removal of this
> blot on the general community.[20]

Characterizations of "problem families" drew, in part, on reports from the wardens of the large institutions, but also on the familiar rhetoric of the Family Service Units, who were presumed to be experts on the problem. For example, when Edward Bligh, Chief Welfare Officer, described problem families to the LCC, he quoted at length from a Family Service Units pamphlet that cataloged their offenses. The following description was not based on observations of families in the welfare homes. Nonetheless, the Welfare Department incorporated the pamphlet's expression of visceral antipathy to the unacceptable poor into its social policies on homelessness:

> The lives of problem families are characterised by dirt, degradation
> and disorder; they are shiftless, lazy and irresponsible, often to an
> incredible degree; financial mismanagement is rife; as a result of . . .
> misspending they are constantly in debt and in arrears; their sleeping
> habits are bad. They sleep many to a room and many to a bed; their
> meals are irregular and insufficient; food is inappropriate, badly pre-
> pared and badly presented; what clothing they have is rarely washed
> and often the mother does not know how to mend, sew or knit; the
> children suffer most; they are dirty and verminous; discipline is absent
> or varies erratically; among problem families juvenile delinquency is
> common and child neglect is nearly always present.[21]

As evidenced by this passage and countless others like it, Welfare Department officials focused on women's failures as domestic managers and mothers. The composition of the occupants of the welfare homes reinforced this preoccupation. The Welfare Department allowed only women and children to stay in the welfare homes; men were separated from their families and told to find outside lodging on their own. As a result, women and their children—whether affiliated with a man or not—were the most visible burdens on a reluctant Welfare Department. It is not surprising, then, that the disgust of welfare officials, as well as rehabilitation efforts, increasingly targeted women. This revulsion was reflected in the comments of Edward Bligh who asserted in 1950 that "the women [in the welfare homes] are feckless, lazy, coarse and quarrelsome, and they neglect their responsibilities to their children."[22] Moreover, he argued, they were to blame for the deteriorating health of occupants of the large homes, an opinion echoed by the visiting medical officer, who attributed the high incidence of infectious diseases not only to overcrowding, but also to "the poor average standard of the mothers."[23]

Throughout the LCC's tenure, widowed, divorced, deserted, separated, or unmarried women (collectively referred to as "lone women") and their children made up about 40% of the population of homeless families in temporary accommodations. Most of these women were separated from their husbands.[24] Officials included most lone women among the problem families,[25] although some officers allowed that some of the lone women in the welfare homes were capable of heading normal families.[26] Three of the welfare homes had separate mother and baby units. Pregnant women were encouraged to give up their babies for adoption, but most refused.[27] Under the National Assistance Act, the Welfare Department was obliged to provide accommodation for pregnant and nursing women. The bulk of this "moral welfare work" was undertaken by voluntary organizations (heavily subsidized by the LCC), who ran about thirty mother-and-baby homes in London. The voluntary organizations, though, refused to take women who were not "of reasonably good character"; for example, women who had previously had another illegitimate child. These more difficult cases (about 300 in 1955) were handled by the Welfare Department.[28]

Although Welfare Department officials generally attributed the chaos of the large welfare homes to the deviance of the families living there, the facilities themselves were simply inadequate. The conditions in the large homes were miserable, as was recognized by one member of a visiting subcommittee in 1951:

> My tour of this unit horrified me. A small room nine or ten feet square, had just room for 3 beds, small chest and window, with a common floor space in the centre of 3 or 4 feet square, in which a mother and two growing children must live . . . others are in dormitories which it has become necessary to crowd so closely with beds and cots that there is little or no space even to stand between them; more beds and cots are in the centre of the floor and even then there are not enough beds to go round—others have to sleep on the floor at night and in the day their pallets must be cleared away . . . These women's lives—in the same room with a dozen other women, with old and young children and babies, nappies, potties, in perpetual pandemonium, and in all the 24

hours not one minute of privacy . . . the husbands may visit them after work and in the evening must go away. Little wonder that they become subdued, tend to neglect themselves and are content to sit in bovine indifference until the next meal is served to give some small variety.[29]

This focus on the structural flaws of an overcrowded temporary accommodation system was atypical. Far more common was the conclusion that the women of problem families were unwilling and/or unable to behave responsibly. The warden at King's Mead in Chelsea, one of the large homes, commented in 1951 that the women

are only too ready to grasp at the present 'everything laid-on' conditions as an escape from the mental and physical effort necessary to run a household. I believe there are many who fear an offer of outside accommodation rather than hope for it.[30]

The wardens of the other large homes lambasted their charges in more scathing terms, invariably blaming mothers for the families' offenses. The disgusted warden at Luxborough Lodge complained that "the children run wild, dirty, foulmouthed, insolent, lacking all the elements of common decency."[31] His counterpart at Southern Grove Lodge similarly objected to "the low and disgraceful behaviour of many of the married women," whose children were "most unruly—rude, vile-mouthed, and very destructive."[32] These sorts of opinions were expressed quite consistently by the officials who had the most control over temporary accommodations.

REHABILITATION OF PROBLEM FAMILIES

Early on, the Welfare Department decided that one way to rid itself of problem families was to reform them, and its rehabilitation projects reflected the assumption that the pathology of such families was due, in large part, to the domestic deficiencies of mothers. The Welfare Department's efforts closely resembled similar projects that proliferated in the nineteenth and early twentieth centuries, when both volunteers and government workers entered the homes of the poor to instruct women about proper domestic and childcare practices.[33] When it became evident in the late 1940s that the number of homeless families was increasing at a rapid pace, the Chief Officer of the Welfare Department recommended the formulation of a long-term plan to rehabilitate problem families.[34] By the early 1950s, authorities had launched a coordinated effort to reform the mothers residing in the large welfare homes. The plan began with attempts to foster domesticity in the homes themselves. The council's officers advised mothers on childcare, hygiene, and general conduct, and held classes in dressmaking and mending.[35]

In 1952, the LCC began thinking about creating residential rehabilitation centers for problem families. Welfare officials believed that housing the entire family together would be important in conditioning the participants to normal family circumstances. Authorities viewed the special units as more than way stations on the road to permanent housing—they would be sites for socializing homeless families in the norms of proper family life, which necessarily included a responsible male breadwinner and a skilled female house manager. The families would purchase and cook their own food and would "in other respects be encouraged to live under conditions approaching those of a normal home."[36] In May 1953, two "special units" were opened. At Trenmar Lodge and Nazareth House, homeless mothers and their children rejoined the men they had been separated from when they entered the large welfare homes. Lone women with children were not eligible for the program.

The Welfare Department selected thirty-two families who appeared "unlikely to be acceptable to a housing authority because of lack of proper standards of behaviour, cleanliness, financial responsibility or care and control of children."[37] Officials believed that sometimes the man was "the main cause of his family's troubles by slackness and improvidence" and that at the special units it was "possible to get him work and persuade him to keep it."[38] The wardens and social workers at the rehabilitation centers closely monitored the employment of the male residents. Those who had "occasional lapses . . . responded to warning and advice."[39] Although officials in the special units encouraged and pressured men with poor employment records to find steady work, mothers were the primary focus of intensive correction and training efforts. Officials emphasized the importance of direct supervision over most aspects of the women's lives. The National Institute of Houseworkers held weekly classes in home-making, including dressmaking and alteration of garments. In addition, special officers saw that children were properly cared for by their mothers; encouraged the women to follow an orderly routine in domestic matters; and advised them about the economic layout of their money, methods of cooking, and the maintenance of proper standards in their homes. Health visitors kept an eye on families and urged women to take the children to clinics.[40] C. S. Petheram, Chief Welfare Officer in 1955, had strong praise for the wardens of the special rehabilitation units, who monitored the families constantly. The wardens were:

> on duty 24 hours, so at all times and in all circumstances, as for example, early in the morning to see that husband and children get off to work and school in time, properly fed and clad; late in the evening to see that a proper meal is given to the husband when he returns, and to ensure that the children are adequately cared for and get to bed at a reasonable hour.[41]

Officials prepared detailed "before and after" reports on each family, with an emphasis on dramatic success, measured by adherence to exacting standards of domestic propriety. The documented metamorphosis of "Family H.B." was typical. Before their stint at Nazareth House, the family was:

> very poor as to cleanliness . . . the woman must be a great trial to the man who appears to be patient. An irresponsible woman, married to a man who is sure he could keep her straight if only they could be together. Certainly needing training in looking after the children and running a home.

After retraining, however, the family could be placed in permanent housing, and the warden issued a glowing report. As indicated in the warden's comments, the sign of success and eligibility for permanent housing was a well-kept home:

> Today I visited Mrs. B in her flat in Homerton. The place was spotlessly clean and at 3:45 p.m. the table was already laid and ready for the two children returning from school, there was a nice clean cloth on the table, cut bread and butter, jam and home made cakes, made from a recipe she was given when attending one of our cookery classes. They have some furniture on hire purchase at 16 s. per week, curtains at all the windows. At the moment they are without floor covering, but the boards were well scrubbed and mats put down, they are buying lino this week for one room, and will do so each week until all the floors are covered, they have lino in the hall. The beds were new, and had ample bedding on them . . . The flat was wholesome and fresh. They have bought a very good nursery fireguard and there was a bright fire burning. I was very satisfied with all I saw.[42]

The same features of a successful home life appear again and again in the accounts of the transformations of problem families—an attractively set table, well-chosen décor, and properly prepared food. Mastery of these skills was the key to obtaining permanent housing. Also, though not discussed by officials, becoming a decent family required an income sufficient to purchase the prescribed trappings of respectability. Not only were the Welfare Department's standards of behavior largely unrelated to the ability to pay the rent, but they also went beyond concerns about cleanliness and responsible child care. One family, a rare failure of the special units, drew criticism from officials because "the place was clean but drab with no attempt at home-making."[43] A rigorous standard of women's domesticity lay at the heart of the Welfare Department's vision of proper family life. Local officials contended that achievement of this standard would lift poor families into decent society, notwithstanding the presence of a range of other ills such as poverty, mental and physical disability, and domestic abuse.

Due to the perceived success of the special units, in 1955, thirty houses were transferred from the Housing Department to be used as additional rehabilitation sites for problem families.[44] In reviewing the achievements of the special units, the Chief Officer of the Welfare Department stressed the importance of allowing men to live with their families, which was crucial in restoring a sense of family unity, independence, and self-respect. He also reiterated that women's behavior was the key to insuring the decency and productivity of the whole family. Work-shy men, he asserted, would be cured by their wives' newfound ability to provide a proper home life. Rehabilitation was based on the assumption that family defects were the result of ignorance; they could be corrected by showing mothers a routine and a method of housekeeping and child control they could follow.[45]

The special units quickly caught the eye of other local authorities and central government ministries. In September 1955, authorities from Manchester came to London to see the rehabilitation units, and in November 1955, officials from Southport followed suit. The Minister of Health broached the possibility of extending the rehabilitation scheme to problem families who were not homeless.[46] The enthusiasm for reforming problem families reflected the growing feeling among statutory and voluntary welfare workers that rehabilitation of such families could further all sorts of objectives. In June 1952, for example, the Medical Officer of Health for London initiated a small-scale program for the "rehabilitation of mothers." Carried out by health visitors and funded by the LCC, the rehabilitation plan aimed to use "mothercraft training" to improve the health of the family as a whole.[47] Improved home circumstances, the Medical Officer of Health claimed, would allow the family to benefit from a wide range of welfare services that an unreformed mother would not be inclined to seek out. The Children's Department shared the belief that, without rehabilitation, problem families were incapable of grasping the safety net of social security provided by the post-war welfare state. The Children's Chief Welfare Officer cited with approval a statement from the Association of Family Case-Workers arguing that problem families would "if ignored, multiply and produce yet more problem families in each successive generation."[48]

Intensive casework was seen as the only way to avert this disaster, and in 1956, a child welfare officer initiated a program to go into the homes of problem families. The *London Times* reported that as a result of the officer's attention to basic problems such as marital disharmony and character defects, twenty children who would otherwise have come into the care of the LCC were able to remain with their parents. The *Times* concurred with the Children's Department's conclusion that in the absence of training in moral standards, the benefits of the welfare state could have a perverse effect. "Practical and material help alone," claimed the Children's Department, "would, in many cases, only worsen matters, because it can have the effect of increasing the parents' tendency to depend on others."[49] Since proper domestic practices of women were seen as a precondition of full participation in the welfare state, part of the state's mission became the rehabilitation of mothers.

LONE MOTHERS

The program of domesticity advanced in the special units and in other similar schemes turned on the presence of a husband to provide financial support. Forty percent of the families in temporary accommodation, however, had no male breadwinner. The Welfare Department recognized the different problems facing these families:

> In the case of "lone" women, while they can normally manage in employment or with help from the National Assistance Board while they have a roof over their heads, once they lose their homes they have great difficulty in re-establishing themselves in another and in obtaining fresh employment. It is important therefore that these mothers should have individual and special help from a welfare officer.[50]

In the mother-and-baby units, rehabilitation focused not so much on domestic propriety as on economic self-sufficiency. The women received instruction in childcare and budgeting, but these tutorials were of little use if lodging and childcare were unavailable. The Children's Department and voluntary organizations, fearing that children of lone women would ultimately come into the care of the LCC, lobbied for increased hostel and day nursery provision for lone mothers.[51] The LCC largely ignored their requests, even converting one of the few hostels for working mothers into temporary accommodation for homeless families in 1961. For the Welfare Department, it was easier to rail against "the tendency of some mothers . . . to 'settle down' and to make little effort towards a return to independent life" than to provide solutions to foster women's autonomy.[52] Moreover, though welfare officials could enumerate the difficulties facing the women who tried to leave temporary accommodations, in the late 1950s and early 1960s, they pushed to shorten the stays of lone women in the Part III homes. In 1960, D. C. R. Munro, the Chief Welfare Officer, argued that lone women's dependence on any state aid was inappropriate, and he insisted that financial independence was preferable to reliance on the government, even if it necessitated placing children in the care of the Children's Department. "If [lone mothers] are required to leave the unit and to find work," Munro contended:

> the fact of their being in work and self-supporting, even if it entails the temporary reception of their children into care, is surely better than the demoralizing effects of living a communal life on National Assistance and losing all inclination for independence.[53]

As evidenced in the Welfare Department's policies concerning lone mothers, rehabilitation had always shared the policy arena with other, more punitive methods to reduce the burden on the large welfare homes. Welfare officers and wardens of the large homes tried to deter families from coming into Part III accommodation by separating men from their families, refusing to admit families who might stay with relatives, and sending women back to husbands with whom they had had domestic disputes. The crux of the Welfare Department's policy was its resolve to provide temporary accommodation only to those who were "actually homeless." Wardens and admitting officers had strict instructions to admit only those families who would have to sleep on the street if they were turned away. Welfare officials were especially interested in refusing admission to women who had "quarreled with their husbands or other relatives." Like the officers at the NAB who handled the claims of recently separated women (see Chapter 2, this volume), officials at the Welfare Department believed that such women ought to rely on their spouses, rather than the government, for support and lodging. Their need for housing was not seen as legitimate, and, moreover, officials feared that without the backing of male wage-earners, they would become permanent charges of the welfare homes. The Welfare Department also made clear that temporary accommodation was only for Londoners. In a practice reminiscent of the settlement laws, families who applied for admission shortly after arriving in London from other areas were told to return home immediately. If the family had no money, they were sent to the local office of the NAB, where they were given a railway voucher for their return journey.[54]

EVICTIONS

The most controversial of the Welfare Department's practices was the eviction of families from the large homes. Stressing economic self-sufficiency rather than domestic propriety, the Welfare Department contended that the remedy for homelessness was to eject women and their children from Part III accommodation so that parents would be forced to take responsibility for their own lives. Governmental responsibility should be limited to caring for children temporarily until parents could provide a home for their children. Consequently, throughout 1950 and 1951, the Welfare Department began urging the Children's Department of the LCC to take the children of homeless families in Part III accommodation into care, arguing that their parents would be able to become financially independent, find lodging, and take the children back into a more stable environment. In contrast to the rationales offered for their rehabilitation programs, welfare officials suggested that homeless mothers' first task was to secure their families' economic self-reliance. What the proposal meant in practice, of course, was that the Welfare Department could lighten its load by evicting the children's mothers from temporary accommodation once the children had been taken by the Children's Department. In effect, much of the financial and administrative burden of homeless families would be shifted from the Welfare Department to the Children's Department.

Officials at the Children's Department, who wanted to avoid the added responsibility entailed in the Welfare Department's plan, claimed the proposal undermined the general social interest in family unity. One official said:

> I do think it wrong that our service is to be used to facilitate the breaking up of families—a breaking up which is apparently to be enforced by another department. All modern arguments seem to favour keeping the child with the family and welfare is a service for the family.[55]

Children's Department officials frequently invoked the childhood development theories of John Bowlby, a prominent children's psychologist, to support their position that children should be kept with their mothers. They contended that mothers evicted from temporary accommodation were not likely to reclaim their children and that "the welfare [department's] proposals are likely to create problem children (if modern child care ideas are right) and thus sacrifice the long term interests of the children in favour of a short term palliative."[56]

Despite the Children's Department's objections, the Welfare Department opted for the short-term palliative and in 1952 began evicting families (i.e., mothers with children) from Part III accommodation after a specified period, and instead offered accommodation on a night-by-night basis only. Mothers and children who had stayed too long were evicted from the various welfare homes and were provided shelter only at night in Newington Lodge in Southwark, the worst of the welfare facilities. Because they had nowhere to go during the day, many women (between forty and fifty per month) took their children to the Children's Department to be received into care. Children's officers lambasted this policy, pointing out that many mothers did not want to place their children in care and that the cost to the LCC of providing care in children's establishments was greater than the cost of housing families in welfare establishments.[57]

The situation worsened in 1956, when the Housing Department, in an effort to accelerate its slum clearance program, slashed the number of permanent units made available to homeless families housed by the Welfare Department from 450 to 50 per year. In response, the Welfare Department tightened its admissions policies and made conditions more unpleasant. Officers became more vigilant in refusing temporary accommodation to women who had "marital quarrels" or disagreements with other relatives. "Promising" families who had been placed in halfway houses (sometimes called "short-stay" accommodation) were informed that re-housing was no longer guaranteed and that they were responsible for finding their own permanent housing. Beginning in May 1956, homeless families who sought accommodation were only admitted to the recently expanded night shelter at Newington Lodge. The Chief Welfare Officer ordered that Newington Lodge be used only for nighttime accommodation. Between nine o'clock in the morning and five o'clock in the afternoon, mothers and children were not allowed inside the facility, regardless of weather conditions. In effect, homeless mothers with children no longer had access to daytime accommodation. In the following year, admissions into Part III accommodation dropped from twenty to eight per week.[58]

The Chief Officer of the Welfare Department viewed the reduction in the number of homeless families in the large homes with satisfaction, and in 1957 he credited the warden and his staff at Newington Lodge (the reception point for all new homeless families) with "solv[ing] the immediate problem of homelessness."[59] The Welfare Department also redoubled its efforts to move families who had been in the large homes in May 1956 out of Part III accommodation. Some were evicted, some left in 1958 after rates were increased by 20% (for the stated purpose of forcing residents out), and others left after the Welfare Committee set up panels to pressure "long-stay" cases to move on in 1959. Of the 566 homeless families who left Part III accommodation in the year following the implementation of the new policies in 1956, only 20% were transferred to the LCC's short-stay accommodations, where they had a chance to secure permanent council housing. The Welfare Department implied that the remainder of the mothers and their children had found their own accommodation, but provided no information about where the families had gone.[60] Like the National Assistance Board's unsubstantiated claims that men who left the assistance rolls had found permanent work (see Chapter 3, this volume), the Chief Welfare Officer's suggestion that the families who left temporary accommodation found suitable lodging obscured more probable, and troublesome, scenarios. The housing situation in London had not improved, and many families forced out of temporary accommodation likely returned to overcrowded, substandard, and/or temporary housing arrangements with friends, relatives, or estranged spouses.

As an officer of the Children's Department remarked in a hand-written notation on the Chief Welfare Officer's report, many children forced from Part III accommodations probably ended up being taken into care by the LCC.[61] The Children's Department, of course, viewed the Welfare Department's renunciation of responsibility for homeless families with dismay, since it meant an increase in the number of children who had to be taken into care—children who left the welfare homes and children whose parents were deterred from seeking admission in the first place. Children's Department officers emphasized the value of family unity, both to children and to public funds: "The public care of deprived children away from their parents is expensive and emotionally damaging," one official commented, "and although it may be convenient for many homeless people to have their children in care, it is the children who suffer."[62]

The continuing demand for temporary accommodation prevented the Welfare Department from clearing homeless families from the welfare homes as quickly as had been anticipated, and by 1960, the number of homeless families in Part III accommodations had increased again. In the early 1960s, the number of homeless people seeking shelter continued to climb. Twenty-three homeless families sought temporary accommodation in London each week in October 1960, and a year later, the number rose again to forty-five. In the fall of 1961, the *Times* ran a sympathetic story on the plight of homeless families in London, saying that most were not problem families, but "ordinary decent people, couples with several small children and incomes under £12 a week."[63] Conditions in the temporary accommodation facilities were much the same as they had been a decade earlier.

> Squashed into close communal quarters, with sometimes only a piece of hardboard or cloth to give restricted privacy, they live in conditions that one sociologist described as the "nth degree of tattiness." They tell stories of conditions that should have gone out with Oliver Twist—of dining rooms with wooden tables and chairs, unwashed walls and ceilings, dirty lavatories, no curtains or floor coverings, and inadequately lighted rooms, in which even at midday it is often too dark to write a letter. As someone remarked who had recently left one of these institutions, "the only thing in generous supply is advice."[64]

In 1962, the Welfare Department announced a new plan for the management of homeless families, shifting the focus of its efforts to a new Reception Center in Morning Lane, Hackney, where families applying for temporary accommodation were quickly interviewed and redirected. Many applicants—more than half of all who applied in 1962—were refused help altogether. All new applicants for temporary accommodation would be placed in short-stay accommodation. Short-stay units allowed mothers and children to live with fathers, but would no longer be a stepping stone to permanent council housing. Families would be allowed to stay only a few weeks. A special unit for lone women with children was created at Newington Lodge, but the maximum stay for all residents was three months. The Welfare Department also abandoned much of its ongoing work in counseling and rehabilitating its charges, including problem families. It ceded these responsibilities to caseworkers from the Public Health and Children's Departments and some voluntary organizations, particularly the Family Service Units.[65] The Welfare Department retained some of the special rehabilitation units, but its primary objective was to move families out of the temporary accommodation facilities as quickly as possible. Homeless families were to find housing as best they could. Though not acknowledged by the Welfare Department, the intractable housing problems for poor families remained. The removal of even the inadequate temporary accommodation facilities offered in the 1950s forced homeless families to resort to unsatisfactory living arrangements of various sorts: moving into overcrowded lodgings with relatives or friends, returning to abusive spouses, living rough on the streets of London, or giving children up for reception into care or adoption.

The dilemmas faced by homeless families and the consequences of temporary accommodation policies were vividly brought to life in the BBC television special, "Cathy Come Home," first broadcast in November 1966 and watched by a quarter of the British population. Directed by Ken Loach and shot in April 1966, the film was based on a story written in the early 1960s by Jeremy Sandford, who had researched homelessness and interviewed residents in hostels and in the most notorious of the Part III facilities, Newington Lodge. A documentary–drama, the film combines a fictional narrative with voice-overs by homeless people Sandford had interviewed. The story traces the descent of what the authorities would have called a decent family: a young married couple with three small children. Though Cathy's husband Reg works, they cannot find affordable housing and are trapped in a downward spiral—after being evicted, they move to an empty derelict building, then to a caravan, and, as a last resort, into the LCC's temporary accommodation facilities. The final scenes were filmed at Newington Lodge, which appears as grim and demoralizing as it did when described by the *Times* in 1961. Not allowed to live at Newington Lodge with Cathy and the children, Reg eventually abandons the family. Cathy is evicted after three months, and in the wrenching closing scene, her children are forcibly taken from her. The broadcasting of the film, which illustrated the conditions faced by many homeless families quite accurately, heightened awareness of homelessness and represented part of the rediscovery of poverty that occurred in the mid-1960s. A few weeks after "Cathy Come Home" aired, the charity Shelter was launched to remedy the problems of the homeless and poorly housed.

CHILDLESS ADULTS

The temporary accommodation facilities run by the LCC only admitted adults with dependent children. Homeless adults without dependent children had recourse to an entirely different system, with a different history and objectives. Whereas the provision of temporary lodging for families arose from the post-war housing shortage, maintaining facilities for people known variously as casuals or vagrants or tramps had long been a responsibility of the Poor Law authorities. In an attempt to reduce stigma, the National Assistance Act of 1948 revised the terminology, introducing the more cumbersome term, "persons without a settled way of living." Under the Act, the NAB replaced the Poor Law authorities and was required to "make provision whereby persons without a settled way of living may be influenced to lead a more settled way of life" and to provide and maintain "reception centers, for the provision of temporary board and lodging for such persons."[66] The National Assistance Act thereby grafted a requirement for reform and rehabilitation on to the obligation to provide shelter.

Prior to 1948, most local authorities managed "casual wards" as part of the workhouse system.[67] The NAB inherited 300 of these institutions in 1948 and immediately decided that maintaining all of them would be inefficient. A process of consolidation began, in which most Reception Centers (the former casual wards) were closed throughout the 1950s and early 1960s. By 1965, only nineteen Reception Centers remained. Many towns, some with substantial populations, did not have Reception Centers, but the NAB argued that the fairly comprehensive coverage of the old casual wards was undesirable. The NAB's annual report for 1964 responded to criticisms that the need for accommodation was not being met:

> To establish a network of small centers providing free accommodation, with few questions asked, all over the country could easily have a positively bad effect by encouraging the perpetual aimless wandering which it is the intention of section 17 [of the National Assistance Act] to remedy.[68]

NAB officials were also opposed to spending funds to transform the old casual wards into more modern, inviting institutions. Improving accommodation for homeless people without children was low on the list of the NAB's priorities, and this budgetary reality meant that little money would be spent on upgrading the few centers in operation.

The vast majority of those who used Reception Centers—like those who had used the casual wards before them—were men. And like the Poor Law authorities, the NAB continued to treat the homelessness of "unsettled" adults as a male social problem. As a consequence of this thinking, NAB policies and strategies in this area envisioned an almost exclusively male clientele. *Ad hoc* arrangements were made for the few women who came to Reception Centers, which were set up to house men, usually with dormitory sleeping arrangements. The only Reception Center exclusively for women was in London in Southwark, and it was closed down in 1961. Though the center could accommodate sixty women, the average nightly population in the early 1960s fell below twenty, and the NAB made arrangements to send homeless women to a hostel run by a voluntary organization near King's Cross Station.[69]

The NAB retained Reception Centers only in urban areas where, it was argued, vagrants tended to congregate. By far the largest Reception Center in the country was in Camberwell in London; the facility was an old workhouse built in the 1870s with a "grim appearance" that deterred many men from seeking refuge there.[70] Though the Board was responsible for funding and management of Reception Centers, it could delegate administration to local authorities, and this was the course it chose in London. The LCC, subject to the oversight of the NAB, handled the daily operations of Camberwell, which could house about 600 men, as well as the handful of much smaller centers that were used intermittently in the 1950s and 1960s. Men who came to Camberwell spent the night in large dormitories and were required to work, usually cleaning the facility, until noon the next day. At noon, the men were free to leave, but any who stayed were required to keep working. Those who lingered in the Center could also expect counseling on "leading a more settled life." Men estranged from their wives were encouraged to reconcile, youths who had run away from home were urged to return, and older men in poor health were sent to the LCC's institutions for the infirm and elderly. The primary form of resettlement work, however, involved employment. Caseworkers from the LCC joined with officers from the Ministry of Labour to place men in jobs. Men who found work were allowed to stay in the Camberwell Center until they found lodging, but those who did not were sent to lodging houses as soon as possible.[71]

From the moment it took control of the Reception Centers, the NAB set out to reduce the number of men who made use of them. In conjunction with local authorities, the NAB succeeded in this effort, reporting a steady decline in the number of occupants throughout the 1950s and 1960s. NAB officials claimed that the fact that fewer men came to the Reception Centers meant that fewer deserving men needed their services. The reduction also meant, according to NAB officials, that proper management of the Centers had allowed authorities to weed out those users who did not deserve help. NAB officials held up the Camberwell Reception Center as a particularly good example of the firm administration that was ideal in the centers. Camberwell's insistence that the men work while at the Center "kept numbers [of occupants] under reasonable control in spite of the constant drift of persons of all sorts to the metropolis."[72] The NAB contended that many men who might think of using the Center "have, or could earn, the means to pay for a bed in a lodging house, and do so when they can no longer regard the Centre as an easy-going, free lodging house."[73]

As in so many aspects of the NAB's work, officials worried constantly that public provision was being abused, and they, along with their LCC counterparts, gravitated toward deterrence in policymaking. In 1953, the LCC opened a small Reception Center at Woolwich that would allow more rigorous, workhouse-style discipline for men who turned up repeatedly at Camberwell. Men who made persistent use of Camberwell were sent to Woolwich, where the Superintendent could detain them for two nights and require them to work.[74] Anyone who left before the end of the forty-eight-hour period could be criminally prosecuted by the NAB. In most cases, however, the discipline at Camberwell was sufficiently tight to keep men from returning too often. A. A. Bell, a long-time member of the

NAB's Surrey Advisory Committee, visited Camberwell in April of 1959 and reported favorably on the discipline imposed on the men there. He was satisfied, he told the other members of the Advisory Committee, that "the casuals were now having a fair crack of the whip."[75]

Though NAB and local officials were satisfied with the operations of its Reception Centers, in 1962, an unwelcome spotlight was cast on the provision for the homeless in London. The presence of more and more men sleeping rough in parks and railway stations and outside Employment Exchanges received attention from the press, which in turn focused attention on the adequacy of London's facilities for the homeless. In February 1962, the *Times* reported that men were sleeping in London's railway terminals.[76] On August 17, 1962, the *Times* again carried an article on the increasing visibility of homeless men in public places, reporting that over 1,000 men slept rough in London every night. The figure came from a survey carried out by the Voluntary Hostel Conference, a group concerned about the shortage of affordable lodging for the poor.[77] A spate of articles on the problem appeared in the fall of 1962. In October, the *Daily Mail* carried the story of an undercover investigator who had lived among the homeless, both on the street and at Camberwell. The report painted a disturbing picture of Camberwell as a deteriorating facility with a staff that treated its residents badly.[78] G. W. Cole, one of the top civil servants at the NAB, was undisturbed by the criticism, remarking that if Camberwell were more welcoming, it would become overcrowded.[79] Others at the NAB, however, quietly acknowledged that Camberwell presented the wrong image, and one official made discreet inquiries about the possibility of purchasing new property for the Reception Center. "I very much dislike the idea of the Board continuing to be associated with this barrack-like place for presumably years to come," he commented, "the more so as the place has acquired over the years a bad name among social workers and others interested in the problem of homelessness in London."[80]

Publicly, however, the NAB and LCC maintained that the *status quo* was perfectly acceptable, even in the face of substantial evidence that homelessness was on the rise. The intensified pressures on Camberwell became apparent in November 1962, when the Reception Center admitted more men than it had in any month in the previous ten years. The Board responded to criticism in three ways: 1) by claiming that the reports of men sleeping rough were exaggerated; 2) by insisting that the men who slept rough were not its responsibility; and 3) by ratcheting up its efforts to reduce the number of men at Camberwell. The voluntary organizations that provided lodging for homeless men were also anxious to dispel the image of an epidemic of homelessness. The Salvation Army, in particular, bristled at allegations that it had failed the community, and it hastily arranged a survey of its own to count the number of men sleeping rough. On the night of December 21, 1962, Salvation Army officers said they found only 69 men sleeping out, and the NAB aggressively promoted this figure as the accurate barometer of homelessness, rather than the estimates of over 1,000 that had been advanced earlier in the fall.[81] Almost a year later, the NAB scrambled to rebut the allegations of rampant homelessness, citing a survey conducted by the Welfare Department of the LCC that had discovered only 114 people sleeping out one night in November 1963. "The problem is nothing like so large as has sometimes been represented," claimed the NAB's 1963 Annual Report, but the report also noted that the survey had been fairly cursory, disregarding private property and abandoned buildings. [82] These omissions, according to critics, made the count hopelessly inaccurate.[83]

In addition to insisting that there was no homelessness problem, officials argued that even if more men were sleeping rough, the NAB was under no obligation to house them. The NAB acknowledged that the ever-decreasing supply of cheap lodging houses made it extraordinarily difficult for low wage-earners to find accommodation. These men often turned to voluntary organizations such as the Salvation Army and Church Army for temporary lodging, and in late 1962, these organizations asked the NAB and LCC for funding to expand their temporary housing capacity. In refusing the Salvation Army's requests for subsidies, G. W. Cole tightly circumscribed the NAB's role in the provision of shelter for the homeless. Noting that the National Assistance Act only mandated furnishing Reception Centers for "persons without a settled way of living," Cole renounced responsibility for the constituency served by the voluntary organizations. "There is no legislative mandate [to help the voluntary organizations]," he argued, "given the fact that so few of the lodgers there are 'casuals.'"[84] Men who lacked housing not because of an "unsettled life," but because of the housing shortage and low wages, he concluded, were outside the purview of the NAB.

By all accounts, the growing number of men sleeping out included a large proportion of men whose "unsettled" lives clearly brought them within the bounds of the NAB's jurisdiction, even as narrowly defined by G. W. Cole and other officials. But the NAB claimed that it had no duty to assist many of these men because they had chosen their rootless existence. Depicting a large slice of the urban homeless population as improvident and hedonistic, NAB officials denied any responsibility for addressing the problems of such men. The NAB and LCC would only help men if they submitted themselves to the resettlement program at Camberwell. NAB officials argued that they could not "be held accountable if men would rather spend the night in a café in Soho or Fleet Street or sleep outside."[85]

Meanwhile, the NAB and LCC continued to tighten admissions policies at Camberwell. Because of the exceptionally large increase in the number of men seeking accommodation at the end of 1962 and in the early part of 1963, a team of NAB officers joined the LCC's resettlement officers already at Camberwell to steer as many men as possible away from the Reception Center. The freshly fortified resettlement corps focused on men who did not appear to have "an unsettled way of living," interviewing them to determine whether they should be sent to find private lodging on their own, even if that would require filing for cash assistance from the NAB. As a result of the efforts to divert men away from Camberwell, the number of men using the Center was substantially reduced.[86] Because of the continuing pressures on Camberwell, NAB and LCC officials retained the teams of interviewers to keep admissions down and to move occupants out as quickly as possible. In 1965, the teams were still working with officers of the Ministry of Labour to assess the employment potential of the men and, where practicable, to place them in work.[87]

In 1964, a social caseworker from the LCC, Miss Paige, spent four months at Camberwell to determine the need for social work support at the institution. She concluded that the immense pressures to dispose of cases by rapidly transferring men out seriously compromised the possibilities of meaningful rehabilitation.

> The present system of "disposal" at the Reception Centre often seems an artificial one—a passing of the buck; e.g., if a man is seriously disturbed and unsettled, a quick placement in a Salvation Army hostel is really an avoidance of looking at his problem, and is unlikely to be of very great value to him. On the other hand, the alternatives are often ludicrously inadequate; e.g., to place him somewhere where he could receive individual care and help may involve a wait of many months. Where?[88]

As Paige pointed out, the problems were largely systemic, resulting from inadequate social services in the community and poor coordination between providers. The mentally ill fared especially poorly in the shuffle in and out of Camberwell. Of the six cases Paige described to illustrate her work at the facility, five involved psychiatric impairments. One man, "Mr. Y," was so depressed on admission to Camberwell that he was sent to a mental hospital. When he returned to Camberwell a week later, Paige arranged for him to stay in a "slightly protected situation" for a few weeks. The permanent staff members objected to the longer-than-usual stay, arguing that "a good kick in the pants would help Mr. Y more!"[89]

In general, "the kick in the pants" approach prevailed at Camberwell, and in 1965, as the NAB prepared to turn the facility over to local authorities, its officers still focused on keeping the number of residents down. The nagging fear that men would take advantage of the facility persisted. As an official at headquarters commented:

> There is a danger that the centre is looked upon by the less scrupulous fringes of society as a useful sort of place at which to obtain free accommodation while the men concerned can devote their resources to their personal pleasures.[90]

Meanwhile, the number of homeless rose. In a nationwide count conducted by the NAB on the night of December 6, 1965, about 1,000 people were found sleeping rough in England, Scotland, and Wales, 275 (almost 30%) of them in London. Forty percent of them were employed.[91] After 1965, the administration of Reception Centers would change, as both the NAB and the LCC were dissolved. The Camberwell borough authority took over responsibility for the Reception Center, guided by the NAB's successor, the Supplementary Benefits Commission. However, as these organizational changes took place, it was clear that homelessness had become an intractable problem. A survey of men admitted to Camberwell in 1965 showed that 70% sometimes slept rough, whereas in 1960, less than half had done so. The proportion of Camberwell residents who said they frequently slept rough doubled (from 10% to 20%) between 1960 and 1965.[92] Though the need for temporary shelter for men was increasing, the NAB and LCC adamantly refused to assume more than peripheral responsibility. Through deterrence and restrictive admissions practices, officials at Camberwell made the Reception Center available to only the poorest and most desperate homeless men.

* * *

The limits of the government's capacity to remedy the homelessness of both families and individuals were thrown into sharp relief in the 1950s and 1960s. Increasing pressure on available resources revealed a basic unwillingness of both the NAB and the LCC to treat homelessness as a legitimate concern of the government. The limited extent to which government agencies did get involved, however, presented opportunities for reform and rehabilitation, the content of which were determined by marital status and family position. In families with male breadwinners, women's domesticity was fostered, whereas lone women with children were pushed toward the labor market. The reform of "unsettled" men without children, less systematic than that of families, focused on instilling a work ethic. But though gendered reform figured prominently in government strategies, the overriding imperative in dealing with the homeless was minimizing governmental responsibility; thus, reform often took a back seat to more direct methods of nudging people away from the temporary accommodation supplied by the state. Despite growing awareness of the terrible conditions in which homeless families lived, there was insufficient political will to address the problem. Discussing the impact of his 1966 film about homelessness, "Cathy Come Home," Ken Loach commented that although many public figures and politicians (including Labour Housing Minister Anthony Greenwood) commended the film's exploration of the issue, they "clearly had no intention of doing anything."[93] In the end, both reform projects and the abandonment of the homeless to fend for themselves had the same objective—to move people away from dependence on state aid.

Epilogue
The New Right, New Labour, and Welfare

In the 1980s, the British welfare state—once the pride of politicians—drew venomous criticism from Margaret Thatcher and her supporters in the New Right. They blamed the welfare state for a host of national ills: economic decline, unemployment, the deterioration of the nuclear family, a collective loss of ambition and initiative, and the rise of a class of parasitic freeloaders. The corrosive force of the welfare state, Thatcher claimed, lay in its distortion of the normal relationships that enfolded individuals into families and connected families to the labor market. By providing income support indiscriminately, the welfare state encouraged unjustifiable dependence on the government and compromised work incentives and family obligations. In short, it allowed people to disregard the relationships and behavior that formed the basis of civil society.

Accompanied by cuts in public expenditure that extended into the 1990s, Margaret Thatcher's bold rhetorical attacks on the British welfare state occasioned a reassessment of the status of social policy in post-war Britain. Many pundits and academics concluded that the era of consensus posited by Paul Addison had ended, that the Conservative pledge to "roll back the state" marked the end of bipartisan political agreement about the role of the welfare state and popular support for it. The problems with the post-war welfare state dated back to the late 1960s, when lagging economic growth and rising unemployment meant that escalating demand for social services coincided with a declining ability to pay for them. Political uncertainty about the role of welfare in the 1970s gave way to open hostility from some quarters in the 1980s and 1990s. During this "crisis" of the welfare state, which continues today, two groups of its poorest constituents, the unemployed (usually depicted as male) and lone parents (usually female), have been particularly maligned in public and political discourse.[1] Both groups have been blamed for their unnecessary dependence on the government, a reliance attributed more or less explicitly to their gendered inadequacies: for men, their failure as breadwinners; for women, their failure to secure or retain the support of a breadwinner for themselves and their children.

The vigor with which the government sought to stigmatize and subvert the state's provision of income to the undeserving in the 1980s led many scholars of social policy to investigate the punitive and disciplinary policies that had begun to emanate from Whitehall. In developing its rhetoric and policies, the Conservative government proceeded as if the post-war welfare state had been designed to undermine the mutual support obligations of families and the responsibility for self-sufficiency through labor. But the premise of Conservative policy—that the unreconstructed welfare state of the post-war era had fostered deviations from the traditional dependencies of family and labor market—was unfounded. The post-war welfare state had always regulated individuals' relationships within families and to the labor market, often in punitive and coercive ways. The literature's emphasis on the depredations of the Thatcher era creates the impression that the government's efforts to mold relationships and behavior in a systematic way and minimize state provision in the last quarter of the twentieth century were unprecedented, and that they grew out of the crisis of the welfare state precipitated by economic decline and Thatcherism. But this was not the case. The mechanisms of welfare distribution that emerged after the Second World War created a bureaucratic language and logic that anticipated the more publicized, politicized anxieties that surfaced as the welfare state itself came under attack in the 1970s.

The rhetoric and policies of "welfare reform" have proven to be quite resilient. The New Labour governments of Tony Blair and Gordon Brown, in their own way, have embraced the notion of tightening the reigns of the welfare state. In October 2000, David Blunkett, then Secretary of State for Education and Employment, said, "In order to develop a welfare state fit for the 21st century, we must recognize the adverse impact of previous policies and learn from the lessons of the past."[2] In his admonition to be mindful of past mistakes, Blunkett was not referring, as one might expect, to the policies of Margaret Thatcher and John Major, against which the Labour Party railed in the 1980s and 1990s. Although the Labour Party had roundly criticized Conservative attempts to roll back the welfare state, after coming to power in 1997, its leaders fretted about the same issues that so exercised the New Right. New Labour traced the difficulties with welfare to the principles set out after World War II, which were dutifully carried forward by successive post-war governments, both Labour and Conservative. The "lessons of the past," David Blunkett argued, came from the "old" welfare state, in which:

> Rights were not accompanied by responsibility. State intervention stifled the creativity and innovation that individuals and families craft in finding their own solutions to particular difficulties. Despite the best intentions, the actions of the State ultimately encouraged dependency

instead of offering support to those in need while encouraging future independence.[3]

In October 1998, Prime Minister Tony Blair asserted that "there is no greater challenge than reform of the welfare state." Reform was necessary, according to Blair, because the institution was outdated, inflexible, and ill-prepared for the new millennium. In short, the welfare state cried out for modernization, which the Blair government promised to deliver in short order. In typical New Labour fashion, a flurry of initiatives, slogans, and plans appeared with great fanfare in green papers, reports, and speeches. Modernity was the inescapable watchword: the Department of Social Security pledged to create "an active modern service for the next century" by "modernizing the structure of decision making" and "developing, in partnership with the private sector, the modern technology to deliver a transformed service."[4] Part of the modernization effort came in the form of organizational and equipment changes: more service by telephone, more computers, more use of the internet, and greater integration. But the most important dimension of modernization—more important even than the technology of which Blair was so enamored—was "chang[ing] the whole culture of the benefits system."[5] The post-war welfare state had locked people into dependency and eroded their sense of personal responsibility, Blair and his ministers argued; people wanted something for nothing. New Labour would change that dynamic, insisting on a "new contract for welfare" that required "something for something." Under New Labour, demoralizing welfare dependency would be attacked by moving claimants into work. Thus, the official slogan for welfare reform, articulated first in a green paper in March 1998 and endlessly repeated thereafter, was "work for those who can and security for those who cannot."[6]

The themes of individual responsibility and hard work championed by Blair shared a great deal with the New Right's prescriptions for a broken welfare state. But what distinguished New Labour's welfare policy at the turn of the century was the dizzying array of rhetoric and reorganization, inflected not by the Victorian conservatism of Margaret Thatcher, but the sunny optimism and self-styled progressivism of Tony Blair. Welfare reform began the day after Blair's election in May 1997, when he asked Frank Field to be Minister for Welfare Reform and to "think the unthinkable" in heading the government's effort to overhaul social security. Field, embroiled in internecine battles with other ministers from the beginning, did not last, but the project of welfare reform has endured, gaining momentum as Blair included it more explicitly in the ideology of the "Third Way."[7]

The undertaking began in earnest in March 1998 with the green paper, *New Ambitions for our Country: A New Contract for Welfare*, which set out the principles of reform. First and foremost, the new welfare contract would promote employment and independence from state aid and would encourage increased private provision for foreseeable risks and retirement. Reformed welfare would also shift resources from cash benefits to the education and health budgets. Disabled people would be encouraged to focus on their capacity for work rather than their incapacity. Children in the very poorest families would enjoy increased benefits, but, in general, parents would be forced to face up to their responsibilities to their children. Finally, additional resources would be committed to stop benefit fraud.[8]

Subsequent green papers outlined how reform would be implemented, but the overarching objective—"to forge an entirely new culture which puts work first"[9]—was never far from view. The "welfare to work" initiatives thus assumed the greatest importance in the government's plans. The government promoted its plans for benefit recipients as the "New Deal," launching a £10 million advertising campaign to publicize it.[10] The Department of Social Security (DSS) started several "New Deal" programs for different classes of people of working age who were receiving benefit: young people, lone parents, the long-term unemployed, the partners of unemployed people, and disabled people. In addition, the DSS merged the Employment Service and Benefits Agency to ensure that the welfare state's relationship with its constituents would never be limited to the distribution of money. At the new ONE Service (later renamed JobCentre Plus), claimants interacted with the state through a "single work-focused gateway." When a claimant first applied for benefit, he or she was assigned to a New Deal personal advisor, who conducted an initial work-focused interview and continued to monitor the claimant's job search.[11] All these measures were enacted into law in the Welfare Reform and Pensions Act of 1999, which received royal assent in November 1999.

The upshot of the new deals, contracts, advisors, and gateways was that Blair's government got more directly involved in moving people off the welfare rolls. Like the "reformed" welfare policy in the United States, which served as the model for the British changes, the welfare policy of New Labour has been primarily concerned with reducing the number of welfare claimants. The state's role is not so much to provide benefits as to facilitate entry or return to the labor market. This position has become increasingly clear throughout New Labour's governance, in both its rhetoric and practices. In October 2000, David Blunkett argued that the welfare state needed to be redefined in a way that increased the role of other components of civil society.

> We need to examine and clarify the roles and responsibilities of the state, ensuring it supports rather than ignores or partly replaces the roles and responsibilities of individuals and families; or in the wider context, the local community, the trade union or the employer. It is a combination of these building blocks which make up our society that form the true welfare state. The Government is the "enabler," sometimes providing services itself, but increasingly the Government offers a

framework for services and support, acting as regulator or information giver or the catalyst for activity. It is not, alone, the "welfare state."[12]

In practice, this residual role for the state has been confined to promoting employment, not through job creation, but by enhancing the employability of benefit recipients. Relying on another ubiquitous term in the lexicon of New Labour, government officials constantly invoke the need for "flexibility," which in the context of dealing with unemployed claimants means allowing for both "supportive follow-up, or a tougher approach where people are unwilling to help themselves." [13] The tough approach became increasingly evident in New Labour's New Deal for welfare recipients. In a speech in June 1999, Tony Blair noted that the unemployed were not as amenable to the job-readiness program at the ONE Service's gateway as they should be, but he assured his audience that the situation would be rectified. "New steps are also being taken to make the gateway more intensive, more effective in preparing people for work," Blair said. "In some cases that may mean young people coming in five days a week to learn what it's like to hold down a steady job."[14]

In the first year of Gordon Brown's Labour government, he has committed himself to the same principles of welfare reform endorsed by Tony Blair. Like Blair, Brown has promised to transfer resources from welfare to education, and his Work and Pensions Secretary called his plan to move the long-term unemployed into work "the next radical phase of welfare reform."[15] In January 2008, Brown asked David Freud, an investment banker who wrote a 2007 report on welfare reform for the Blair government, to advise the Department of Work and Pensions in its efforts to cut the number of people receiving incapacity benefit, lone parent benefit, and jobseekers allowance. More compulsion, tougher sanctions for the unemployed, and privatization of some parts of benefit administration headed the list of tactics to reduce the welfare rolls. And like Blair, Brown has also emulated some of the disciplinary aspects of welfare reform found in the United States. His "Contracts out of Poverty" plan, for example, is based on a New York City welfare program that terminates benefits to poor families if work targets set by the government are not met.[16]

Continuities running through policy and practice over the last sixty years abound. Promoting employability and job-readiness, of course, was the *raison d'etre* of the Re-Establishment Centers in the 1950s and 1960s, and the "get tough" approach now espoused by New Labour typified the Advisory Subcommittees' dealings with the long-term unemployed. The personal advisor of New Labour's welfare state serves the same purpose, as the unemployment review officers found at the National Assistance Board in the 1950s and 1960s. And just as the National Assistance Board did in the 1950s, the Blair government instituted medical reviews, called Personal Capability Assessments, in 2000 for those claimants who had previously been found to be physically or mentally incapable of working.[17] In late

2005, before scandals forced him out of the government, Work and Pensions Secretary David Blunkett pushed ahead with a plan to dramatically reduce the number of people receiving incapacity benefit. Angering Labour backbenchers, Blunkett told disabled people "sitting at home watching daytime television" to go out and find work.[18] Gordon Brown's advisor for welfare reform, David Freud, has gone further, saying that two-thirds of those receiving incapacity benefit are either capable of working or are doing so already and fraudulently collecting money from the government. "If you're disabled," Freud insisted, "work is good for you and not working is bad for you."[19]

The current resolution to crack down on benefit "fraud," which has always been broadly defined, also has parallels in the early years of postwar welfare. Special investigations of women thought to be cohabiting in the 1950s and 1960s ended in numerous benefit terminations and deterred many other women from seeking government help. The state's reluctance to take responsibility for lone women with children is as evident under New Labour as it was fifty years ago. In December 1997, Harriet Harman, then Secretary of State for Social Security, announced that she would press ahead with the cuts in lone-parent benefit that had been proposed by her Tory predecessor, a move that made her notorious among advocates for the poor.[20] Tony Blair, meanwhile, at the Labour Party conference that year called the dissolution of marriages "a modern crisis," a view that provided the context for various "pro-marriage initiatives" and the demand that absent parents be held accountable for support of their children.[21] As was the case in the 1940s, 1950s, and 1960s, this approach has proven only marginally successful in shifting the financial burden for lone-parent families from the state to absent fathers. Consequently, an important component of the New Deal for Lone Parents has been the introduction of job counseling, which is intended to "to help these families make the transition back into the mainstream."[22] In 2002, Blair claimed that his government had succeeded in changing the very culture of the welfare state by winning universal support for the notion that lone parents should work if at all possible.[23] In September 2007, the Department of Work and Pensions announced a plan to use lie detectors to reduce fraud. If implemented, telephone calls from benefit claimants will be subjected to "voice risk analysis," and those whose voice patterns are suspicious will be required to provide additional evidence to substantiate their claims.[24]

Current law requires local authorities to supply temporary accommodation to certain categories of homeless people until permanent housing can be found. Because of an exacerbation of the shortage of affordable housing, particularly in London, the number of households in temporary accommodation has increased dramatically since the mid-1990s, rising 150% between 1997 and 2005. In March 2005, about 100,000 households were in temporary accommodation in England, 60% of these in London.[25] Conditions in temporary accommodation are far better now than they were in the 1960s, and the Labour government has succeeded in moving most families with children into self-contained units. Still, the quality of the accommodation is very poor, sometimes lacking heat. The quality of temporary accommodation provided for single homeless people—whose housing needs are viewed as low priority—is even worse, most of it in dormitory-style hostels. The Blair government pledged to reduce the number of households in temporary accommodation by half by 2010, but realistic plans for accomplishing this goal have not been presented.[26]

Welfare benefits also continue to be used as instrument to control and deter immigration, as political and economic refugees have sought asylum in the United Kingdom in growing numbers over the last ten years. In 2003, the Labour government began denying assistance to refugees who did not file claims for asylum immediately upon arrival in the country. The Home Office brushed aside criticism of the denial of food and shelter to destitute asylum-seekers, saying that the measure was needed to combat "abuse of the system" by people who "claim asylum as a way of staying in the UK at the taxpayers' expense."[27]

The legacy of New Labour is yet to be seen, but the basic imperatives of the post-war welfare state—personal responsibility, familial obligation, work discipline—will continue to direct its general course. For Gordon Brown, these principles, which date back to the earliest days of the Poor Law, are essential in modernizing British social policy. In connecting welfare reform to national progress, Brown explained, "just as we are modernizing transport, planning and science policy, we are redefining the British welfare state for a wholly new world."[28]

Notes

NOTES TO THE INTRODUCTION

1. Michael Lipsky used this term to describe the interactions between social workers and clients in the United States. Michael Lipsky, *Street-Level Bureaucracy: Dilemmas of the Individual in Public Services*, New York: Russell Sage Foundation, 1980.
2. T. H. Marshall, *Class, Citizenship and Social Development: Essays by T. H. Marshall*, Garden City, NY: Doubleday, 1964; Dorothy Thompson, "The Welfare State: An Historical Approach," *New Reasoner*, 1957, vol. 4, pp. 127–128. More nuanced analyses include that of Cronin and Weiler, who argue that organized labor did not support social reform through the state until the 1930s; their influence in the 1940s, however, determined the character of the post-war welfare state. J. E. Cronin and P. Weiler, "Working-Class Interests and the Politics of Social Democratic Reform in Britain, 1900–1940," *International Labor and Working-Class History*, 1991, vol. 40, pp. 47–66.
3. Ralph Miliband, *The State in Capitalist Society*, London: Weidenfeld and Nicolson, 1969; Richard Flanagan, *"Parish-Fed Bastards": A History of the Politics of the Unemployed in Britain, 1884–1939*, New York: Greenwood Press, 1991; Ian Gough, *The Political Economy of the Welfare State*, London: Macmillan, 1979.
4. The middle classes were the primary beneficiaries of post-war welfare legislation, both in terms of cash benefits and in their opportunities for employment by the welfare state. Peter Baldwin, *The Politics of Social Solidarity: Class Bases of the European Welfare State, 1875–1975*, Cambridge: Cambridge University Press, 1990.
5. William Beveridge, *Social Insurance and Allied Services*, New York: MacMillan, 1942.
6. The debates of the 1940s show that citizenship in the welfare state was tied to the rights conferred by national insurance, as opposed to means-tested relief. Avoidance of the means test was paramount in the public's priorities for welfare. See Howard Glennerster, *British Social Policy Since 1945*, Oxford: Blackwell, 1995, pp. 15–17.
7. Elizabeth Wilson, *Women and the Welfare State*, London: Tavistock, 1977.
8. Rodney Lowe, *The Welfare State in Britain Since 1945*, New York: St. Martin's Press, 1999; Jane Lewis, *Women in Britain Since 1945: Women, Family, Work and the State in the Postwar Years*, Cambridge, MA: Basil Blackwell, 1993; Gillian Pascall, *Social Policy, A New Feminist Analysis*, New York: Routledge, 1997; Brian Abel-Smith, "Sex Equality and Social Security," in Jane Lewis (ed.) *Women's Welfare Women's Rights*, London: Croom Helm,

1983, pp. 86–102; Dulcie Groves, "Members and Survivors," in Jane Lewis (ed.) *Women's Welfare Women's Rights*, London: Croom Helm, 1983, pp. 38–63.

9. Viola Klein, *Britain's Married Women Workers*, London: Routledge & Kegan Paul, 1965, pp. 24–26, 84–85; Audrey Hunt, *A Survey of Women's Employment: A Survey Carried Out on Behalf of the Ministry of Labour by the Government Social Survey in 1965*, London: H.M.S.O., p. 22.

10. Seebohm Rowntree and G. R. Lavers, *Poverty and the Welfare State*, London: Longmans Green, 1951.

11. Brian Abel-Smith and Peter Townsend, *The Poor and the Poorest*, London: G. Bell and Sons, 1965.

12. Peter Golding and Sue Middleton, *Images of Welfare: Press and Public Attitudes to Poverty*, Oxford: Basil Blackwell, 1984, p .5.

13. Chris Jones and Tony Novak, *Poverty, Welfare and the Disciplinary State*, London: Routledge, 1999; Alan Deacon and Jonathan Bradshaw, *Reserved for the Poor, The Means Test in British Social Policy*, Oxford: Basil Blackwell and Martin Robertson, 1983; Kathleen Kiernan, Hilary Land, and Jane Lewis, *Lone Motherhood in Twentieth-Century Britain: From Footnote to Front Page*, Oxford: Clarendon Press, 1998; Beatrix Campbell, *Wigan Pier Revisited, Poverty and Politics in the Eighties*, London: Virago, 1984; K.D.M. Snell and Jane Millar, "Lone-Parent Families and the Welfare State: Past and Present," *Continuity and Change*, 1987, no. 2, pp. 387–422; Carol Walker, *Managing Poverty, The Limits of Social Assistance*, London: Routledge, 1993.

14. Kiernan, Land, and Lewis, *Lone Motherhood in Twentieth-Century Britain*, p. 185.

15. Claire Callender, "Redundancy, Employment and Poverty," in Caroline Glendinning and Jane Millar (eds.) *Women and Poverty in Britain*, Brighton: Wheatsheaf Books Ltd., 1987, pp. 137–158.

16. Jones and Novak, *Poverty, Welfare and the Disciplinary State*, pp. 58–62.

17. Ibid., pp. 66–70.

18. Kiernan, Land, and Lewis, *Lone Motherhood in Twentieth-Century Britain*.

19. See, for example, Pat Thane, *Foundations of the Welfare State*, London: Longman, 1996, for the pre-1948 period; and Gough, *The Political Economy of the Welfare State*, for the crisis of the welfare state.

20. See, for example, Walker, *Managing Poverty: The Limits of Social Assistance*; and Novak and Jones, *Poverty, Welfare and the Disciplinary State*.

21. Susan Pedersen, *Family, Dependence, and the Origins of the Welfare State: Britain and France, 1914–1945*, New York: Cambridge University Press, 1993; Wilson, *Women and the Welfare State*.

22. Pascall, *Social Policy, A New Feminist Analysis*; Ruth Lister, *As Man and Wife? A Study of the Cohabitation Rule*, London: Child Poverty Action Group, 1973; Callender, "Redundancy, Employment, and Poverty."

23. Peter Taylor-Gooby counters the notion that there was widespread commitment to the welfare state in principle; he argues that people have always been selective about what programs they supported (e.g., those providing direct benefits, such as pensions, and those for the "deserving," like the disabled). Peter Taylor-Gooby, *Public Opinion, Ideology, and State Welfare*, London: Routledge and Kegan Paul, 1985.

24. Gough, *The Political Economy of the Welfare State*.

25. The government's reluctance in the 1950s and 1960s to support women separated from their husbands stands in sharp contrast to the government's willingness during World War I to provide separation allowances to women

whose husbands served in the military. War was one of the rare circumstances that justified a woman living on her own; thus, the state was willing to step in to provide support. See Susan Pedersen, "Gender, Welfare, and Citizenship in Britain During the Great War," *American Historical Review*, 1990, vol. 95, pp. 983–1006.

NOTES TO CHAPTER 1

1. Labour Party Election Manifesto, 1951, quoted in L. J. Macfarlane, *Issues in British Politics since 1945*, London: Longman, 1986, p. 52.
2. Peter Baldwin, "Beveridge in the *Longue Duree*" in J. Hills et al. (eds.) *Beveridge and Social Security*, Oxford: Oxford University Press, 1994, p. 40.
3. Rodney Lowe, *The Welfare State in Britain Since 1945*, New York: St. Martin's Press, 1999, pp. 13–14.
4. Elizabeth Wilson, *Women and the Welfare State*, London: Tavistock, 1977; Susan Pedersen, *Family, Dependence, and the Origins of the Welfare State: Britain and France, 1914–1945*, New York: Cambridge University Press, 1993; Jane Lewis, "Dealing with Dependency: State Practices and Social Realities, 1870–1945," in Jane Lewis (ed.) *Women's Welfare, Women's Rights*, London: Croom Helm, 1983, pp. 17–37; Gillian Pascall, *Social Policy, A New Feminist Analysis*, London: Routledge, 1997.
5. Non-contributory, means-tested old-age pensions (for men and women over age seventy) had been introduced in 1908.
6. Bentley B. Gilbert, *The Evolution of National Insurance in Great Britain, The Origins of the Welfare State*, London: Michael Joseph Limited, 1966, p. 287.
7. Gilbert, *The Evolution of National Insurance in Great Britain*, p. 269.
8. Between 1925 and 1928, two-and-a-half times as many women as men were disallowed benefit under the "genuinely seeking work" and means-test clauses. Jane Lewis, "Dealing with Dependency," pp. 25–29; Alan Deacon, *In Search of the Scrounger: The Administration of Unemployment Insurance in Britain, 1920–1931*, London: G. Bell & Sons, 1976, pp. 54–68, 98–101.
9. Pedersen, *Family, Dependence, and the Origins of the Welfare State*, pp. 126–127.
10. In 1919, the Women's Employment Committee of the Ministry of Reconstruction argued that every effort should be made to keep mothers at home. Lewis, "Dealing with Dependency," p. 24.
11. Lewis, "Dealing with Dependency," pp. 17–37; Sylvia Walby, *Patriarchy at Work*, Cambridge: Polity Press, 1986; Mike Savage, "Trade Unionism, Sex Segregation, and the State: Women's Employment in 'New Industries' in Inter-War Britain," *Social History*, 1988, vol. 13, pp. 209–230. Miriam Glucksmann, *Women Assemble: Women Workers and the New Industries in Inter-War Britain*, London: Routledge, 1990, pp. 216–225.
12. Deacon, *In Search of the Scrounger*.
13. *Final Report of the Royal Commission on Unemployment Insurance*, 1931–1932, Cmd. 4185, p. 472; Deacon, *In Search of the Scrounger*, p. 109.
14. Pedersen, *Family, Dependence, and the Origins of the Welfare State*, p. 306; J. D. Tomlinson, "Women as 'Anomalies': The Anomalies Regulations of 1931, Their Background and Implications," *Public Administration*, 1984, vol. 62, pp. 423–437; Keith Laybourne, *Unemployment and Employment Policies Concerning Women in Britain, 1900–1951*, New York: Edwin Mellen Press, 2002.

15. Historians, too, have focused on the indignities suffered by unemployed men. See Jeremy Seabrook, *Unemployment*, New York: Quartet Books, 1982.
16. J. B. Priestly, *English Journey*, London: William Heinemann, 1934, p. 407.
17. Ross McKibbin, *Classes and Cultures: England 1918–1951*, New York: Oxford University Press, 1998, p. 117.
18. William Beveridge, *Social Insurance and Allied Services*, New York: MacMillan, 1942 (hereinafter referred to as the *Beveridge Report*).
19. *Beveridge Report*, p. 153.
20. Quoted in William Beveridge and A.F. Wells, *The Evidence for Voluntary Action*, London: Allen & Unwin, 1949, p. 59; see also Geoffrey Finlayson, *Citizen, State, and Social Welfare in Britain, 1830–1990*, Oxford: Clarendon Press, 1994, p. 302.
21. T. H. Marshall, *Citizenship and Social Class*, Cambridge: Cambridge University Press, 1950.
22. *Beveridge Report*, p. 6.
23. Carole Pateman sees the denial of full citizenship rights to women as a common feature of the welfare states of liberal democracies. Carole Pateman, "The Patriarchal Welfare State," in Amy Gutman (ed.) *Democracy and the Welfare State*, Princeton, NJ: Princeton University Press, 1988, pp. 231–260.
24. *Beveridge Report*, p. 49.
25. *Beveridge Report*, Appendix.
26. The TUC did not object to the Family Allowance Act of 1945 because the benefits were too meager to threaten the family wage. John Macnicol, *The Movement for Family Allowances, 1918–1945*, London: Heinemann, 1980; Pedersen, *Family, Dependence, and the Origins of the Welfare State*.
27. Pedersen, pp. 353–354. These arguments are set out in detail in Elizabeth Abbott and Katherine Bompas, *The Woman Citizen and Social Security*, London: Women's Freedom League, 1943.
28. The National Archives (hereafter TNA): Public Record Office (hereafter PRO), PIN 8/136, "Beveridge Report, Housewife's Policy," Memorandum dated July 14, 1943.
29. TNA: PRO, PIN 49/27, "Paper 18 of the National Insurance Advisory Committee: Note by Secretary on the Effect of the Proposed Amendments, Part-Time Employment (Classification and Liability for Contributions) Question."
30. Fawcette Library, 5/NWC/H.14, Women's Group on Public Welfare, Report from Conference, October 12–13, 1962.
31. TNA: PRO, PIN 49/27, Minutes of Meeting of National Insurance Advisory Committee, February 20, 1957.
32. The wage-centric character of the Anglo-American social security systems discriminates against women since they are less likely to have wage-earning patterns that maximize various kinds of benefits. In effect, a two-tiered system is created of preferable insurance-based benefits on one hand, and means-tested and stigmatized benefits on the other. See Linda Gordon, *Pitied But Not Entitled: Single Mothers and the History of Welfare, 1890–1935*, Cambridge, MA: Harvard University Press, 1994.
33. Viola Klein, *Britain's Married Women Workers*, London: Routledge & Kegan Paul, 1965, pp. 24–26, 84–85. Between 1950 and 1963 the number of single, widowed, and divorced women who were employed declined from 4.1 million to 3.8 million. By 1963, over 4.3 million married women were employed. Klein relies on Department of Labour statistics rather than census returns because census returns understated the number of married women involved in part-time work. The census questionnaire did not include women

who were "chiefly occupied in unpaid domestic duties at home" among the employed. There was no census in 1941.

34. Audrey Hunt, *A Survey of Women's Employment: A Survey Carried Out on Behalf of the Ministry of Labour by the Government Social Survey in 1965*, London: H.M.S.O., p. 22.

35. Klein, *Britain's Married Women Workers*, pp. 36–44.

36. TNA: PRO, PIN 49/27, "Paper 18 of the National Insurance Advisory Committee: Note by Secretary on the Effect of the Proposed Amendments, Part-Time Employment (Classification and Liability for Contributions) Question."

37. TNA: PRO, PIN 49/197, "Classification. Wives of Managers of Off-License Premises. Carlos & Thrale, Ltd.," 1957–1958.

38. TNA: PRO, CT 1/15, Decisions of the Deputy Commissioners, 1950.

39. Klein, *Britain's Married Women Workers*, pp. 25, 101–103. Estimates for the percentage of part-time work vary. The 1951 figure is based on the census results, which almost certainly underestimated the number of part-timers. The 1957 figure is based on two studies conducted by Klein. In one sample of 56,000 women, 40% of the employed married women worked part-time. In another sample, including fewer women but a wider range of occupations, 50% of the employed married women were in part-time work. Young and Willmott's study of forty-five families in the working-class borough of Bethnal Green showed that of the nineteen wives who were employed, 42% worked part-time. See Michael Young and Peter Willmott, *Family and Kinship in East London*, London: Routledge & Kegan Paul, 1986, pp. 37–38. Ministry of Labour statistics indicate that by 1961, nearly one-fourth of all married women working in the manufacturing industries—and a higher proportion of those working outside—were in part-time employment.

40. The contribution schedule was dependent on sex, however. In the early 1950s, employers paid 6 shillings (s.) 0 pence (d.) for men and 4s. 11d. for women. Employee contributions were similarly sex-based: men paid 6s. 9d., while women paid 5s. 6d.

41. TNA: PRO, PIN 49/27, "Report of National Advisory Committee on the Employment of Older Men and Women," February 11, 1955; Hunt, *A Survey of Women's Employment*, p. 9.

42. Klein, *Britain's Married Women Workers*, p. 32. In Klein's 1957 sample, 45% of the married women working part-time were employed in these jobs.

43. Klein, *Britain's Married Women Workers*, pp. 127–135. Laundries, dyers, and cleaners used part-time workers in the summer months; confectionery manufacturers during holidays; and department stores during the lunch-hour and on Saturdays.

44. Klein, *Britain's Married Women Workers*, p. 33. The proportion of unskilled workers among married women working full-time was smaller: 60% held unskilled positions.

45. TNA: PRO, PIN 49/27 "Part-Time Employment of Women: A Review of Present-Day Schemes." Industrial Welfare Society, March 1955.

46. Alva Myrdal and Viola Klein, *Women's Two Roles*, London: Routledge & Kegan Paul, Ltd., 1956, p. xii. Viola Klein also undertook elaborate surveys of married women and their employers in 1956 and 1957. See Klein, *Britain's Married Women Workers*.

47. Klein, *Britain's Married Women Workers*, pp. 124–125.

48. Klein, *Britain's Married Women Workers*, pp. 126–134.

49. Klein, *Britain's Married Women Workers*, p. 127.

50. TNA: PRO, PIN 49/27, "Letter from G. Walley (Ministry of Pensions and National Insurance) to H.W. Stockman, Esq. (Ministry of Labour)," undated, probably 1955.
51. Complaints and proposals were also filed with the NIAC by the Institution of British Launderers, the National Union of Small Shopkeepers of Great Britain and Northern Ireland, and numerous individual employers.
52. TNA: PRO, PIN 49/27, Minutes of Meeting of National Insurance Advisory Committee, Remarks of L.E. Kenyon of the British Employers Confederation, February 20, 1957.
53. TNA: PRO, PIN 49/27, Minutes of Meeting of National Insurance Advisory Committee, Remarks of Retail Distributive Trades Conference, February 20, 1957.
54. TNA: PRO, PIN 49/27, Letter from Frank C. Ros, Personnel Manager at Marks & Spencer. Ltd. to NIAC, August 9, 1955.
55. TNA: PRO, PIN 49/27, "Representation from South Midland Secretarial Services, Ltd.: Insurance of Part-Time and Temporary Clerical Workers," July 22, 1955.
56. TNA: PRO, PIN 49/27, Minutes of Meeting of National Insurance Advisory Committee, Remarks of Douglas Houghton, M.P. (Trades Union Congress), February 20, 1957.
57. TNA: PRO, PIN 49/27, "Representation from British Federation of University Women, Ltd.," July 28, 1955; "Representation from National Council of Women of Great Britain," July 8, 1955; "Resolution of National Council of Women," October 1957.
58. TNA: PRO, PIN 49/27, Minutes of Meeting of National Insurance Advisory Committee, February 20, 1957; "Report of National Advisory Committee on the Employment of Older Men and Women," February 11, 1955; Ministry of National Insurance Report on the Effects of National Insurance Arrangements on Part-Time Work, April 1951; Letter from J.R. Davis of Ministry of Labour and National Service to J. P. Corswell, Esq., of the Ministry of Pensions and National Insurance, December 1, 1955.
59. TNA: PRO, PIN 49/27, "Memorandum from the Ministry of National Insurance on Part-Time Employment Question," undated, probably 1957.
60. Mrs. Wright was told that she was eligible for Class II insurance, which did not provide unemployment benefits and had a higher contribution rate for employees. To qualify, however, she would have had to pay arrears for nine years of the higher Class II rate. Class II insurance was primarily designed for self-employed people, but could also be invoked by workers who worked a total of eight or more hours, but could not meet the eight-hour rule at any one job. TNA: PRO, PIN 49/198, "Classification: School Meals Worker. London County Council," undated, probably 1959.
61. TNA: PRO, PIN 7/340, "Ministry of Labour Inquiry Regarding the Operation of Anomalies Regulation 4," September 1947.
62. Ibid.
63. TNA: PRO, PIN 7/340, "Report from Northern Region on AR4 Application," January 2, 1948.
64. TNA: PRO, PIN 7/340, "Ministry of Labour Inquiry Regarding the Operation of Anomalies Regulation 4," September 1947. Not all local insurance officers assumed married women would not be able to find work. The 1947 review suggested considerable variation in the way the rule was applied, even in districts that appeared to have similar employment patterns. Some regional controllers and insurance officers also felt that, as a general matter of policy planning, the anomalies regulations should not be used to disallow

claims. They noted that economic growth would soon make the widespread employment of married women necessary.

65. TNA: PRO, PIN 7/340, "Report of a Conference of Regional Insurance Officers," October 28, 1947; Circular P2/651, December 24, 1947.

66. TNA: PRO, PIN 7/340, "Married Women's Anomalies Regulations," C.I.O. Memorandum No. 39, March 1, 1948.

67. TNA: PRO, PIN 7/340, Letter from Gilbert Williams to A.J.G. Crocker, April 22, 1952.

68. TNA: PRO, PIN 7/340, "Ministry of Labour Inquiry Regarding the Operation of Anomalies Regulation 4."

69. TNA: PRO, PIN 7/340, Letter from D. D. Ward to A.J.G. Crocker, March 31, 1952.

70. TNA: PRO, CT 1/15, Decision of Deputy Commissioner Barrington, September 11, 1950.

71. The analysis in this chapter is based on my review of the 1,583 individual decisions on London-area cases issued by the deputy commissioners of the Ministry of National Insurance between 1949 and 1963. These decisions are found at TNA: PRO, CT 1/4 through 1/92.

72. Frances Fox-Piven and Richard Cloward, *Regulating the Poor: The Functions of Public Welfare*, New York: Random House, 1971.

73. Gosta Esping-Andersen, *The Three Worlds of Welfare Capitalism*, Princeton, NJ: Princeton University Press, 1990.

74. Lewis, "Dealing with Dependency," pp. 17–37.

75. Michael Hill, *The Sociology of Public Administration*, New York: Crane, Russak & Company, Inc., 1972, p. 80.

76. Geoffrey S. King, *The Ministry of Pensions and National Insurance*, London: George Allen and Unwin Ltd., 1958, pp. 87–88.

77. King, *The Ministry of Pensions and National Insurance*, pp. 82–89.

78. Kathleen Bell, *Tribunals in the Social Services*, London: Routledge & Kegan Paul, 1969.

79. Hill, *The Sociology of Public Administration*, p. 80.

80. TNA: PRO, CT 1/83, Decision of Deputy Commissioner Nelson, November 7, 1962.

81. TNA: PRO, CT 1/90, Decision of Deputy Commissioner D'Allembuerque, October 10, 1963.

82. TNA: PRO, CT 1/21, Decision of Deputy Commissioner D'Allembuerque, May 15, 1951.

83. TNA: PRO, CT 1/16, Decision of Deputy Commissioner Barrington, October 11, 1950.

84. TNA: PRO, CT 1/10, Decision of Deputy Commissioner D'Allembuerque, March 30, 1950.

85. Young and Willmott, *Family and Kinship in East London*, pp. 37–38.

86. A finding that a worker had "just cause" for restrictions placed on hours or working conditions was legally necessary.

87. TNA: PRO, CT 1/28, Decision of Deputy Commissioner George, June 9, 1952.

88. TNA: PRO, CT 1/57, Decision of Deputy Commissioner Safford, September 26, 1958.

89. TNA: PRO, CT 1/15, Decision of Deputy Commissioner D'Allembuerque, July 26, 1950.

90. TNA: PRO, CT 1/21, Decision of Deputy Commissioner Barrington, June 19, 1951.

91. TNA: PRO, CT 1/33, Decision of Deputy Commissioner D'Allembuerque, August 6, 1953.

92. TNA: PRO, CT 1/32, Decision of Deputy Commissioner D'Allembuerque, February 24, 1953.
93. TNA: PRO, CT 1/15, Decision of Deputy Commissioner Duffes, August 8, 1950.
94. TNA: PRO, CT 1/21, Decision of Deputy Commissioner George, June 18, 1951.
95. TNA: PRO, CT 1/64, Decision of Deputy Commissioner Neligan, July 3, 1959.
96. TNA: PRO, CT 1/76, Decision of Deputy Commissioner Neligan, September 20, 1961.
97. TNA: PRO, CT 1/29, Decision of Deputy Commissioner D'Allembuerque, January 20, 1953.
98. TNA: PRO, CT 1/29, Decision of Deputy Commissioner D'Allembuerque, December 12, 1952.
99. TNA: PRO, CT 1/1, Decision of Deputy Commissioner, D'Allembuerque, November 23, 1948.

NOTES TO CHAPTER 2

* This chapter was first published as "Not the Normal Mode of Maintenance": Bureaucratic Resistance to the Claims of Lone Women in the Postwar British Welfare State, *Law & Social Inquiry*, 2004, vol. 29, no. 2, pp. 343–371.
1. The National Archives (hereafter TNA): Public Records Office (hereafter PRO), AST 12/59, "Minutes of the Conference of Regional Controllers, 10 March 1953, Appendix I, Area Officer Circular Minute, Recovery From Liable Relatives."
2. Pat Thane, "Women and the Poor Law in Victorian and Edwardian England," *History Workshop Journal*, 1978, no. 6, pp. 29–51; K.D.M. Snell and Jane Millar, "Lone-Parent Families and the Welfare State: Past and Present," *Continuity and Change*, 1987, no. 2, pp. 387–422; Lynn Hollen Lees, *The Solidarities of Strangers, The English Poor Laws and the People, 1700–1948*, New York: Cambridge University Press, 1998.
3. Susan Pedersen, *Family, Dependence, and the Origins of the Welfare State: Britain and France, 1914–1945*, New York: Cambridge University Press, 1993; John Macnicol, *The Movement for Family Allowances, 1918–1945*, London: Heinemann, 1980.
4. Linda Gordon, *Pitied But Not Entitled: Single Mothers and the History of Welfare, 1890–1935*, Cambridge, MA: Harvard University Press, 1994.
5. Alan Deacon and Jonathan Bradshaw, *Reserved for the Poor: The Means Test in British Social Policy*, Oxford: Basil Blackwell and Martin Robertson, 1983; Ruth Lister, *As Man and Wife? A Study of the Cohabitation Rule*, London: Child Poverty Action Group, 1973; Elizabeth Wilson, *Women and the Welfare State*, London: Tavistock, 1977. For a rare discussion of NAB policy, see John Veit-Wilson, "The National Assistance Board and the 'Rediscovery' of Poverty," in H. Fawcett and R. Lowe (eds.), *Welfare Policy in Britain: The Road from 1945*, London: Macmillan, 1999, pp. 116–157.
6. Land argues that lone mothers became visible as a significant category of welfare recipients only in the mid-1960s, in the context of the "rediscovery of poverty" inspired by Peter Townsend's research. Concern about children's poverty resulted in improvements in the treatment of lone mothers in the 1970s (apart from the always contentious cohabitation rule). Hilary Land, "Social Security and Lone Mothers," in Kathleen Kiernan, Hilary Land, and

Jane Lewis (eds.), *Lone Motherhood in Twentieth-Century Britain: From Footnote to Front Page*, Oxford: Clarendon Press, 1998, pp. 151–210.

7. Section 4 of the National Assistance Act of 1948 required the NAB to "assist persons in Great Britain who are without resources to meet their requirements, or whose resources (including benefits receivable under the National Insurance Act of 1946) must be supplemented in order to meet their requirements." Under section 9(1) of the Act, a person who was engaged in remunerative full-time work was disqualified from receiving assistance (except in an emergency).

8. If a husband was not earning full-time wages and the family qualified for an assistance allowance, the national assistance claim was filed by the man, and assistance was paid to him for the entire family.

9. This obligation originally grew out of the doctrine of unity of legal personality of husband and wife, which deprived wives of the capacity to hold property or to enter into contracts. Since wives could not own or enter into a binding agreement to buy necessities, their husbands were legally obliged to provide necessities for them.

10. Separated women who had young children and were on assistance outnumbered unmarried mothers on assistance by roughly two to one, and divorced women with children by three to one.

11. In its early years, the NAB did not keep statistics on divorced women. Between 1959 and 1965, the number of divorced women with children claiming benefit increased from 6,000 to 14,000.

12. The statistics in this paragraph are based on data from the annual reports of the NAB from 1949 through 1965.

13. TNA: PRO, AST 12/58, Regional Controller Conference Minutes, July 12, 1950.

14. For a discussion of black female immigrants' assigned identities as "workers" rather than mothers, see Wendy Webster, *Imagining Home: Gender, "Race" and National Identity, 1945–64*, London: University of Central Lancashire Press, 1998, esp. pp. 129–147.

15. TNA: PRO, AST 7/1535, Report on Coloured Applicants for National Assistance, October 29, 1958.

16. TNA: PRO, AST 12/71, Regional Controller Conference Minutes, July 20, 1965.

17. Examples of such cases can be found in TNA: PRO, AST 7/1646, National Assistance Board, London (South) Region, Surrey Advisory Committee, "Cases of Special Interest Considered Between March and August 1958" and AST 7/1646, National Assistance Board, London (South) Region, Surrey Advisory Committee, "Examples of Cases Considered by Area Sub-Committees, 1 March 1959 to 17 August 1959."

18. *Report of the National Assistance Board for 1949*, Cmd. 8030, p. 5.

19. These statistics were drawn from data in the annual reports of the NAB from 1948 through 1965. For national assistance classification purposes, the "elderly" included men over sixty-five and women over sixty.

20. *Report of the National Assistance Board for 1948*, Cmd. 7767, p. 23.

21. Dennis Marsden, *Mothers Alone, Poverty and the Fatherless Family*, London: Allen Lane, 1969, pp. 178–180.

22. *Report of the National Assistance Board for 1949*, p. 21.

23. Maintenance amounts were capped, and in the mid-1950s, a husband could not be compelled to pay more than £5 per week for his wife and 30 shillings per week for each of his children. After 1950, if a married woman pursued a claim in the high court under the Matrimonial Causes Act, she could secure an order for "reasonable" maintenance that was not subject

to the caps imposed on magistrates' courts. However, the vast majority of women who sought relief, especially poor women, turned to the magistrates' courts, which were more accessible. P.M. Bromley, *Family Law*, London: Butterworth, 1957.

24. Marsden, *Mothers Alone.*
25. Hilary Land has minimized the NAB's concern over liable relative cases in the 1950s, saying that there was no significant feeling that lone mothers were abusing the system. Hilary Land, "Social Security and Lone Mothers." This conclusion, however, is based almost exclusively on the NAB's published annual reports, which gloss over many of the difficulties discussed more fully in their internal documents.
26. TNA: PRO, AST 12/57, "Minutes of Regional Controllers' Conference," October 5–6, 1949; TNA: PRO, AST 12/58, "Minutes of Regional Controllers' Conference," March 8, 1950.
27. TNA: PRO, AST 7/1450, "Instructions for Visiting Officers," February 1952.
28. TNA: PRO, AST 12/59, "Conference of Regional Controllers, Note: Enforcement of Liability for Maintenance of Wives and Children," February 28, 1953.
29. TNA: PRO, AST 12/59, "Minutes of Regional Controllers' Conference, 10 March 1953."
30. TNA: PRO, AST 12/59, "Minutes of the Conference of Regional Controllers, 10 March 1953, Appendix III, Draft A Code Changes, Default in Keeping up Payments."
31. Marsden, *Mothers Alone*, pp. 152, 187.
32. TNA: PRO, AST 12/59, "Minutes of the Conference of Regional Controllers, 10 March 1953, Appendix III, Draft A Code Changes, Default in Keeping up Payments."
33. TNA: PRO, AST 12/59, "Minutes of Regional Controllers' Conference, 10 March 1953."
34. TNA: PRO, AST 12/59, "Conference of Regional Controllers, Note: Enforcement of Liability for Maintenance of Wives and Children," February 28, 1953.
35. Technically, adultery terminated the right to maintenance, whereas desertion suspended the right, which was restored if the woman returned to her husband.
36. *Culley v. Charman*, 7 QBD 89 [1881].
37. *National Assistance Board v. Wilkinson*, 2 All E.R. 255 [1952].
38. *Wilkinson*, 1952, p. 258.
39. *Wilkinson*, 1952, p. 259.
40. Stephen Parker (in *Informal Marriage, Cohabitation and the Law, 1750–1989*, New York: St. Martin's Press, 1990) argues that, in the post-war period, the concept of marital fault gradually lost its force, in part because of the burden posed on the public purse when husbands were not liable for maintenance. However, marital fault continued to negate women's maintenance rights into the 1970s.
41. *National Assistance Board v. Parkes*, 3 W.L.R. 347 [1955].
42. *Parkes*, 1955, p. 353.
43. The court also held that a husband's compliance with a separation agreement providing for payments to the wife was similarly not a bar to a claim for maintenance (see also *National Assistance Board v. Prisk*, 1 All E.R. 400 [1954]).
44. 13 All E.R. 792 [1957].

45. TNA: PRO, AST 7/1811, Report by Roger Winn, Solicitor to the NAB, May 16, 1957.

46. Scotland had made use of a similar procedure for many years. The procedure was new, however, in England and Wales.

47. Margaret Wynn, *Fatherless Families: A Study of Families Deprived of a Father By Death, Divorce Separation or Desertion Before or After Marriage*, London: Michael Joseph Limited, 1964, pp. 58–60.

48. These statistics were drawn from data in the annual reports of the NAB from 1954 through 1965.

49. Virginia Wimperis, *The Unmarried Mother and Her Child*, London: Allen and Unwin, 1960; Wynn, *Fatherless Families*.

50. Wynn, *Fatherless Families*.

51. TNA: PRO, AST 7/1931, "Draft Brief for the Government Spokesman in the House of Lords" (on Lady Summerskill's Bill), February 5, 1965.

52. Ibid.

53. TNA: PRO, AST 12/57, "Minutes of Regional Controllers' Conference," October 5–6, 1949.

54. TNA: PRO, AST 12/58, "Minutes of Regional Controllers' Conference," March 8, 1950.

55. TNA: PRO, AST 7/1450, "Instructions for Visiting Officers," February 1952.

56. *Report of the National Assistance Board for 1953*, Cmd. 9210, pp. 20–21.

57. *Report of the National Assistance Board for 1952*, Cmd. 8900, pp. 18–19.

58. *Report of the National Assistance Board for 1953*, p. 20. The source of such proposals was not identified, but given the tenor and content of agency discussions about reconciliation, they likely emanated, in part at least, from within the NAB's own ranks.

59. *Report of the Departmental Committee on Grants for the Development of Marriage Guidance*, 1948, Cmd. 7566.

60. *Report of the Royal Commission on Marriage and Divorce*, 1956, Cmd. 9678. For a history of the National Marriage Guidance Council, see Jane Lewis, "Public Institution and Private Relationship, Marriage and Marriage Guidance," *Twentieth Century British History*, 1990, vol. 1, pp. 233–263.

61. Marsden, *Mothers Alone*.

62. Wynn, *Fatherless Families*, p. 79.

63. *Report of the National Assistance Board for 1954*, Cmd. 9530, p. 20.

64. Ibid.

65. Ibid.

66. The husband always had an obligation to support his children, even if the wife could make no claim on the husband for her own support.

67. *Report of the National Assistance Board for 1954*, p. 20.

68. Concern about this kind of fraud was not new; Poor Law guardians had employed various measures to verify that wives seeking relief had really been deserted. Women who claimed they had been deserted were denied relief for twelve months by local guardians. Thane, "Women and the Poor Law in Victorian and Edwardian England."

69. TNA: PRO, AST 12/59, "Minutes of the Conference of Regional Controllers, 10 March 1953, Appendix I, Area Officer Circular Minute (1953), Recovery From Liable Relatives."

70. Ibid.

71. TNA: PRO, AST 7/1820, "Women Cohabiting with Men in Full-Time Work. Qualification for Assistance Under Section 9(1)," October 1964.

72. TNA: PRO, AST 7/1585, Letter from Miss S.H.M. Peek (NAB Headquarters) to Mr. Beard, December 9, 1959.
73. TNA: PRO, AST 7/1820, Minutes of the Regional Controllers' Conference, October 20, 1964.
74. Social Security Act of 1966, (schedule 2, Pt. I, para. 3[I]).
75. TNA: PRO, AST 7/1535, Report on Coloured Applicants for National Assistance, October 29, 1958.
76. Applicants' names have been changed.
77. TNA: PRO, AST 7/1585, Memorandum from Regional Controller of London (North) Region to NAB Secretary at Headquarters, June 30, 1961.
78. *Report of the National Assistance Board for 1959*, Cmnd. 1085, p. 34.
79. Ibid.
80. *Report of the National Assistance Board for 1965*, Cmnd. 3042. Of the 525 women prosecuted, 481 (91%) were convicted; punishment ranged from fines to imprisonment. The 525 prosecutions of women for fraud concerning support they received constituted almost a quarter of all criminal charges brought by the NAB. Other grounds for fraud prosecutions included non-disclosure of earnings and giving false information to NAB officers in order to collect more than one assistance allowance.
81. *Report of the National Assistance Board for 1964*, Cmnd. 2674; *Report of the National Assistance Board for 1965*.
82. TNA: PRO, AST 7/1590, Regulation A.1551–1554, "Women Acting as Housekeepers to Relatives."
83. TNA: PRO, AST 7/1590, "Audit Report on Kingston Area Office, Restriction of Allowance," December 24, 1958.
84. TNA: PRO, AST 7/1590, "London (South) Region Audit Report," July 16, 1959.

NOTES TO CHAPTER 3

1. Alan Deacon and Jonathan Bradshaw, *Reserved for the Poor, The Means Test in British Social Policy*, Oxford: Basil Blackwell and Martin Robertson, 1983, p. 108; see also Peter Golding and Sue Middleton, *Images of Welfare: Press and Public Attitudes to Poverty*, Oxford: Martin Robertson, 1982.
2. Chris Jones and Tony Novak, *Poverty, Welfare and the Disciplinary State*, London: Routledge, 1999, esp. pp. 66–70.
3. Adrian Webb, "The Abolition of National Assistance," in Phoebe Hall (ed.) *Change, Choice and Conflict in Social Policy*, London: Heinemann, 1975, p. 467.
4. Alan Deacon, "Unemployment and Politics in Britain Since 1945," in Brian Showler and Adrian Sinfield (eds.) *The Workless State, Studies in Unemployment*, Oxford: Martin Robertson, 1981, p. 69.
5. The National Archives (hereafter TNA): PRO, AST 7/1049, Minute from the Regional Officer, London, to the Secretary, National Assistance Board, London, on Advisory Committees, January 29, 1949, Appendix A.
6. TNA: PRO, AST 7/1049, Minute from the Regional Officer, London, to the Secretary, National Assistance Board, London, on Advisory Committees, January 29, 1949, Appendix B.
7. Criticism of the unemployed and the policies responding to such criticism focused on unemployed men, who made up 90% of the unemployed applicants for national assistance.
8. "Abuse of Public Assistance," *London Times*, January 29, 1953, p. 9.

9. Letter to the Editor from B. E. Astbury, General Secretary, Family Welfare Association, *London Times*, January 31, 1953, p. 7.

10. Letter to the Editor from F. E. S. Hatfield, *London Times*, February 2, 1953, p. 9.

11. TNA: PRO, LAB 8/2487, Area Officer Circular Minute No. 30: The Revised Voluntary Unemployment Instructions, December 4, 1958.

12. TNA: PRO, LAB 8/2487, Minute to all Regional Controllers (Ministry of Labour) from B. M. Grainger, January 20, 1961; Ministry of Labour Minute, November 21, 1960; Letter from Miss J. Hope-Wallace (NAB) to C. J. Maston, Esq., Ministry of Labour, November 17, 1960; Letter from R. P. Snow (Ministry of Labour) to S. B. Kibbey, Esq., Ministry of Pensions and National Insurance, May 9, 1961; "Abuse of National Assistance," *London Times*, May 8, 1961.

13. TNA: PRO, AST 7/1646, Minutes of the Meeting of the Surrey Advisory Committee, April 22, 1959.

14. *Report of the National Assistance Board for 1965*, Cmnd. 3042, p. vii.

15. *Report of the National Assistance Board for 1951*, Cmd. 8632, p. 8.

16. *Report of the National Assistance Board for 1952*, Cmd. 8900, p. 13.

17. TNA: PRO, AST 12/57, Minutes of Regional Controllers' Meeting, July 5, 1951.

18. *Report of the National Assistance Board for 1952*, pp. 13–14.

19. *Report of the National Assistance Board for 1951*, p. 15.

20. The re-establishment regime is strikingly similar to the "remotivation" courses introduced in the mid-1990s. Claimants who refuse to attend have their "jobseekers allowance" (the successor of unemployment benefit and national assistance) suspended. See Jones and Novak, *Poverty, Welfare and the Disciplinary State*, p. 70.

21. *Report of the National Assistance Board for 1951*, p. 15.

22. *Report of the National Assistance Board for 1952*, p. 13. The attendance rate under section 10 orders did not improve; throughout the 1950s and early 1960s, it ranged from 10% to 30%.

23. *Report of the National Assistance Board for 1952*, p. 17.

24. *Report of the National Assistance Board for 1956*, Cmnd. 181, p. 17.

25. *Report of the National Assistance Board for 1953*, Cmd. 9210, p. 15.

26. *Report of the National Assistance Board for 1956*, p. 15.

27. *Report of the National Assistance Board for 1956*, p. 17.

28. Ibid.

29. *Report of the National Assistance Board for 1953*, p. 16.

30. *Report of the National Assistance Board for 1957*, Cmnd. 444, p. 22.

31. TNA: PRO, AST 7/1712, Report by London (North) Region of NAB on Experimental Non-Residential Re-Establishment Center, undated, probably late 1961.

32. TNA: PRO, AST 7/1712, Confidential Memorandum 1,178 of the National Assistance Board, London Day Re-Establishment Center, circulated January 26, 1962.

33. Ibid.

34. TNA: PRO, AST 7/1712, Leaflet by W. J. Botwright (Warden of Brady House) on Brady House, undated.

35. "Under the Affluence," *The Economist*, July 6, 1963.

36. *Report of the National Assistance Board for 1965*, p. 32.

37. TNA: PRO, AST 7/1646, National Assistance Board, London (South) Region, Surrey Advisory Committee, "Examples of Cases Considered by Area Sub-Committees, 1 March 1960 to 31 August 1960."

38. TNA: PRO, AST 7/1646, National Assistance Board, London (South) Region, Surrey Advisory Committee, "Examples of Cases Considered by Area Sub-Committees, 1 March 1960 to 31 August 1960."
39. TNA: PRO, AST 7/1646, National Assistance Board, London (South) Region, Surrey Advisory Committee, "Examples of Cases Considered by Area Sub-Committees, 1 September 1963 to 29 February 1964."
40. Ibid.
41. Ibid.
42. Ibid.
43. TNA: PRO, AST 7/1646, Minutes of the Meeting of the Surrey Advisory Committee held on April 22, 1959. Disagreements in this area between the local Advisory Committees and NAB staff members continued. In 1965, the Regional Controller for the South London Region tried to smooth over the hurt feelings of Subcommittee members who felt their recommendations to terminate allowances were being ignored by local NAB managers. TNA: PRO, AST 7/1646, Minutes of the Meeting of the Surrey Advisory Committee, April 29, 1965.
44. TNA: PRO, AST 7/1646, Minutes of the Meeting of the Surrey Advisory Committee, April 22, 1959.
45. TNA: PRO, AST 7/1646, National Assistance Board, London (South) Region, Surrey Advisory Committee, "Examples of Cases Considered by Area Sub-Committees, 1 March 1961 to 31 August 1961."
46. TNA: PRO, AST 7/1646, Minutes of the Meeting of the Surrey Advisory Committee, October 16, 1958.
47. *Report of the National Assistance Board for 1961*, Cmnd. 1730, p. 35.
48. Ibid.
49. Ibid.
50. TNA: PRO, LAB 8/2635, Voluntary Unemployment Specialisation Report (NAB), undated, probably early 1964.
51. *Report of the National Assistance Board for 1962*, Cmnd. 2078, p. 41.
52. TNA: PRO, AST 7/1646, Minutes of the Meeting of the Surrey Advisory Committee, October 3, 1963; TNA: PRO, LAB 8/2635, Voluntary Unemployment Specialisation Report (NAB), undated.
53. *Report of the National Assistance Board for 1965*, p. 32; TNA: PRO, LAB 8/2635, Voluntary Unemployment Specialisation Report.
54. *Report of the National Assistance Board for 1961*, p. 33.
55. Ibid.
56. *Report of the National Assistance Board for 1960*, Cmnd. 1410, p. 51.
57. Though 17% were referred to Industrial Rehabilitation Units, most were not accepted because of their physical condition and vocational prospects. Thirty-five men (3.5% of those examined) were referred to the NAB's Re-Establishment Centers, but only seven attended. As discussed above, the Re-Establishment Centers offered no vocational training or any specific services for the disabled. *Report of the National Assistance Board for 1960*, pp. 51–52.
58. The NAB reported that 324 had found work, but as was typical of NAB reports, no information was provided about how long the work was sustained, or if the men reappeared on the rolls. *Report of the National Assistance Board for 1960*, p. 51.
59. Ibid.
60. Ibid.
61. TNA: PRO, AST 7/1646, National Assistance Board, London (South) Region, Surrey Advisory Committee, "Examples of Cases Considered by Area Sub-Committees, 1 September 1964 to 28 February 1965."
62. *Report of the National Assistance Board for 1952*, p. 14.
63. Ibid.

64. *Report of the National Assistance Board for 1955*, Cmd. 9781, p. 30.
65. *Report of the National Assistance Board for 1953*, p. 12.
66. *Report of the National Assistance Board for 1961*, p. 36.
67. The NAB prosecuted 180 men in 1961, as opposed to 88 the year before. Ibid.

NOTES TO CHAPTER 4

1. Henry Hopkinson, Minister of State for Colonial Affairs, House of Common Debates, November 5, 1954, col. 830.
2. The National Archives (hereafter TNA): Public Record Office (hereafter PRO), AST 7/1210, Note to Secretary of the NAB from Osbert Peake (Chairman, NAB), July 8, 1952.
3. See, for example, Ian R. G. Spencer, *British Immigration Policy Since 1939: The Making of Multi-Racial Britain*, New York: Routledge, 1997; Kathleen Paul, *Whitewashing Britain: Race and Citizenship in the Postwar Era*, Ithaca, NY: Cornell University Press, 1997; Laura Tabili, *We Ask For British Justice: Workers and Racial Difference in Late Imperial Britain*, Ithaca, NY: Cornell University Press, 1994.
4. Harry Goulbourne, *Ethnicity and Nationalism in Post-Imperial Britain*, New York: Cambridge University Press, 1991; Harry Goulbourne, *Race Relations in Britain Since 1945*, New York: St. Martin's Press, 1998; Paul Gilroy,"*There Ain't No Black in the Union Jack*": *Cultural Politics of Race and Nation*, London: Hutchinson, 1987; Stuart Hall, *Policing the Crisis: Mugging, the State, and Law and Order*, London: Macmillan, 1978; Chris Waters, "'Dark Strangers' in Our Midst: Discourses of Race and Nation in Britain, 1947–1963," *Journal of British Studies*, 1997, vol. 36, pp. 207–238.
5. Spencer, *British Immigration Policy Since 1939*, pp. 38, 90–91; Colin Holmes, *John Bull's Island: Immigration and British Society, 1871–1971*, Basingstoke, UK: Macmillan, 1988.
6. Spencer, *British Immigration Policy Since 1939* and Paul, *Whitewashing Britain*.
7. Holmes, *John Bull's Island*, p. 221; Spencer, *British Immigration Policy Since 1939*.
8. Spencer, *British Immigration Policy Since 1939*,p. 60.
9. Holmes, *John Bull's Island*, p. 221.
10. TNA: PRO, AST 7/1210, Minute from NAB Officer, Birmingham, to J. Gaskell, Esq., NAB Regional Office, Birmingham, July 9, 1952; Minute from NAB officer, Birmingham, to F. Jackson, Esq., NAB Regional Office, Birmingham, July 16, 1952.
11. TNA: PRO, AST 7/1880, Report on "Commonwealth Immigrants-Welfare," from Manager, Brixton NAB to Miss V. M. Baker, London (South) Region, November 15, 1962.
12. Ibid.
13. Ibid.
14. TNA: PRO, AST 7/1880, Minute from Manager Slough Area Office to London (South) Regional Controller, November 15, 1962.
15. TNA: PRO, AST 7/1880, Report on "Commonwealth Immigrants-Welfare," from Manager, Lambeth NAB to Miss V. M. Baker, London (South) Region, November 14, 1962; TNA: PRO, AST 7/1210, Minute from NAB Officer, Birmingham, to J. Gaskell, Esq., NAB Regional Office, Birmingham, July 9, 1952.
16. TNA: PRO, AST 7/1880, Minute from Manager Slough Area Office to London (South) Regional Controller, November 15, 1962.

17. TNA: PRO, AST 7/1210, Minute from NAB Officer, Birmingham, to F. Jackson, Esq., NAB Regional Office, Birmingham, July 16, 1952.
18. TNA: PRO, AST 7/1614, Letter from Regional Controller, Birmingham, to Miss J. Hope-Wallace, C. B. E., NAB Headquarters, May 19, 1958; Confidential Memorandum from Sir Alexander Symon, July 1958.
19. Ibid.
20. Ibid.
21. TNA: PRO, AST 7/1210, "Coloured Immigrants and National Assistance," July 18, 1952; Letter to D. J. Hope-Wallace from the Home Office Aliens Department, July 23, 1952; Memorandum from R. Dronfield (Ministry of National Insurance) to J. E. Bullard, Esq., National Assistance Board, July 28, 1952.
22. "Coloured Work-Shys Find Paradise in Britain and We Have to Keep Paying Them," *Sunday Chronicle*, December 14, 1952.
23. TNA: PRO, AST 7/1210, Letter from Regional Controller, Birmingham, to G. W. Cole, December 20, 1952.
24. TNA: PRO, AST 7/1211, Letter from T. H. Brain to Sir H. Fieldhouse, Secretary, National Assistance Board, January 6, 1954.
25. TNA: PRO, AST 7/1211, Minute on "Coloured Colonials" from Regional Controller for the London Inner Region to the Secretary of the NAB, January 18, 1954.
26. TNA: PRO, AST 7/1211, Postcard from J. L. Corney to Capt. Henry Kerby, M. P., undated, probably 1957.
27. TNA: PRO, AST 7/1211, Letter from Miss M. Johnson, Acting Hon. Secretary, Battersea Ratepayers' Association, to Rt. Hon. Major Lloyd-George, M. P., November 6, 1954.
28. TNA: PRO, AST 7/1211, Letter to Hendrie D. Oakshott, M. P., April 5, 1957.
29. Other answers to the survey question in 1961: "they congregate in a neighbourhood and turn it into a slum," 39%; "some of them become landlords and charge terrible rents," 36%; "they take away work from Britishers," 27%; "they exploit vice and crime for gain," 16%; "they undercut wages," 14%; none of the above, 7%. World Political Opinion and Social Surveys, Series One: British Opinion Polls, Part 1: 1960–1988, Gallup Political Index, Report No. 90, October 1967.
30. TNA: PRO, AST 7/1878, Letter from Geoffrey Hutchinson, NAB chairman, to Michael Hughes-Young, M. P., April 7, 1961.
31. TNA: PRO, AST 7/1878, Extract from Area Officers' Conference (Northern Region), August 18, 1959.
32. TNA: PRO, AST 7/1878, Minute from Shoreditch Manager to the Regional Controller, London (North) Region, March 29, 1961; Minute from the Regional Controller, London (North) Region to the Secretary, Headquarters, London, April 7, 1961.
33. TNA: PRO, AST 7/1878, Minute from W. J. Scott, Manager Paddington to Regional Controller, London (North), February 10, 1960; Minute from Regional Controller, London (North) to the Secretary, Headquarters, London, February 16, 1960.
34. There were, however, provisions to allow deportation after a criminal conviction.
35. TNA: PRO, AST 7/1210, Letter from J. E. Bullard to R. Dronfield, Esq., Ministry of National Insurance, July 12, 1952.
36. Ibid.
37. TNA: PRO, HO 376/133, Minute from J. Hope-Wallace, National Assistance Board, undated, probably August 1964.

38. TNA: PRO, HO 376/133, Minute from W. H. Lee, Home Office, January 7, 1965.
39. TNA: PRO, HO 376/133, "Repatriation of Commonwealth and Colonial Immigrants by the National Assistance Board," undated, probably late 1964; Letter from NAB to W. M. Lee, Esq., Home Office, March 15, 1966.
40. TNA: PRO, AST 7/1249, Minute from D. D. Jameson, NAB Headquarters, July 12, 1961.
41. TNA: PRO, AST 7/1249, Minute from H. S. Jones to D. D. Jameson, NAB Headquarters, July 12, 1961.
42. TNA: PRO, AST 7/1882, Minute from M. A. Brougham, NAB Headquarters to the Manager, Birmingham (South) Area Office, June 27, 1963.
43. TNA: PRO, AST 7/1878, "Coloured Applicants," from Birmingham Regional Controller to R. E. Higginson, Esq., NAB Headquarters, August 31, 1959.
44. TNA: PRO, AST 7/1445, Confidential Memorandum for the Use of the Advisory Panel of the Metropolitan Boroughs' Standing Joint Committee, "The Coloured Population of London," January 21, 1952.
45. Cited in Ruth Glass, *London's Newcomers, The West Indian Migrants*, Cambridge, MA: Harvard University Press, 1961, Appendix B.
46. London Metropolitan Archives (hereafter LMA): LCC/CL/GP/1/219, J. M. Sainsbury, Minutes of Welfare Department Conference on the Colour Problem in London, February 17, 1955.
47. *The London Times*, November 6, 1954.
48. TNA: PRO, AST 7/1210, Minute from Area Officer, Bristol North to Regional Controller, Bristol on "Coloured Stowaways," November 23, 1950. In 1965, 25% of lodging houses in Britain would not accept "coloured persons." British Library (hereafter BL): OP-GPA/16765, National Assistance Board, "Homeless Single Persons: Report on a Survey Carried out by the NAB between October 1965 and March 1966," 1966, p. 26.
49. LMA: LCC/CL/GP/1/219, Memorandum from R. J. Allerton to the Clerk of the Council, March 4, 1955.
50. Ibid.
51. LMA: LCC/CL/GP/1/219, Memorandum from R. J. Allerton (Director of Housing) to Clerk of the Council, April 14, 1959.
52. LMA: LCC/CL/GP/1/219, Minutes from Meeting of the Consultative Committee on the Homeless Poor, October 26, 1954.
53. LMA: LCC/GP/1/219, Memorandum from LCC Welfare Department on Coloured Immigrants, undated, probably 1955.
54. LMA: LCC/CL/GP/1/219, Mr. Barton, Minutes of Welfare Department Conference on the Colour Problem in London, February 17, 1955.
55. LMA: LCC/MIN/7681, Report from Director of Housing on Overseas Immigrants Living in Overcrowded Conditions, March 15, 1956.
56. LMA: LCC/CL/GP/1/219, Letter from Lambeth Town Clerk to Clerk of LCC, March 1, 1955. Similar opinions were expressed by a representative from Paddington. LMA: LCC/CL/GP/1/219, Mr. Barton, Minutes of Welfare Department Conference on the Colour Problem in London, February 17, 1955.
57. Sheila Patterson, *Immigration and Race Relations in Britain, 1960–67*, London: Oxford University Press, 1969, p. 211.
58. LMA: LCC/CL/GP/1/219, Minutes of the Meeting of the Consultative Committee on the Homeless Poor, February 21, 1950.
59. TNA: PRO, AST 7/1210, Letter from J. E. Bullard to C. J. Bentley, Esq., Regional Office Birmingham, March 10, 1954.

60. LMA: LCC/CL/GP/1/219, Minutes of the Meeting of the Consultative Committee on the Homeless Poor, October 26, 1954.
61. Different allowances for rent turned on a distinction between "householders," who were assumed to have direct responsibility for rent, and "non-householders," who were paid a different (slightly higher) assistance rate, but were assumed not to have a direct rent obligation and were therefore paid a low fixed allowance for their share of rent.
62. TNA: PRO, AST 7/1878, "Coloured Applicants—Problems," from W. L. Lidbury, London (North) Regional Controller, July 23, 1959.
63. TNA: PRO, AST 7/1535, Memorandum from Mr. Lidbury on "Coloured Applicants," October 29,1958.
64. TNA: PRO, AST 7/1880, Letter from Regional Controller, Birmingham to C. G. Beltram, Esq., NAB Headquarters, November 15, 1962.
65. TNA: PRO, AST 7/1445, Letter from J. L. Keith of the Colonial Office to the Lambeth Town Clerk, September 3, 1951.
66. Neither women nor the old or sick were counted because the numbers were thought to be too small to be of significance.
67. Of the 1,870 men receiving assistance, about 500 (26%) had dependents (wives and children) whose needs were also met out of the man's assistance payment. Men with dependents received larger grants than those without.
68. TNA: PRO, AST 7/1210, National Assistance Board Memorandum 804: Assistance to Coloured Men, October 16, 1953.
69. TNA: PRO, AST 7/1210, Minute from Secretary to NAB Chairman, March 25, 1955.
70. Another 687 were claiming unemployment benefit (earned through national insurance contributions) but did not meet the means test for additional national assistance. Statistics of Unemployed Coloured Workers Claiming Unemployment Benefit and National Assistance During Week Commencing July 18, 1955, TNA: PRO, AST 7/1210.
71. For discussions of discrimination encountered by immigrants, see Dilip Hiro, *Black British, White British: A History of Race Relations in Britain*, London: Grafton, 1991, p. 144; Holmes, *John Bull's Island*, p. 382.
72. TNA: PRO, AST 7/1210, Minute from Area Officer, Bristol North to Regional Controller, Bristol on "Coloured Stowaways," November 23, 1950.
73. LMA: LCC/CL/GP/1/219, Minutes of the Meeting of the Consultative Committee on the Homeless Poor, February 21, 1950.
74. TNA: PRO, AST 7/1445, Confidential Memorandum for the Use of the Advisory Panel of the Metropolitan Boroughs' Standing Joint Committee on "The Coloured Population of London," January 21, 1952.
75. TNA: PRO, AST 7/1210, Memorandum on Coloured Applicants to F. Jackson, Esq., Regional NAB Office, Birmingham, July 16, 1952.
76. TNA: PRO, AST 7/1210, Letter from H. S. Jones (NAB) to V. Harris, Esq., Colonial Office, Welfare Department, March 6, 1953.
77. Ibid.
78. TNA: PRO, AST 7/1614, Letter from Regional Controller, Leeds, to A. G. Beard Esq., NAB Headquarters, March 5, 1958.
79. TNA: PRO, AST 7/1614, Letter from Regional Controller, Leeds, to Miss J. Hope-Wallace, NAB Headquarters, April 9, 1958.
80. "Strike Brings Problem to Head," *Haslingdon Observer*, May 11, 1958; "Unions to Act," *Haslingdon Observer*, April 26, 1958.
81. "Unions to Act," *Haslingdon Observer*.
82. TNA: PRO, AST 7/1614, Minute (Reference 14883 B), May 6, 1958.
83. TNA: PRO, AST 7/1614, Letter from Regional Controller, Leeds, to Miss J. Hope-Wallace, NAB Headquarters, April 9, 1958.

84. "Fear Keeps 'Slaves' Silent," *Daily Express*, April 25, 1958.

85. TNA: PRO, AST 7/1878, Minute from J. Hope-Wallace to Secretary and Chairman, December 12, 1960.

86. TNA: PRO, AST 7/1880, Memorandum from National Assistance Board to Commonwealth Immigrants Advisory Council, undated, probably late 1962.

87. For example, see Ronald Kershaw, "Pakistanis Swell Number of Jobless: Grave Consequences Feared," *Yorkshire Post*, February 21, 1962; and "More Jobless Immigrants," *Daily Telegraph*, February 16, 1962.

88. Ibid; and TNA: PRO, HO 376/133, Letter from Miss J. Hope-Wallace to K. B. Paice, Home Office, July 13, 1964.

89. TNA: PRO, AST 7/1880, Report on "Commonwealth Immigrants-Welfare," from Manager, Brixton NAB to Miss V. M. Baker, London (South) Region, November 15, 1962.

90. TNA: PRO, AST 7/1880, Report on "Commonwealth Immigrants-Welfare," from Manager, Lambeth NAB to Miss V. M. Baker, London (South) Region, November 14, 1962.

91. TNA: PRO, AST 7/1880, Memorandum from National Assistance Board to Commonwealth Immigrants Advisory Council, undated, probably late 1962.

92. TNA: PRO, HO 376/133, Letter from Miss J. Hope-Wallace to K. B. Paice, Home Office, July 13, 1964.

93. Ruth Glass, *London's Newcomers, The West Indian Migrants*, Cambridge, MA: Harvard University Press, 1961.

94. TNA: PRO, AST 7/1535, Memorandum from Mr. Lidbury on "Coloured Applicants," October 29, 1958.

95. LMA: LCC/CL/GP/1/219, Minutes from Meeting of the Consultative Committee on the Homeless Poor, October 26, 1954.

96. Ibid.

97. TNA: PRO, AST 7/1646, National Assistance Board, Surrey Advisory Committee, Examples of Cases Considered by Area Sub-Committees, March 1, 1964 to August 31, 1964.

98. For a discussion of black female immigrants' assigned identities as "workers" rather than mothers, see Wendy Webster, *Imagining Home: Gender, "Race" and National Identity, 1945–64*, London: University of Central Lancashire, 1998, esp. pp. 129–147.

99. TNA: PRO, AST 7/1879, Letter from J. W. Grove (Transport & General Workers' Union) to Sir Geoffrey Hutchinson (NAB Chairman), September 8, 1961.

100. TNA: PRO, AST 7/1879, Extract from Report by the Manager, Nottingham (North) on the Area Sub-Committee for the Year Ended June 30, 1961.

101. TNA: PRO, AST 7/1878, Letters from E. M. Scott (NAB) to Immigrants Advisory Committee, June 2, 1961 and June 13, 1961.

102. TNA: PRO, AST 7/1880, Minute from London (South) Manager on Commonwealth Immigrants-Welfare, November 15, 1962.

103. *Report of the National Assistance Board for 1949*, Cmd. 8030, p. 39.

104. TNA: PRO, AST 7/1535, Memorandum from Mr. Lidbury on "Coloured Applicants," October 29, 1958.

105. Laura Tabili, *"We Ask for British Justice": Workers and Racial Difference in Late Imperial Britain*, Ithaca, NY: Cornell University Press, 1994, chp. 7; Sonya Rose, *Which People's War? National Identity and Citizenship in Britain, 1939–1945*, New York: Oxford, 2003.

106. TNA: PRO, AST 7/1445, Letter from R. L. Jones of the Home Office to J. E. Thomas, Esq., of the Colonial Office (Welfare Department), August 23, 1951.

107. TNA: PRO, AST 7/1445, Confidential Memorandum for the Use of the Advisory Panel of the Metropolitan Boroughs' Standing Joint Committee on "The Coloured Population of London," January 21, 1952.
108. LMA: LCC/CL/GP/1/219, Mr. Petheram, Minutes of Welfare Department Conference on the Colour Problem in London, February 17, 1955.
109. Similar resentment, the regional controller wrote, resulted when houses were "bought by coloured people with the result that white residents are 'crowded' out." TNA: PRO, AST 7/1535, Report on Coloured Applicants for National Assistance, October 29, 1958.
110. TNA: PRO, AST 7/1472, Letter from Miss Reed to Mr. Newman, March 18, 1959; Memorandum from Regional Controller for London North to Miss Jill Morton, March 16, 1959; Letter from R. J. Newman to Regional Controller for London North, March 24, 1959; Letter from Regional Controller for London North to Miss Morton, April 16, 1959.
111. TNA: PRO, AST 7/1880, Report on "Commonwealth Immigrants-Welfare," from Manager, Lambeth NAB to Miss V. M. Baker, London (South) Region, November 14, 1962.
112. TNA: PRO, AST 7/1445, Letter from Almoner of Lambeth Hospital to V. Harris, Secretary, Committee for the Welfare and Employment of Nonstudents, Colonial Office, July 22, 1952.
113. TNA: PRO, AST 7/1445, Letter from Miss M. W. McK. Cochrane, NAB London Inner Region, to H. S. Jones, NAB Headquarters, August 14, 1952.
114. TNA: PRO, AST 7/1880, Memorandum from National Assistance Board to Commonwealth Immigrants Advisory Council, undated, probably late 1962.
115. TNA: PRO, AST 7/1880, Memorandum from National Assistance Board to Commonwealth Immigrants Advisory Council, undated, probably late 1962.
116. TNA: PRO, AST 7/1535, Report on Coloured Applicants for National Assistance, October 29, 1958.
117. Ibid.
118. Ibid.
119. TNA: PRO, AST 7/1878, Extract from report by the Chief Constable of Derby, December 20, 1960.
120. TNA: PRO, AST 7/1878, Minute from G. Beltram, Esq., NAB Headquarters to J. H. Bradley, Esq., North-Midland Regional Office, March 27, 1961; Letter from J. H. Bradley, North-Midland Regional Controller, to G. Beltram, Esq., NAB Headquarters, April 4, 1961.
121. TNA: PRO, AST 7/1445, Confidential Memorandum for the Use of the Advisory Panel of the Metropolitan Boroughs' Standing Joint Committee, "The Coloured Population of London," January 21, 1952.

NOTES TO CHAPTER 5

1. London government was restructured, and individual borough councils took over the welfare services that had been handled by the LCC, which was dissolved. In 1965, the NAB also faced dissolution, and was replaced the following year by the Supplementary Benefits Commission.
2. John Greve, Dilys Page, and Stella Greve, *Homelessness in London*, Edinburgh: Scottish Academic Press, Ltd., 1971, p. 58.
3. London Metropolitan Archives (hereafter LMA): LCC/CL/WEL/1/53, Report by Chief Officer of the Welfare Department to Welfare Committee on Homeless Families, October 12, 1949.

4. LMA: LCC, Report of Research Team to the Committee of Inquiry into Homelessness, General Purposes Committee Report (No. 3), July 1962; Greve, Page, and Greve, *Homelessness in London*, p. 90.
5. National Assistance Act of 1948, Section 21(1).
6. Greve, Page, and Greve, *Homelessness in London*, pp. 123–125.
7. LMA: LCC, Report on Homelessness to London County Council, p. 25.
8. John Macnicol, "From 'Problem Family' to 'Underclass,' 1945–95," in Helen Fawcett and Rodney Lowe (eds.) *Welfare Policy in Britain: The Road from 1945*, New York: St. Martin's Press, 1999, p. 79.
9. In June 1950, the Welfare Department reported that the average length of stay for non-problem families was less than 8 weeks, whereas 90% of "problem families" stayed at least 3 months, and 70% stayed longer than 6 months. LMA: LCC/CL/WEL/1/53, Report by Chief Officer of the Welfare Department on Problem Families, June 30, 1950.
10. Macnicol, "From 'Problem Family' to 'Underclass,'"; John Welshman, "The Social History of Social Work: The Issue of the 'Problem Family,' 1940–70," *British Journal of Social Work*, 1999, vol. 29, pp. 457–476.
11. LMA: LCC/CH/M/31/2, Report by Chief Officer of the Welfare Department on Temporary Accommodation of Homeless Families, July 3, 1957.
12. LMA: LCC/CL/WEL/1/53, Report by Chief Officer of Welfare Department to Welfare Committee on Homeless Families, Appendix: Reports from Wardens, June 6, 1951.
13. Though the LCC administered the rest centers and halfway houses, they were requisitioned by the Ministry of Health and transferred to the LCC on an agency basis. The Ministry of Health set the rates charged. Halfway houses were usually requisitioned by individual borough councils.
14. If the husband did not pay the weekly charges, the LCC could ask a magistrate for a judgment against him. In 1951, the Welfare Department initiated legal action for non-payment in fifty-two cases. LMA: LCC/CL/WEL/1/53, Report by the Chief Officer of the Welfare Department on Homeless Families in Part III Accommodation—Legal Proceedings for Recovery of Charges: Eviction, June 6, 1951.
15. LMA: LCC/CL/WEL/1/53, Report by Chief Officer of the Welfare Department to Welfare Committee on Homeless Families, October 12, 1949.
16. Ibid.
17. LMA: LCC/CL/WEL/1/53, Report by Chief Officer of Welfare Department to Welfare Committee on Homeless Families, November 10, 1949.
18. Ibid.
19. LMA: LCC/CL/WEL/1/53, Housing Report, September 30, 1954.
20. LMA: LCC/CL/WEL/1/53, Family Service Units Pamphlet, quoted in Report by Chief Officer of the Welfare Department on Problem Families, June 30, 1950.
21. Ibid.
22. LMA: LCC/CL/WEL/1/53, Report by Chief Officer of the Welfare Department on Problem Families, June 30, 1950.
23. LMA: LCC/CL/WEL/1/53, Report by Chief Officer of Welfare Department to Welfare Committee on Homeless Families, June 6, 1951.
24. In 1959, for example, nearly 75% of the "lone women" in temporary accommodation in London were separated from their husbands. The proportion of "lone women" in temporary accommodation stayed fairly constant throughout the 1960s. Greve, Page, and Greve, *Homelessness in London*; LMA: LCC/CL/WEL/1/15, Report by Chief Officer of Welfare Department on Homeless Families, January 9, 1962.

25. In November 1949, the wardens of the Part III establishments reported that of the 360 families living there, 100 (30%) were problem families. Of these, thirty-six were "lone women" with children. LMA: LCC/CL/WEL/1/53, Report by Chief Officer of Welfare Department to Welfare Committee on Homeless Families, November 10, 1949.
26. LMA: LCC/CL/WEL/1/15, Report by Chief Officer of Welfare Department on Homeless Families, January 9, 1962.
27. In 1956, about 25% of the 686 mothers in residence at the Welfare Department's mother-and-baby unit in Southwark chose to give their babies up for adoption. LMA: LCC/CH/M/26/1, Notes from Conference on Moral Welfare Work and the Care of the Unmarried Mother and Her Child, October 17, 1963.
28. LMA: LCC/CL/WEL/1/15, Report by Chief Officer of Welfare Department on Mothers and Babies—Accommodation, November 2, 1962; LCC/CH/M/26/1, Memorandum from Children's Department, January 4, 1956.
29. LMA: LCC/CL/WEL/1/53, Statement of Member of Visiting Subcommittee, quoted in Report by Chief Officer of Welfare Department to Welfare Committee on Homeless Families, June 6, 1951.
30. LMA: LCC/CL/WEL/1/53, Report by Chief Officer of Welfare Department to Welfare Committee on Homeless Families, Appendix: Reports from Wardens, June 6, 1951.
31. Ibid.
32. Ibid.
33. Ellen Ross, *Love and Toil: Motherhood in Outcast London, 1870–1918*, New York: Oxford University Press, 1993; George K. Behlmer, *Friends of the Family: The English Home and Its Guardians, 1850–1940*, Stanford, CA: Stanford University Press, 1998.
34. LMA: LCC/CL/WEL/1/53, Report by Edward Bligh, Chief Officer of the Welfare Department, October 12, 1949.
35. LMA: LCC/CL/WEL/1/53, Report of the Housing Committee on Unsatisfactory Tenants and Housing Applicants, September 30, 1954.
36. LMA: LCC/CL/WEL/1/53, London County Council Response to Questionnaire on Problem Families, September 25, 1952.
37. LMA: LCC/CL/WEL/1/53, Report of the Housing Committee on Unsatisfactory Tenants and Housing Applicants, September 30, 1954.
38. LMA: LCC/CL/WEL/1/53, Report by Chief Officer of the Welfare Department, Homeless Families: Special Units, April 27, 1955.
39. LMA: LCC/CL/WEL/1/53, Report by the Chief Officer of the Welfare Department, Homeless Families: Special Units, September 22, 1954.
40. LMA: LCC/CL/WEL/1/53, Report of the Housing Committee on Unsatisfactory Tenants and Housing Applicants, September 30, 1954; LMA: LCC/CL/WEL/1/53, Report by Chief Officer of the Welfare Department, Homeless Families: Special Units, April 27, 1955.
41. LMA: LCC/CL/WEL/1/53, Report by Chief Officer of the Welfare Department, Homeless Families: Special Units, April 27, 1955.
42. LMA: LCC/CL/WEL/1/53, Report by the Chief Officer of the Welfare Department, Homeless Families: Special Units, Appendix, September 22, 1954.
43. Ibid.
44. LMA: LCC/CL/WEL/1/53, Report by the Director of Housing and the Chief Officer of the Welfare Department on Problem Families—Provision of Accommodation, April 27, 1955.
45. LMA: LCC/CL/WEL/1/53, Report by Chief Officer of the Welfare Department, Homeless Families: Special Units, April 27, 1955.

46. Ibid.
47. LMA: LCC/CL/WEL/1/15, Report on Rehabilitation of Mothers by the Medical Officer of Health, June 19, 1952.
48. LMA: LCC/CH/M/29/5, Memorandum from Conference of Association of Family Case-Workers, May 15, 1954.
49. *London Times*, June 4, 1956.
50. LMA: LCC/CL/WEL/1/15, Report by the Chief Officer of the Welfare Department on Mothers and Babies—Accommodation, October 10, 1960.
51. LMA: LCC/CH/M/26/1, Memorandum from Children's Officer for Area 3, March 10, 1955; Memorandum from Children's Department, January 4, 1956.
52. LMA: LCC/CL/WEL/1/15, Report by the Chief Officer of the Welfare Department on Mothers and Babies—Accommodation, October 10, 1960.
53. Ibid.
54. LMA: LCC/CL/WEL/1/53, Report by Chief Officer of Welfare Department to Welfare Committee on Homeless Families, November 10, 1949.
55. LMA: LCC/CH/M/30/7, Memorandum from Mr. Carr on Homeless Families, July 17, 1951.
56. Ibid.
57. LMA: LCC/CH/M/30/7, Letter from Children's Officer of Area 8 to Chief Officer of Children's Department, October 5, 1952; Report by Chief Officer of Children's Department, October 22, 1952; Notes of Discussion Between Chief Officer of the Children's Department and Deputy Clerk of the LCC, August 22, 1952; Memorandum from Chief Officer of Children's Department to Mr. Ford, Chairman of the Children's Committee, June 20, 1952.
58. LMA: LCC/CH/M/31/2, Report by Chief Officer of the Welfare Department on Temporary Accommodation of Homeless Families, July 3, 1957.
59. Ibid.
60. Ibid.
61. Ibid.
62. LMA: LCC/CH/M/31/2, Letter from Children's Officer to Welfare Department, August 21, 1956.
63. "Homeless Families in London," *London Times*, October 27, 1961.
64. Ibid.
65. LMA: LCC/CL/WEL/1/15, Report by the Chief Officer of the Welfare Department on Homeless Families, January 9, 1962; and Report by the Chief Officer of the Welfare Department on Mothers and Babies—Accommodation, October 10, 1960.
66. National Assistance Act of 1948, Section 17.
67. Scotland, unlike England and Wales, had not dealt with "casuals" as a special class. The English-type casual ward (a separate unit within the workhouse) was rare in Scotland. *Report of the National Assistance Board for 1949*, Cmd. 8030, p. 31.
68. *Report of the National Assistance Board for 1964*, Cmnd. 2674, p. 46.
69. The National Archives (hereafter TNA): Public Record Office (hereafter PRO), AST 7/1757, Memorandum from N. E. Clark on Hostels for Homeless Women, June 5, 1961.
70. TNA: PRO, AST/7/1718, Memorandum on Proposed Replacement of Camberwell Reception Centre, undated.
71. *Report of the National Assistance Board for 1948*, Cmd. 7767, pp. 29–31.
72. *Report of the National Assistance Board for 1949*, p. 32.
73. Ibid., p. 33.

74. *Report of the National Assistance Board for 1953*, Cmd. 9210, p. 23. Woolwich was a "designated" Center under section 18 of the National Assistance Act of 1948, which provided that "a Reception Centre may be 'designated' by the Minister of Pensions and National Insurance, and that a person who persistently uses Reception Centres when capable of maintaining himself may be made subject to a direction that he shall only be admitted to the designated Centre on condition that he remains at the Centre for a period up to 48 hours and during that time does work allotted to him."

75. TNA: PRO, AST 7/1646, Minutes of the Meeting of the Surrey Advisory Committee held on April 22, 1959.

76. *London Times*, February 5, 1962.

77. *London Times*, August 17, 1962.

78. *Daily Mail*, October 31, 1962.

79. TNA: PRO, AST 7/1726, undated. Memorandum on Vagrancy: Persons Sleeping Rough In London from G. W. Cole, undated, probably December 1962.

80. TNA: PRO, AST 7/1718, Letter from NAB to Ministry of Public Building and Works, December 13, 1962.

81. TNA: PRO, AST 7/1726, Memorandum from G. W. Cole at the National Assistance Board, December 27, 1962.

82. TNA: PRO, AST 7/1726, Report on Survey of November 1963 on Persons Sleeping Out in London; *Report of the National Assistance Board for 1963*, Cmnd. 2386, p. 45.

83. Greve, Page, and Greve, *Homelessness in London*.

84. TNA: PRO, AST 7/1726, Memorandum from G. W. Cole, December 27, 1962.

85. TNA: PRO, AST 7/1726, Report from London County Council Welfare Department's Consultative Committee on Homeless Poor, October 25, 1962.

86. *Report of the National Assistance Board for 1963*, p. 44.

87. *Report of the National Assistance Board for 1965*, Cmnd. 3042, p. 37

88. LMA: PH/GEN/2/26, Report by Miss P. Paige, Reception Centre Caseworker, January 28, 1964–May 6, 1964.

89. Ibid.

90. TNA: PRO, LAB 8/2635, Letter from L. E. Clarke to Miss B. M. Grainger, Ministry of Labour, October 15, 1963.

91. British Library: OP-GPA/16765, National Assistance Board, "Homeless Single Persons: Report on a Survey Carried out by the NAB between October 1965 and March 1966," p. 80.

92. *Report of the National Assistance Board for 1965*, Appendix XXVIII, p. 87.

93. Ken Loach, Commentary on *Cathy Come Home*, British Broadcasting Company, 2003.

NOTES TO THE EPILOGUE

1. Chris Jones and Tony Novak, *Poverty, Welfare and the Disciplinary State*, London: Routledge, 1999; Alan Deacon and Jonathan Bradshaw, *Reserved for the Poor, The Means Test in British Social Policy*, Oxford: Basil Blackwell and Martin Robertson, 1983; Alan Deacon, "Unemployment and Politics in Britain Since 1945," in Brian Showler and Adrian Sinfield (eds.) *The Workless State, Studies in Unemployment*, Oxford: Martin Robertson,

1981; Ruth Lister, *As Man and Wife? A Study of the Cohabitation Rule*, London: Child Poverty Action Group, 1973; Kathleen Kiernan, Hilary Land, and Jane Lewis, *Lone Motherhood in Twentieth-Century Britain: From Footnote to Front Page*, Oxford: Clarendon Press, 1998; Beatrix Campbell, *Wigan Pier Revisited , Poverty and Politics in the Eighties*, London: Virago, 1984; K.D.M. Snell and Jane Millar, "Lone-Parent Families and the Welfare State: Past and Present," *Continuity and Change*, 1987, no. 2, pp. 387–422; Carol Walker, *Managing Poverty, The Limits of Social Assistance*, London: Routledge, 1993.

2. David Blunkett, Secretary of State for Education and Employment, "Enabling Government: The Welfare State in the 21ˢᵗ Century," Keynote Speech to the Policy Studies Institute Seminar, October 11, 2000, http://www.dfee.gov.uk/speech/ (printed copy is on file with author).

3. Ibid.

4. Department of Social Security (hereafter DSS), *A New Contract for Welfare: Principles Into Practice*, Cm. 4101, London: Her Majesty's Stationary Office (hereafter HMSO), October 1998, p. 7.

5. DSS, *A New Contract for Welfare: Principles Into Practice*, Foreword from the Prime Minister, p. iii.

6. DSS, *New Ambitions for our Country: A New Contract for Welfare*, Cm. 3805, London: HMSO, March 1998.

7. John Lloyd and Steve Richards, "Finished, or Just Getting Started: Analysis of UK Welfare Reform Formulated by Frank Field," *New Statesman*, vol. 127, no. 4370, January 30, 1998, pp. 10–14.

8. DSS, *New Ambitions for Our Country: A New Contract for Welfare*.

9. Ibid.

10. Jones and Novak, *Poverty, Welfare and the Disciplinary State*, p. 197.

11. David Blunkett, Secretary of State for Education and Employment, "Enabling Government: The Welfare State in the 21ˢᵗ Century."

12. Ibid.

13. Ibid.

14. Tony Blair, Speech on the New Deal, June 22, 1999, http://www.number-10.gov.uk/news.asp?NewsId=394

15. Peter Hain, quoted at www.thesun.co.uk/sol/homepage/news/article512508, November 27, 2007 (printed copy is on file with author).

16. Nicholas Watt, "Tough New York Welfare Scheme for U.K.," *The Guardian*, April 17, 2008, www.guardian.co.uk (printed copy is on file with author).

17. David Blunkett, Secretary of State for Education and Employment, "Enabling Government: The Welfare State in the 21ˢᵗ Century."

18. Helene Mulholland, "Switch off the TV and Get on Your Bike, Blunkett Tells Long-Term Sick," *The Guardian*, October 10, 2005, www.guardian.co.uk

19. David Freud, quoted in "1.9 m on Benefit 'Should Go Back to Work'," *The Telegraph*, February 7, 2008, www.telegraph.co.uk

20. "Tony Blair's Big Idea," *The Economist*, vol. 344, no. 8046, December 6, 1997, pp. 59–60.

21. Scarlett McGwire, "A Family Policy Tony Can Live With," *New Statesman*, vol. 127, no. 4378, March 27, 1998, pp. 18–19.

22. David Blunkett, Secretary of State for Education and Employment, "Enabling Government: The Welfare State in the 21ˢᵗ Century."

23. Tony Blair, Speech on Welfare Reform, October 6, 2002, www.pm.gov.uk

24. Amelia Hill, "Lie Detectors Target Benefit Claim Cheats," *The Guardian*, September 2, 2007, www.guardian.co.uk.

25. Rita Diaz, *Housing and Homelessness*, London: Shelter, 2005.
26. Marc Francis, *Building Hope: The Case for More Homes Now*, London: Shelter, 2005.
27. Angelique Chrisafis, "Destitute: Asylum Seekers Pushed on to the Street by an Official Letter," *The Guardian*, August 18, 2003, www.guardian.co.uk.
28. Gordon Brown, quoted at www.thesun.co.uk, *The Sun*, November 27, 2007.

Bibliography

Abbott, Elizabeth and Bompas, Katherine, *The Woman Citizen and Social Security*, London: Women's Freedom League, 1943.

Abel-Smith, Brian, "Sex Equality and Social Security," in Jane Lewis (ed.) *Women's Welfare Women's Rights*, London: Croom Helm, 1983, pp. 86–102.

Abel-Smith, Brian and Townsend, Peter, *The Poor and the Poorest*, London: G. Bell and Sons, 1965.

Baldwin, Peter, *The Politics of Social Solidarity: Class Bases of the European Welfare State, 1875–1975*, Cambridge, 1990.

Baldwin, Peter, "Beveridge in the *Longue Duree*" in J. Hills et al. (eds.) *Beveridge and Social Security*, Oxford: Oxford University Press, 1994, pp. 37–55.

Behlmer, George K., *Friends of the Family: The English Home and Its Guardians, 1850–1940*, Stanford, CA: Stanford University Press, 1998.

Bell, Kathleen, *Tribunals in the Social Services*, London: Routledge & Kegan Paul, 1969.

Beveridge, William, *Social Insurance and Allied Services*, New York: MacMillan, 1942.

Beveridge, William and Wells, A. F., *The Evidence for Voluntary Action*, London: Allen & Unwin, 1949.

Bromley, P. M., *Family Law*, London: Butterworth, 1957.

Callender, Claire, "Redundancy, Employment and Poverty," in Caroline Glendinning and Jane Millar (eds.) *Women and Poverty in Britain*, Brighton: Wheatsheaf Books Ltd., 1987, pp. 137–158.

Campbell, Beatrix, *Wigan Pier Revisited, Poverty and Politics in the Eighties*, London: Virago, 1984.

Cronin, J. E. and Weiler, P., "Working-Class Interests and the Politics of Social Democratic Reform in Britain, 1900–1940," *International Labor and Working-Class History*, 1991, vol. 40, pp. 47–66.

Culley v. Charman, 7 QBD 89 [1881].

Davison, R.B., *Black British: Immigrants to England*, London: Oxford University Press (for the Institute of Race Relations), 1966.

Deacon, Alan, *In Search of the Scrounger: The Administration of Unemployment Insurance in Britain, 1920–1931*, London: G. Bell & Sons, 1976.

Deacon, Alan, "Unemployment and Politics in Britain Since 1945," in Brian Showler and Adrian Sinfield (eds.) *The Workless State, Studies in Unemployment*, Oxford: Martin Robertson, 1981, pp.

Deacon, Alan and Bradshaw, Jonathan, *Reserved for the Poor, The Means Test in British Social Policy*, Oxford: Basil Blackwell and Martin Robertson, 1983.

Diaz, Rita, *Housing and Homelessness*, London: Shelter, 2005.

Esping-Andersen, Gosta, *The Three Worlds of Welfare Capitalism*, Princeton, NJ: Princeton University Press, 1990.

Finlayson, Geoffrey, *Citizen, State, and Social Welfare in Britain, 1830–1990*, Oxford: Clarendon Press, 1994.

Flanagan, Richard, *"Parish-Fed Bastards": A History of the Politics of the Unemployed in Britain, 1884–1939*, New York: Greenwood Press, 1991.

Fox-Piven, Frances and Cloward, Richard, *Regulating the Poor: The Functions of Public Welfare*, New York: Random House, 1971.

Francis, Marc, *Building Hope: The Case for More Homes Now*, London: Shelter, 2005.

Gilbert, Bentley B., *The Evolution of National Insurance in Great Britain, The Origins of the Welfare State*, London: Michael Joseph Limited, 1966.

Gilroy, Paul, *"There Ain't No Black in the Union Jack": Cultural Politics of Race and Nation*, London: Hutchinson, 1987.

Glass, Ruth, *London's Newcomers, The West Indian Migrants*, Cambridge, MA: Harvard University Press, 1961.

Glennerster, Howard, *British Social Policy Since 1945*, Oxford: Basil Blackwell, 1995.

Glucksmann, Miriam, *Women Assemble: Women Workers and the New Industries in Inter-War Britain*, London: Routledge, 1990.

Golding, Peter and Middleton, Sue, *Images of Welfare: Press and Public Attitudes to Poverty*, Oxford: Martin Robertson, 1982.

Gordon, Linda, *Pitied But Not Entitled: Single Mothers and the History of Welfare, 1890–1935*, Cambridge, MA: Harvard University Press, 1994.

Gough, Ian, *The Political Economy of the Welfare State*, London: Macmillan, 1979.

Goulbourne, Harry, *Ethnicity and Nationalism in Post-Imperial Britain*, New York: Cambridge University Press, 1991.

Goulbourne, Harry, *Race Relations in Britain Since 1945*, New York: St. Martin's Press, 1998.

Greve, John, Page, Dilys, and Greve, Stella, *Homelessness in London*, Edinburgh: Scottish Academic Press, Ltd., 1971, p. 58.

Groves, Dulcie, "Members and Survivors," in Jane Lewis (ed.) *Women's Welfare Women's Rights*, London: Croom Helm, 1983, pp. 38–63.

Hall, Stuart, *Policing the Crisis: Mugging, the State, and Law and Order*, London: Macmillan, 1978.

Hill, Michael, *The Sociology of Public Administration*, New York: Crane, Russak & Company, Inc., 1972.

Hiro, Dilip, *Black British, White British: A History of Race Relations in Britain*, London: Grafton, 1991.

Holmes, Colin, *John Bull's Island: Immigration and British Society, 1871–1971*, Basingstoke, UK: Macmillan, 1988.

Hunt, Audrey, *A Survey of Women's Employment*, Government Social Survey, 1968.

Jones, Chris and Novak, Tony, *Poverty, Welfare and the Disciplinary State*, London: Routledge, 1999.

Kiernan, Kathleen, Land, Hillary, and Lewis, Jane, *Lone Motherhood in Twentieth-Century Britain: From Footnote to Front Page*, Oxford: Clarendon Press, 1998.

King, Geoffrey S., *The Ministry of Pensions and National Insurance*, London: George Allen and Unwin, Ltd., 1958.

Klein, Viola, *Britain's Married Women Workers*, London: Routledge & Kegan Paul, 1965.

Laybourne, Keith, *Unemployment and Employment Policies Concerning Women in Britain, 1900–1951*, New York: Edwin Mellen Press, 2002.

Lees, Lynn Hollen, *The Solidarities of Strangers, The English Poor Laws and the People, 1700–1948*, New York: Cambridge University Press, 1998.

Lewis, Jane, "Dealing with Dependency: State Practices and Social Realities, 1870–1945," in Jane Lewis (ed.) *Women's Welfare, Women's Rights*, London: Croom Helm, 1983, pp. 17–37.

Lewis, Jane, "Public Institution and Private Relationship, Marriage and Marriage Guidance," *Twentieth Century British History*, 1990, vol. 1, pp. 233–263.

Lewis, Jane, *Women in Britain Since 1945: Women, Family, Work and the State in the Post-War Years*, Cambridge, MA: Basil Blackwell, 1993.

Lipsky, Michael, *Street-Level Bureaucracy: Dilemmas of the Individual in Public Services*, New York: Russell Sage Foundation, 1980.

Lister, Ruth, *As Man and Wife? A Study of the Cohabitation Rule*, London: Child Poverty Action Group, 1973.

Lowe, Rodney, *The Welfare State in Britain Since 1945*, New York: St. Martin's Press, 1999.

Macfarlane, L. J., *Issues in British Politics since 1945*, London: Longman, 1986.

Macnicol, John, *The Movement for Family Allowances, 1918–1945*, London: Heinemann, 1980.

Macnicol, John, "From 'Problem Family' to 'Underclass,' 1945–95," in Helen Fawcett and Rodney Lowe (eds.) *Welfare Policy in Britain: The Road from 1945*, New York: St. Martin's Press, 1999, pp. 69–93.

Marsden, Dennis, *Mothers Alone, Poverty and the Fatherless Family*, London: Allen Lane, 1969.

Marshall, T. H., *Citizenship and Social Class*, Cambridge: Cambridge University Press, 1950.

Marshall, T. H., *Class, Citizenship and Social Development: Essays by T. H. Marshall*, Garden City, NY: Doubleday, 1964.

McKibbin, Ross, *Classes and Cultures: England 1918–1951*, New York: Oxford University Press, 1998.

Miliband, Ralph, *The State in Capitalist Society*, London: Weidenfeld and Nicolson, 1969.

Myrdal, Alva and Klein, Viola, *Women's Two Roles*, London: Routledge & Kegan Paul, Ltd., 1956.

National Assistance Board v. Parkes, 3 W. L. R. 347 [1955].

National Assistance Board v. Wilkinson, 2 All E. R. 255 [1952].

Parker, Stephen, *Informal Marriage, Cohabitation and the Law, 1750–1989*, New York: St. Martin's Press, 1990.

Pascall, Gillian, *Social Policy, A New Feminist Analysis*, New York: Routledge, 1997.

Patterson, Sheila, *Immigration and Race Relations in Britain, 1960–67*, London: Oxford University Press, 1969.

Pateman, Carole, "The Patriarchal Welfare State," in Amy Gutman (ed.) *Democracy and the Welfare State*, Princeton, NJ: Princeton University Press, 1988, pp. 231–260.

Paul, Kathleen, *Whitewashing Britain: Race and Citizenship in the Postwar Era*, Ithaca, NY: Cornell University Press, 1997.

Pedersen, Susan, "Gender, Welfare, and Citizenship in Britain During the Great War," *American Historical Review*, 1990, vol. 95, pp. 983–1006.

Pedersen, Susan, *Family, Dependence, and the Origins of the Welfare State: Britain and France, 1914–1945*, New York: Cambridge University Press, 1993.

Priestly, J. B., *English Journey*, London: William Heinemann, 1934.

Ross, Ellen, *Love and Toil: Motherhood in Outcast London, 1870–1918*, New York: Oxford University Press, 1993.

Rowntree, Seebohm and Lavers, G. R., *Poverty and the Welfare State*, London: Longmans Green, 1951.

Savage, Mike, "Trade Unionism, Sex Segregation, and the State: Women's Employment in 'New Industries' in Inter-War Britain," *Social History*, 1988, vol. 13, pp. 209–230.

Seabrook, Jeremy, *Unemployment*, New York: Quartet Books, 1982.

Snell, K. D. M. and Millar, Jane, "Lone-Parent Families and the Welfare State: Past and Present," *Continuity and Change*, 1987, no. 2, pp. 387–422.

Spencer, Ian R. G., *British Immigration Policy Since 1939: The Making of Multi-Racial Britain*, New York: Routledge, 1997.

Tabili, Laura, *We Ask For British Justice: Workers and Racial Difference in Late Imperial Britain*, Ithaca, NY: Cornell University Press, 1994.

Taylor-Gooby, Peter, *Public Opinion, Ideology, and State Welfare*, London: Routledge & Kegan Paul, 1985.

Thane, Pat, "Women and the Poor Law in Victorian and Edwardian England," *History Workshop Journal*, 1978, no. 6, pp. 29–51.

Thane, Pat, *Foundations of the Welfare State*, London: Longman, 1996.

Thompson, Dorothy, "The Welfare State: An Historical Approach," *New Reasoner*, 1957, vol. 4, pp. 127–128.

Tomlinson, J. D., "Women as 'Anomalies': The Anomalies Regulations of 1931, Their Background and Implications," *Public Administration*, 1984, vol. 62, pp. 423–437.

Veit-Wilson, John, "The National Assistance Board and the 'Rediscovery' of Poverty," in H. Fawcett and R. Lowe (eds.) *Welfare Policy in Britain: The Road from 1945*, London: Macmillan, 1999, pp. 116–157.

Walby, Sylvia, *Patriarchy at Work*, Cambridge: Polity Press, 1986.

Walker, Carol, *Managing Poverty, The Limits of Social Assistance*, London: Routledge, 1993.

Webb, Adrian, "The Abolition of National Assistance," in Phoebe Hall (ed.) *Change, Choice and Conflict in Social Policy*, London: Heinemann, 1975.

Webster, Wendy, *Imagining Home: Gender, "Race" and National Identity, 1945–64*, London: University of Central Lancashire Press, 1998.

Welshman, John, "The Social History of Social Work: The Issue of the 'Problem Family,' 1940–70," *British Journal of Social Work*, 1999, vol. 29, pp. 457–476.

Wilson, Elizabeth, *Women and the Welfare State*, London: Tavistock, 1977.

Wimperis, Virginia, *The Unmarried Mother and Her Child*, London: Allen and Unwin, 1960.

Wynn, Margaret, *Fatherless Families: A Study of Families Deprived of a Father by Death, Divorce Separation or Desertion Before or After Marriage*, London: Michael Joseph Limited, 1964.

Young, Michael and Willmott, Peter, *Family and Kinship in East London*, London: Routledge & Kegan Paul, 1986.

Index